Richard T. Hughes

CHRISTIAN AMERICA
and the Kingdom of God

Foreword by Brian McLaren

University of Illinois Press
Urbana and Chicago

© 2009 by the Board of Trustees
of the University of Illinois
All rights reserved
Manufactured in the United States of America
C 5 4 3 2 1
∞ This book is printed on acid-free paper.

Library of Congress Cataloging-in-Publication Data
Hughes, Richard T. (Richard Thomas), 1943–
Christian America and the Kingdom of God /
Richard T. Hughes ; foreword by Brian McLaren.
p.   cm.
Includes bibliographical references (p.   ) and index.
ISBN 978-0-252-03285-1 (cloth : alk. paper)
1. Christianity and politics—United States.
2. Kingdom of God—Political aspects—United States.
3. Particularism (Theology)—Political aspects—United States.
4. Kingdom of God—Biblical teaching.
5. Particularism (Theology)—Biblical teaching.
I. Title.
BR517.H83   2009
277.3'08—dc22   2008050477

This volume is dedicated to Franklin H. Littell, whose book,
The Anabaptist View of the Church,
awakened me to the biblical vision of the kingdom
of God over forty years ago,

To the memory of Barton W. Stone (1772–1844)
and David Lipscomb (1831–1917),
early leaders of Churches of Christ,
whose lives and published works have immeasurably
enriched my understanding of that vision,

And to All Saints Episcopal Church in Pasadena, California,
a congregation whose work embodies that vision
in truly remarkable ways.

Contents

Foreword

I am a citizen of the United States and I love my country. I choke up sometimes when I sing about our land—the purple mountain's majesty and fruited plain, the spacious skies and amber waves of grain, from the Mojave to the Okeefenokee to the oceans white with foam. I love the people, because they're my people, Democrats and Republicans and independents, northerners and midwesterners, southerners and northwesterners, urbanites and suburbanites and ruralites, folks of all skin tones and accents, recent immigrants, long-term settlers, and aboriginals.

I love our sports, our music, our jokes, our cooking, our holidays. There's so much I love. But there's something I'm not so fond of. The thing I don't love is hard to name, hard to describe. It's a flaw in our national character, I think, or maybe not a flaw as much as an immaturity, like an adolescent chip on our shoulder, something we need to grow out of.

You could call it arrogance, a sense of exceptionalism, superiority, and pride. But I often think underneath what seems like conceit, there's really a strong sense of insecurity. Maybe our real problem is a kind of inferiority that we keep overcompensating for, like the short guy who has the toughest attitude, or the preacher's kid who cusses a lot so he won't be taken for a goody-goody, or the lady who fears she's too old and ugly and wears too much makeup to hide, not just her wrinkles, but also her fear.

Why would we be afflicted with such an inferiority? Could it be because we've never faced some of the truths of our collective past? Could it be we haven't faced the truth of land-theft and attempted genocide of our native peoples? Or the truth of slavery too long defended before finally overthrown? Or the truth of an expansionist tendency that wasn't satisfied once we reached from

Atlantic to Pacific, but that tempted us to extend our control to Hawaii and the Philippines—and later to Vietnam and Iraq?

I love my country, and I want my country to be even better than it is by maturing in our national character—maturing enough to face the uncomfortable truths that we try not to know. I don't want us to be like the alcoholic-in-denial who tells himself he's the life of the party, or the blabbermouth who considers himself friendly, or the gossip who sees herself as a good communicator, or the playground bully who mistakes his classmates' fear for respect.

That's why I have come to admire the work of Richard Hughes. In *Myths America Lives By*, and now in *Christian America and the Kingdom of God*, Richard is trying to help us grow up as a nation. As a historian, he is well suited to inform us about our history—including the parts we are tempted to hide or spin, thus helping us face our denial. And as a sincere and committed Christian, Richard is well suited to confront— gently, delicately, but firmly—the besetting sin of religious hypocrisy to which we Christians in America are easily tempted.

Imagine if Great Britain never faced the downsides of the British Empire, if Belgium never came to terms with the holocaust of the Congo under King Leopold, if South Africa practiced amnesia about the apartheid years, if Germany hid rather than faced the nightmare of the 1930s and early 1940s. That imaginative exercise reinforces the importance of the work Richard Hughes is doing—and asking us to do—in this book.

It's easy to demonize, and easy to lionize. In between comes the hard work of sober judgment, and Richard Hughes is one of the best people alive to help us in this national task. To do so, Richard has to explore the idea of a Christian nation, and then offer a solid explanation of what the phrase "kingdom of God" meant in the biblical text, which he does clearly and well in the book's introduction and first three chapters. Then he has to explore the outworking of "kingdom of God" in relation to both church history and American history, which he does concisely and strongly in the fourth chapter.

Finally, he must bring all this to bear on the present moment in the book's final chapter. When I read the final chapter, and especially its last sentence—actually, a question—I felt a kind of chill, along with an urgent sense of responsibility. I felt more strongly that I am a shareholder in the most powerful economy and most deadly weapons arsenal and the most influential mass media industry in the history of history. I felt my responsibility as a shareholder, my stewardship of that wealth and weaponry and influence. I also felt my responsibility as a person of faith. And I felt the tension between those two identities—as a citizen of a rich, well-armed, powerful Western nation and as a follower of a poor, nonviolent peasant from the Middle East. These feelings of urgency, responsibility, and tension have stayed with me for many weeks since reading this book.

As you turn these pages, keep in mind that hundreds of Christian radio and television preachers will simultaneously be broadcasting a message that is exactly the opposite of the one you're reading. If you go to church this Sunday, remember that from thousands of pulpits, preachers will pontificate with none of the insight contained in this book. When you close the book's final page, I hope that you will share my sense of responsibility, and that you will translate that responsibility into action—speaking up when "Christian America" language is casually tossed around, having the courage to differ when U.S. national interest and God's will are treated as one and the same, perhaps buying a copy of this book for the pastors and other influencers in your life, and starting a reading group to help others engage with this message. For much is at stake. And much is possible if we take the next needed steps on our pathway towards national—and spiritual—maturity.

Brian D. McLaren

Acknowledgments

This book could not have become a reality without the support and advice of numerous colleagues.

I wish to thank first the editorial staff at the University of Illinois Press—especially Willis Regier, director, and Elizabeth Dulany, editor—for the invitation they extended to me to write this book, and Geof Garvey for the marvelous job he did in copyediting the manuscript.

Several people contributed financially to free me from some of my teaching duties during the 2005–6 academic year at Pepperdine University, thereby allowing me to complete most of the research for this book during that time frame. I wish to thank in this regard William S. Banowsky, Dwain Evans, Terry Koonce, and Foster Stanback.

Martin Marty was especially helpful with his incisive criticisms of an earlier version of this text. In addition, a variety of friends, colleagues, and family members read various drafts of this material and made helpful suggestions. I owe debts of gratitude especially to Randall Balmer, Gordon Brubacher, Raymond Carr, John Fea, Lareta Finger, Samuel S. Hill Jr., Douglas Jacobsen, Ken Johnson, Donald Kraybill, Bill Leonard, Stuart Love, Kelly Phipps, Brian Smith, James Thomas, John Yeatts, David Weaver-Zercher, and Cynthia Wells. I also wish to thank Melissa Lewis, a Messiah College student, who was extraordinarily helpful with her suggestions for how to improve the flow of the text. Finally, I am especially indebted to my wife, Jan, and our son, Andy, who offered extremely helpful insights as I wrote and rewrote various drafts of this book. Although many people helped me to shape its final version, I take full responsibility for whatever shortcomings it may possess.

CHRISTIAN AMERICA
and the Kingdom of God

Introduction

GETTING
Our Bearings

The idea of Christian America is a powerful, seductive, and potentially destructive theme in American life, culture, and politics. It therefore deserves thoughtful consideration by every citizen of this republic. And one of the most fruitful ways to explore that theme is to compare it with the biblical vision of the kingdom of God.

Throughout this book, the reader will encounter the phrase "the myth of Christian America." When I use the term *myth*, I don't have in mind something that is fundamentally untrue. A myth may be false in certain ways and true in certain ways, but one characteristic of myth remains unchanging: A myth conveys power and deep meaning to people who embrace it.

Our English word *myth* derives from the Greek word *mythos*, whose literal meaning is "story." A myth, therefore, is a story, but not just any story. Rather, a myth is a story so powerful and so rich in meaning that it can orient our lives amidst the chaos and confusion of the world in which we live. The notion of Christian America performs that role for millions of Americans, and in that sense, this book will inquire into "the myth of Christian America."

Many fundamentalist and evangelical leaders routinely promote the idea of Christian America, and millions of Americans—people who represent an array of religious traditions and no religion at all—simply assume the Christian character of the United States. Consider the following examples.

- The platform of the Republican Party of the state of Texas affirmed in 2004 that the United States is "a Christian nation" and rejected the traditional American ideal of "separation of church and state."[1]
- When asked the question "Why does the Arab world hate the United States?" a general in the United States Army—William G. Boykin—responded, "Because we are a Christian nation . . . and the enemy is a guy named Satan."[2]
- Al Gore, while campaigning for the presidency in 2000, pledged to reporters to ask before every major decision, "What would Jesus do?"[3]
- George W. Bush, while campaigning in that same year, named Jesus as his "favorite philosopher." And Franklin Graham, at Bush's 2001 inaugural prayer service, offered this: "May we as a nation again place our hope and trust in the Almighty God and his Son the Lord Jesus Christ, our Savior, our Redeemer and our Friend."[4]
- Addressing a conference of Republican governors in 1992, Mississippi's Kirk Fordice spoke of America as a "Christian nation." When one of his gubernatorial colleagues suggested that he really meant to say "Judeo-Christian nation," Fordice replied, "If I meant that, I would have said it."[5]
- In 1998 Arkansas Governor Mike Huckabee, speaking at a Baptist convention, declared, "I hope we answer the alarm clock and take this nation back for Christ."[6]
- In the days leading up to the Iowa Republican caucus of January 2008, Governors Mitt Romney and Mike Huckabee, along with Senators Fred Thompson and John McCain, outdid one another in their bid to claim the mantle of the most Christian candidate for president of the United States.
- And Senator John McCain, a candidate for the presidency of this nation, claimed in 2007 that "the Constitution established the United States of America as a Christian nation."[7]

The Constitution, of course, did not establish the United States as a Christian nation. In fact, it did just the reverse, making it clear that "Congress shall make no law respecting an establishment of religion, or prohibiting the free exercise thereof"[8]—a provision one would think that United States senators, state governors, members of Congress, candidates for the presidency of the United States, and highly placed military leaders in this country would grasp and understand.

But if people in those positions buy into the myth of Christian America, can we be all that surprised when the sociologist Christian Smith—basing his work on extensive surveys with a broad population sample—reports that "not only conservative Protestants but the majority of Americans believe that America was founded as a Christian nation?"[9]

While this book will point to the obvious truth that the notion of Christian America is alien to the United States Constitution, that is not the primary purpose of this text. Rather, this book will unpack the irony that the myth of Christian America is alien to the one book that Christians claim to prize more than any other—the Bible. It is alien to the New Testament, especially to the teachings of Jesus and Paul, and alien to significant sections of the Hebrew Bible as well, especially the Hebrew prophets who preached to Israel and Judah beginning in the eighth century BCE.

Only two concepts in the Bible even begin to approximate the idea of a Christian nation, and those are the concepts "chosen nation" and "kingdom of God." We will deal with those themes in substantial detail in the next three chapters, but I want to remark briefly in this introductory chapter on the idea of the kingdom of God—a notion that stands in radical opposition to the idea of Christian America.

According to the Bible, the kingdom of God and the nations of the earth embody radically different values and reflect radically different orders of reality. The kingdom of God relies on the power of self-giving love while nations—even so-called "Christian" nations—rely on the power of coercion and the sword. For that reason, nations—even "Christian" nations—inevitably go to war against their enemies while the kingdom of God has no enemies at all. The kingdom of God is universal and those who promote that kingdom care deeply for every human being in every corner of the globe, regardless of race or nationality. But earthly nations—even so-called "Christian" nations—embrace values that are inevitably nationalistic and tribal, caring especially for the welfare of those within their borders. And while the kingdom of God exalts the poor, the disenfranchised, and the dispossessed, earthly nations inevitably exalt the rich and powerful and hold them up as models to be emulated. In fact, in the context of earthly nations—even so-called "Christian" nations—the poor seldom count for much at all.

The very first thesis that drives this book, then, is this: the notion of Christian America and the notion of the kingdom of God are polar opposites whose values could not be further apart. This means that the idea of Christian America is in every key respect an oxymoron—essentially a contradiction in terms—when measured by the most sacred document of the Christian tradition: the Bible itself.

A second theme that drives this book is the devastatingly ironic truth that Christian America so often behaves in such unchristian and even anti-Christian ways. From Indian removal and extermination to African slavery to racial segregation to state-sanctioned killing in wars for dominance and profit to state-sanctioned torture of enemy combatants—in all these ways and more, Christian America has made a mockery of the Christian religion.

This book does not argue that the United States should seek to become more faithful to the Christian religion or that the nation should embrace as its norm the biblical vision of the kingdom of God. Indeed, this book assumes that no nation—whether the United States or any other nation—can possibly measure up to the standards of the kingdom of God as we find those standards spelled out in the biblical text.[10]

But I do argue—and this is the third important thesis of this book—that Christians should behave in ways that are consistent with their profession of faith, especially in America's public square. Millions of American Christians take their political cues from imperial considerations and then justify their political behavior with appeals to the Bible and their religion. That fact is terribly important politically when one considers that Christians—especially evangelical and fundamentalist Christians—represent a significant power bloc in American politics.

When Christians embrace the myth of Christian America but refuse to question the nation when it behaves in ways that are alien—even hostile—to the Christian faith, they implicitly transform their religion into a highly destructive force that erodes justice for the poor and threatens the peace and stability of the world. In this radically perverse scenario, Jesus and the religion that bears his name now sanction war instead of peace, oppression instead of reconciliation, and greed instead of selfless giving.

A fourth theme that defines this book is the fact that biblical and theological illiteracy runs rampant in the United States, even in America's churches, despite the frequent claims that America is a Christian nation. Many Christians base their politics on what they imagine the Bible teaches, or on what someone else—often their pastor—has told them the Bible teaches. But what they imagine the Bible teaches is often quite foreign to biblical reality.

While biblical illiteracy abounds among rank and file church members—a point we will explore more fully in the following chapter—misreadings of the biblical text and, as a result, misrepresentations of biblical theology are common even among Christians who are especially visible in America's public square.

Ann Coulter, a best-selling political author in the early years of the twenty-first century, illustrates this point especially well. In spite of her claims to represent the Christian tradition, her message is so completely alien to the Christian faith that *Pittsburgh Post-Gazette* columnist Tony Norman, after reading her book, *Godless: The Church of Liberalism*, complained, "Her exaggerations, hackery, lies and bad faith are dutifully pointed out by critics every time she hits the book circuit, but the insincerity of her Christian profession is rarely commented upon. . . . I can't be a Christian in a world where Ann Coulter can call herself a Christian without fear of contradiction."[11]

While the apostle Paul argued that "the fruit of the Spirit is love, joy, peace, patience, kindness, generosity, faithfulness, gentleness, and self-control," Coulter has specialized in sarcasm, ridicule, mud-slinging, and hate-mongering. She scorned grieving widows in the aftermath of the 9/11 disaster. She identifies the biblical vision of the kingdom of God with American nationalism ("they [liberals] deny the Biblical idea of dominion and progress, the most ringing affirmation of which is the United States of America"). She slanders those with whom she disagrees ("liberals have fervently believed that human beings are a blight on the earth"), and publicly consigns her political opponents to the fires of hell ("I would be crestfallen to discover any liberals in heaven").[12] Yet she doesn't shrink from identifying her own brand of politics with the Judeo-Christian tradition ("their [the liberals] rage against us is their rage against the Judeo-Christian tradition").

Of all her public proclamations since September 11, 2001, the one most radically out of line with the biblical vision of the kingdom of God was her claim that the United States "should invade their countries [Muslim nations], kill their leaders and convert them to Christianity."[13] Coulter claims that her views are consistent with the Christian tradition, and millions of her fans apparently take her at her word—a clear indication that they, like she, know little about the biblical tradition or the most basic principles of the Christian faith.

The Moral Majority, founded in 1979 by Jerry Falwell (1933–2007) and dissolved in 1989, offers another example. In recent years, perhaps no organization promoted the vision of Christian America more fervently than did this one. Yet, in the name of Christian America, that organization lobbied for American control of the Panama Canal, rejected the Salt II treaty that required the United States to reduce its nuclear arsenal, aggressively promoted a buildup of American military forces, claimed that biblical prophecy demanded unqualified American support for Israel, promoted American dominance in the world, and even called for violence and war as the fulfillment of biblical prophecies.[14] All the while, the Moral Majority operated with the assumption that this brand of politics was somehow in keeping with the biblical message and the Christian tradition. In the pages that follow, I hope to demonstrate that politics like these are utterly foreign to the biblical text and especially to the biblical vision of the kingdom of God.

Finally, the reader should understand several other assumptions and objectives that govern the argument and layout of this book.

- This book does not ask whether the United States is a good nation or a moral nation. Its only concern is with the question, "Is the United States a Christian nation?" The truth is, the United States often behaves in ways that are moral and good, but conventional morality falls woefully short of the biblical vision of the kingdom of God.
- While this book is critical of Christian America, it does not seek to diminish the good that Christians have done over the course of American history. American Christians have been responsible for untold good and have pointed the nation in some spectacularly good directions. As examples, one need only note the substantial role evangelical Christians played in the antislavery crusade of the nineteenth century, the work of Dorothy Day's Catholic Worker Movement in alleviating suffering among marginalized people, the Freedom Movement led by Martin Luther King Jr., who understood his work as a fundamentally Christian undertaking, or the social gospel of the early twentieth century that sought to alleviate domestic poverty on a broad scale.
- Finally, instead of merely referencing biblical passages, I have quoted scripture extensively, especially in chapters two and

three. I have done this out of the conviction that readers will gain a far better understanding of the biblical tradition of the kingdom of God if they can actually read the words of scripture as opposed to relying on my secondhand summary of those words. This book is therefore somewhat like an art book with numerous exhibits, though in this case those exhibits are texts instead of paintings. Those texts are cited from the New Revised Standard Version of the Bible.

Before we examine the notion of Christian America from a biblical perspective, we must acknowledge two other ways one might make the claim that America is a Christian nation: on legal grounds and on cultural grounds. We will briefly examine each of those arguments in turn.

The Claim That America Is Legally a Christian Nation

For the legal claim to carry weight, one would have to demonstrate that the nation's Constitution clearly defines the Christian character of the United States. The Constitution, of course, does not even mention the name of God, much less define the United States as a Christian nation. As a result, the Confederate States of America, whose constitution *did* reference the name of God, routinely claimed moral superiority over the United States.

At the very time the Confederacy was proclaiming its moral superiority, Christian groups in the north began proposing a Christian amendment to the Constitution of the United States. In 1864, for example, a group of evangelical Christians established the National Reform Association designed, as they put it,

> to maintain existing Christian features in the American government, and to secure such an amendment to the Constitution of the United States as will indicate that this is a Christian nation, and will place all the Christian laws, institutions and usages of our government on an undeniable legal basis in the fundamental law of the land.[15]

These evangelicals proposed to President Abraham Lincoln, therefore, that the opening words of the Constitution—"We, the People of the United States, in Order to form a more perfect Union . . ."—be replaced with this:

> Recognizing Almighty God as the source of all authority and power in civil government, and acknowledging the Lord Jesus Christ as the

Governor among the nations, His revealed will as the supreme law of the land, in order to constitute a Christian government. . . .

Lincoln listened, but in the end, refused to act on the proposal, and Congress tabled the resolution for several years running.[16]

In 1946 evangelical Christians launched another effort to write a Christian amendment to the Constitution. This initiative appeared under the auspices of the Christian Amendment Association and sought to insert into the Constitution the following words: "This nation devoutly recognizes the authority and law of Jesus Christ, Saviour and Ruler of nations, through whom are bestowed the blessings of Almighty God."[17] Like the 1864 initiative, this one also came to naught.

Failing to secure a Christian amendment to the Constitution, various states drafted into their own constitutions language that described America as a Christian nation. Those efforts had no legal effect whatsoever. When all was said and done, they were mainly ceremonial expressions of wishful thinking on the part of the many evangelical Christians who helped craft the various state constitutions.

Far more important—and far more telling—was that soon after the creation of the republic, state after state complied with the guidelines of the federal Constitution and voted to eliminate the Christian church as the legally established state religion. Massachusetts—the former stronghold of New England Puritanism—was the last state to disestablish, doing so in 1833.

One state—South Carolina—made a last ditch effort to retain its Christian establishment by writing into its 1778 constitution that "the Christian Protestant religion shall be deemed, and is hereby constituted and declared to be, the established religion of this state." The reluctance of Massachusetts and South Carolina to disestablish suggests that for half a century following the ratification of the Constitution, several states were simply unwilling to abandon the notion of an established Christian state.

Having failed to guarantee the Christian character of the nation in any meaningful legal sense, some Christians sought alternate ways to accomplish that objective. For example, in the early nineteenth century, a Presbyterian pastor named Ezra Stiles Ely proposed the creation of "a Christian party in politics." If all Christians would only unite, Ely believed, they "could govern every public election in our country" in spite of the Constitution's ban on an established church.[18]

Ely also urged Christians to elect to office only those candidates who supported the Christian faith. "We are a Christian nation," Ely proclaimed in one of his sermons. "We have a right to demand that all our rulers in their conduct shall conform to Christian morality; and if they do not, it is the duty and privilege of Christian freemen to make a new and a better election."[19] Americans today are familiar with strategies like those proposed by Ely, having witnessed comparable efforts by Jerry Falwell, Pat Robertson, Paul Weyrich, and others.

As recently as 2008, Congressman Randy Forbes (R-Va.) sponsored House Resolution 888 that called for Americans to honor the nation's "religious history" during a proposed American Religious History Week. According to the preamble of that resolution, "The United States Supreme Court has declared throughout the course of our Nation's history that the United States is 'a Christian country,' 'a Christian nation,' 'a Christian people.'" Based on that premise, House Resolution 888 concluded that the House "rejects, in the strongest possible terms, any effort to remove, obscure, or purposely omit such history from our Nation's public buildings and educational resources." After so many failed efforts over so many years, House Resolution 888 was but one more backdoor attempt to proclaim the Christian character of the United States through formal legislation.[20]

But efforts like these are finally ceremonial, for the simple fact is this: the Constitution of the United States has denied to American citizens the right to create a religious establishment by law or by coercion. That ruling means that any effort to Christianize the nation must do so by persuasion.[21] And to the extent that persuasion is successful, the Christian character of the nation can be enshrined only in ceremonial forms and cultural celebrations.

Accordingly, we look now at the claim that the United States is culturally a Christian nation.

The Claim That America Is Culturally a Christian Nation

It is undeniable that the United States is a Christian nation in a cultural and ceremonial sense. It became so early in its history by virtue of the fact that its people overwhelmingly professed—and continue to profess—an allegiance to the Christian religion. By the early years of the twenty-first century, for example, 76 percent of the American people identified themselves with the Christian faith. Those numbers were low in the years immediately after the Revolution but have remained consistently high from the early nineteenth century to the present.

America is also Christian by virtue of the extraordinary success Christians have achieved in promoting cultural celebrations and ceremonial forms of the Christian faith, from the founding to the present. These ceremonial dimensions include affirmations in various state constitutions, along with affirmations in party platforms, that America is a Christian nation. It includes as well the statement in the Pledge of Allegiance that this nation is "under God," enacted by Congress in 1954, and the statement on American currency, "In God We Trust," authorized in 1956. Indeed, when George W. Bush proclaimed Jesus as his "favorite philosopher," or when Al Gore proposed to govern by asking, "What would Jesus do?" both men paid tribute to the cultural and ceremonial establishment of the Christian religion in the United States.

It is worth noting that the Supreme Court, in a statement issued in 1892, defined the United States as a Christian nation precisely in these cultural and ceremonial terms. When state constitutions affirmed America as a Christian nation, the Court declared, those constitutions bore witness to the common law of the land. The Court then added,

> If we pass beyond these matters to a view of American life as expressed by its laws, its business, its customs and its society, we find everywhere a clear recognition of the same truth. Among other matters note the following: The form of oath universally prevailing, concluding with an appeal to the Almighty; the custom of opening sessions of all deliberative bodies and most conventions with prayers; the prefatory words of all wills, "In the name of God, Amen"; the laws respecting the observance of the Sabbath, with the general cessation of all secular business, and the closing of courts, Legislatures, and other similar public assemblies on that day; the churches and church organizations which abound in every city, town, and hamlet; the multitude of charitable organizations existing everywhere under Christian auspices; the gigantic missionary associations, with general support, and aiming to establish Christian missions in every quarter of the globe. These, and many other matters which might be noticed, add a volume of unofficial declarations to the mass of organic utterances that this is a Christian nation.[22]

The most important term in this statement is the word "unofficial," for this nation can be Christian in no other way. The unofficial Christianity enshrined in the popular culture of the United States is hardly Christian in any classic or orthodox sense. To take but one example, the language that appears on American currency—"In God We Trust"—finally says nothing at all about the nation's allegiance to the Christian faith since many religions—Judaism and Islam among them—can easily make the same confession. It is also worth observing the deep irony involved in placing the phrase, "In God We Trust," on money, especially in light of the pointed statement in the Sermon on the Mount (Matthew 6:24) and repeated in Luke 16:13: "You cannot serve God and wealth."

In 1967 the eminent sociologist and student of American culture Robert N. Bellah wrote an essay that became a classic description of what I am calling in this book the ceremonial and cultural establishment of Christianity in the United States. Bellah referred to that phenomenon as America's "civil religion." "Though much [in that religion] is selectively derived from Christianity," Bellah wrote, "this religion is clearly not itself Christianity"[23] for the simple reason that it so often leaves out so much that is central to the Christian faith—an allegiance to Jesus as the Son of God, for example. At the same time, this religion includes much—an affirmation of the messianic value of war, for example—that is inimical to the Christian faith.

The fact is, America's civil religion—as the German observer Geiko Müller-Fahrenholz points out—"draws heavily on Christian images and symbols, but it can easily include references to Judaism, Islam, and other religious traditions."[24] For this reason, it can speak of God, but it may or may not speak of Christ. It can speak of morality, but it may or may not speak of divine revelation. It can speak of endurance, but it may or may not speak of resurrection or eternal life. And it can speak of community, but it may or may not speak of the community of saints.

There are other ways in which America's civic faith resembles the Christian tradition. Christians worship in church buildings and cathedrals and celebrate sacred days and seasons in the liturgical year. America's civil religion also has its sacred shrines—Gettysburg National Cemetery and the Lincoln Memorial, for example—and its ritual calendar that includes days that are sacred to the memory of Americans—days like Memorial Day, Thanksgiving, and the Fourth of July. The civil religion of the United States also has a well-defined liturgy, including such national hymns as "God Bless America" and the "Battle Hymn of the Republic."[25]

What is crucial to emphasize is this: America's civic faith draws on Christianity at many points. Indeed, it overlaps with the Christian tradition in so many ways that many Christians fail to distinguish the one from the other. A single example of this profound overlapping will suffice: Julia Ward Howe's "Battle Hymn of the Republic," published in the *Atlantic Monthly* in 1862.

The first stanza of that majestic hymn that celebrates America's civic faith equated "the glory of the coming of the Lord" with the cause of the republic in America's Civil War. It then suggested that in the guns of the Union Army, God himself "hath loosed the fateful lightning of His terrible swift sword." Indeed, Howe concluded, in the midst of that war, "His truth is marching on."

The second stanza suggested that God was to be found "in the watch-fires of a hundred circling camps" as the army of the republic retired for the night. And there, in those camps, Howe affirmed, Americans could "read His righteous sentence by the dim and flaring lamps," for "His day is marching on."

The third stanza spoke of a "fiery gospel writ in burnished rows of steel," thereby suggesting some connection between the gospel of Christ and the nation's military agenda. The fourth stanza suggested that it was God who had sounded the trumpet summoning Americans to war, and then confused that war with the final judgment described in the Bible. Thus, through the power of the war, "He is sifting out the hearts of men before His judgment-seat."

But the fifth stanza did the most to confuse America's civic faith with the Christian religion, for it directly linked the work of Christ with the work of the Union army, and the cross of Christ with the cause of temporal freedom.

In the beauty of the lilies Christ was born across the sea;
With a glory in His bosom that transfigures you and me;
As He died to make men holy, let us die to make men free,
While God is marching on.[26]

Over the years, millions of Christians have sung that song, fully convinced that they were singing a Christian hymn, or at least a hymn that was in keeping with the central themes of the Christian gospel. And to the extent that America is a Christian nation both culturally and ceremonially, they were right. But as we shall see in chapter three, the sentiments of "The Battle Hymn of the Republic" are altogether foreign to the message of the Christian faith if we measure those sentiments against the biblical vision of the kingdom of God.

Julia Ward Howe's "Battle Hymn of the Republic" clearly celebrated certain aspects of America's civil religion. But to the extent that it confused America's civic faith with the Christian message, it also celebrated what I describe in this book as the ceremonial and cultural establishment of the Christian religion.

That establishment harks back at least to the Civil War, a time of which Winthrop S. Hudson wrote, "The ideals, the convictions, the language, the customs, the institutions of society were so shot through with Christian presuppositions that the culture itself nurtured and nourished the Christian faith."[27] Hudson might well have added that American Christianity had become by then so thoroughly infused with cultural presuppositions that the faith both nurtured and nourished the culture. Another historian, Robert T. Handy, observed that by the dawn of the twentieth century, "The virtual identification of the Christian way and the American way became axiomatic for many."[28]

It is precisely in this sense that America is a Christian nation. But if we were to measure the United States by the biblical text, and especially by biblical themes like "chosen nation" and "kingdom of God," could we still regard the United States as a Christian nation? That is the question to which we shall turn in chapters one, two, and three.

Chapter 1

CHRISTIAN AMERICA
As God's Chosen People

On the morning of October 2, 2006, a man entered a one-room Amish school house in the community of Nickel Mines, Lancaster County, Pennsylvania, brandishing guns, ammunition, lumber, nails, and sexual paraphernalia. The children in that school—as with all Amish schools—ranged from first to eighth grade. After the teacher and her mother ran from the building to seek help, the man ordered three other adults and the boys to leave. He then boarded the doors and windows to prevent the girls from escaping—and the police from getting in—and began his assault. He bound the hands and feet of ten little girls, ranging in age from seven to thirteen, then lined them up in front of the chalkboard and shot them in the head at point blank range, killing five. He then turned the gun on himself.

Before the day was over, the Amish of Nickel Mines had gathered to process their unspeakable grief. But one by one and two by two, in a completely spontaneous procession that lasted for several weeks, the Amish also made their way to the home of the man who killed their children. There, they offered forgiveness to the killer's family—his parents, his widow, and her parents.[1]

Their forgiveness was more than merely verbal. The Amish also invited the killer's widow to attend the funerals of their children, and over half the people at the killer's burial were Amish.[2]

Only days following the shootings, Sam Stolzfus, a member of the Amish community, explained that the Amish forgave "because that's what we are taught." "If we don't forgive," he said, "we won't be forgiven."[3]

The news that the Amish had rejected retribution and vengeance and had actually forgiven the man who murdered their children shocked the American public fully as much as the murders themselves.[4] And the depth of that shock revealed how shallow the notion of Christian America really is. Without meaning to do so, when the Amish rejected vengeance and embraced forgiveness instead, they held a mirror up to Christian America, and the image that appeared in that mirror was that of a nation that could barely comprehend the fundamental Christian vision that had inspired the Amish to act as they did.

Theological Illiteracy in America

This failure on the part of Christian America to understand the Christian practice of forgiveness should not be surprising since most Americans—whether Christian or not—have little understanding of the most basic contents of the biblical text, much less its deepest teachings. And that has been true for a very long time.

Roughly fifty years ago, Will Herberg reported that between 1949 and 1953, at a time when Bibles were selling at a record rate and 80 percent of Americans believed the Bible to be the "revealed word of God," over 50 percent of those Americans could not name even one of the four gospels.[5] Herberg concluded that while Americans purchased the Bible in record numbers in the early 1950s, they apparently failed to read it.

Fifty years later—in 2005—Bill McKibben reported that Americans still didn't know much about the Bible. While 85 percent of Americans identified themselves as Christians, McKibben wrote, "only 40 percent of Americans can name more than four of the Ten Commandments, and a scant half can cite any of the four authors of the Gospels."

But the most telling fact McKibben reported was this: "Three quarters of Americans believe the Bible teaches that 'God helps those who help themselves.'" The truth is, these words are not in the Bible but came from the mouth of Ben Franklin. And while this notion may be a popular American idea, it runs completely counter to the witness of the biblical text. As McKibben noted, "Not only is Franklin's wisdom not biblical; it is counter-biblical,"[6] since the core message of the Bible focuses on laying down one's life for one's neighbor, not on helping one's self. But that truth is lost on most Americans in this so-called Christian nation.

Not long before McKibben published this information, then-presidential candidate Howard Dean told a reporter that his favorite book in the New Testament was Job—a book that is actually in the Hebrew Bible, not the New Testament. Dean's gaffe might fairly be taken as a metaphor for the extent of biblical illiteracy that prevails in Christian America.

In 2007 Stephen Prothero published a major book that documented that illiteracy in substantial detail. He called that book, *Religious Literacy: What Every American Needs to Know—and Doesn't*. While Prothero examined illiteracy about many world religions, not just Christianity, his study confirmed what others have been reporting for many years on the ignorance of the American people about the Bible. We learn in this book, for example, that "most Americans cannot name the first book of the Bible," that "only one-third know that Jesus . . . delivered the Sermon on the Mount," and that "ten percent of Americans believe that Joan of Arc was Noah's wife."

Most surprising—and appalling—is the fact that religious illiteracy abounds where one would most expect to find a solid knowledge of the biblical text: among evangelical Christians. Prothero argued that "despite their conviction that the Bible is the Word of God, evangelicals show scant interest in learning what scripture has to say or wrestling with what it might mean."[7] Indeed, in the 1990s evangelical theologian David Wells lamented, "I have watched with growing disbelief as the evangelical church has cheerfully plunged into astounding theological illiteracy."[8]

The truth is that, in general terms, American Christians across the board know precious little about the religion they claim to profess. Their factual understanding of the Christian religion is meager, and their grasp of the great theological teachings of the Christian faith is more meager still. That fact alone should call into serious question the notion of Christian America.

Even more alarming, it is no exaggeration to say that theological illiteracy among American Christians translates into misguided political assumptions that can threaten the stability of the world. When American Christians, for example, fail to distinguish between God's chosen people, on the one hand, and the United States of America, on the other; or when they think that Israel, as God's original chosen people, deserves unqualified American support regardless of its behavior; or when they construct a political agenda on such outlandish fabrications as the rapture (a word never mentioned even once in the biblical text and an idea whose current contours were unknown in Christian history until the nineteenth century); or when they advocate the deployment of nuclear weapons on the grounds that God will use those weapons in the final battle of Armageddon, they violate the most fundamental teachings of the Christian faith and invite catastrophic consequences both for the nation and for the world.

Standing at the heart of many of these assumptions is the notion of America as a Christian nation. We saw in the previous chapter that this notion is utterly foreign to the Constitution of the United States, and I suggested that it is foreign to the Bible as well. Our task at this point is to document exactly how foreign to the biblical text the notion of Christian America really is.

Only two biblical themes could be construed—even remotely construed—to support the notion of Christian America. One is the notion of "God's chosen people," a dominant theme in the Hebrew Bible, a text some Christians call the Old Testament. The other is the notion of the kingdom of God, a concept found first in the Hebrew Bible, then designated with the formal name kingdom of God in the Christian New Testament. That phrase—kingdom of God—is found regularly in two of the synoptic gospels of the New Testament—Mark and Luke—and less so in the gospel of John, as well as in the book of Acts and the writings of the apostle Paul.

While this book will focus especially on the motif of the kingdom of God, we will begin our investigation by looking first at the theme of God's chosen people and the relation that notion bears to the idea of America as a Christian nation.

God's Chosen People

From the colonial period to the present, many American Christians have made the claim that God anointed America—first the colonies and then the nation—as his chosen people. Some have argued that God chose America as the formal successor to ancient Israel, or that in a very deliberate way, God chose the United States out of all the nations of the earth for a special mission in the world—to spread freedom and democracy, for example, or to bless the world with the truths of the Christian religion.

Most often, however, the argument for America's chosen status is far more subtle and typically runs something like this: Because America is a Christian nation and a nation "under God," it must be faithful to the will of God revealed in the Holy Bible. While the *New Testament* offers principles for righteous living on the part of *individuals*, the *Hebrew Bible*—focused as it was on the Jewish nation—offers principles for righteous living on the part of *nations*. For that reason, a Christian nation like the United States should model its behavior on principles God revealed to ancient Israel. If, for example, God called ancient Israel to punish evil nations, then God also calls the United States to punish evil nations. If God used Israel as an instrument of His wrath, then God also uses the United States as an instrument of His wrath. And if God demanded faithfulness from ancient Israel, then God also demands faithfulness from the United States, and faithfulness on the part of the United States requires that America nurture and protect its identity as a Christian nation.

Early proponents of a connection between chosen nation and Christian nation—the New England Puritans, for example—typically argued that God chose the colonies *because* of their Christian character. No one made that connection more apparent than Thomas Hooker, who preached a sermon to his British compatriots just before he departed England for the American colonies in 1633. His message was clear: Because England had failed in its Christian profession—or so Hooker surmised—God would turn his back on England and select a new chosen nation that took the Christian faith with the seriousness it deserved. Thus, he explained, "God is packing up his gospel because nobody will buy his wares nor come to his price. O, lay hands on God, and let him not go out of your coasts. He is a going. Stop him, and let not thy God depart."[9] Presumably, Hooker imagined that God was leaving England to take up his abode in a more authentically Christian community, namely, New England.

On the other hand, more recent proponents of a connection between chosen nation and Christian nation have argued, not that God chose America *because* of its Christian character, but that God *intended* the United States to serve as a Christian nation. Thus, when they link the categories, "Christian" and "chosen," they do so not so much out of hope for America's Christian future as out of despair over the nation's rejection of its alleged Christian heritage. And they do so as a way to encourage the nation to return to its alleged Christian roots. They seem to say, "God intended the United States to be a Christian nation, so come on, America, and get with the program."

No one articulated that relationship more clearly than D. James Kennedy (1930–2007), pastor of the Coral Ridge Presbyterian Church from 1959 to 2007 and founder of Coral Ridge Ministries, a radio and television ministry that regularly reached some three million viewers around the world. In a book clearly intended to lament America's apostasy from its Christian calling and to encourage the nation to return to its Christian roots—a book he called, *What If America Were a Christian Nation Again?*—Kennedy wrote,

> Here God established a certain sort of nation, a nation that was founded by the Pilgrims and the Puritans and others who came with evangelical Christianity. Here the Bible was believed and the gospel was preached. It was an evangelical nation. . . . If God, in His providence, ordained that this is what this nation should be, then all down through the ages, in fact from all eternity, God intended that it would be so.[10]

America As Chosen Nation: A Brief History of an Idea

However one might construe the relationship between chosen America and Christian America, the history of that relationship is long and complex and finds its oldest and deepest roots in the Hebrew Bible itself. Indeed, the Hebrew Bible was clear: Israel was God's chosen people. Texts throughout the Hebrew Bible testify to that fact, but none more clearly than Deuteronomy 7:6: "For you are a people holy to the Lord your God; the Lord your God has chosen you out of all the peoples on earth to be his people, his treasured possession."

Central to the Hebrew Bible's vision of the chosen people was the notion of covenant—the idea that God would bless His chosen people if they remained faithful to Him, but would curse them if they abandoned His laws and turned to other gods. Thus, Deuteronomy 7 goes on to explain,

> If you heed these ordinances, by diligently observing them, the Lord your God will maintain with you the covenant loyalty that

he swore to your ancestors; he will love you, bless you, and multiply you; he will bless the fruit of your womb and the fruit of your ground, your grain and your wine and your oil, the increase of your cattle and the issue of your flock, in the land that he swore to your ancestors to give you. (Deut. 7:12–13)

On the other hand, Deuteronomy 8:19 warns, "If you do forget the Lord your God and follow other gods to serve and worship them, I solemnly warn you today that you shall surely perish."

But how did this vision become central to the American self-understanding? That story began in England, long before the European settlement of what would become the United States. It began in the days of Henry VIII, who ruled England from 1509 to 1547. During the course of Henry's reign, a biblical translator named William Tyndale translated and brought to publication two editions of the New Testament, one in 1526 and the other in 1534.

Tyndale believed that a New Testament in the English language, widely distributed among the English people, might contribute to the cause of religious reform in England. So driven with the dream of a Protestant England, or at least of substantial reform of the Catholic Church, he filled both texts with short essays and marginal notes that he hoped would help readers understand the themes that stood at the heart of the New Testament message.

Tyndale argued in his notes to the 1526 edition a lesson he had learned from his theological mentor, the Protestant reformer Martin Luther, that the central message of the New Testament text was justification by grace through faith. The 1526 edition of Tyndale's New Testament, however, never had a chance to shape the English people as Tyndale hoped, since Henry VIII suppressed it almost as soon as it came from the press.

Over the next several years, in the course of translating the Pentateuch (the first five books of the Hebrew Bible), Tyndale encountered, apparently in a life-changing way, the twin themes of chosen people and covenant. He found especially compelling the twenty-eighth chapter of Deuteronomy—a chapter that catalogued in great detail the blessings that would come upon the chosen people (Israel) if they kept their covenant with God but, conversely, the curses with which God would smite the chosen people if they violated that covenant. Tyndale applied that text directly to England, and in an agonizing response to that passage, he wrote, "A Christian man's heart might well bleed for sorrow at the reading of it, for fear of the wrath that is like to come upon us according unto all the curses which thou there readest. For according unto these curses hath God dealt with all nations, after they were fallen into the abomination of blindness."[11]

When Tyndale issued his second edition of the New Testament in 1534, he had substantially rewritten the prologues and prefaces to the 1526 edition. While still maintaining a belief in justification by grace through faith, Tyndale was now convinced that the twin themes of chosen people and national covenant stood at the heart of the biblical text. Thus, in his introduction to the 1534 edition, he wrote

> The general covenant wherein all other are comprehended and included is this. If we meek ourselves to God, to keep all his laws, after the example of Christ: then God hath bound himself unto us to keep and make good all the mercies promised in Christ, throughout all the scripture.[12]

We cannot understand Tyndale's preoccupation with the national covenant unless we first understand how intensely he longed for religious reform in England. Reform had occurred in Switzerland under Zwingli and in Germany under Luther, but England, under the thumb of Henry VIII, had made no meaningful progress toward reform at all.

No text from Tyndale more clearly links his desire for religious reform with the motif of the national covenant than his preface to the book of Jonah, likely published in 1531. There Tyndale lamented that over the years, God had sent numerous prophets to proclaim repentance to England, but England had refused to respond to those indictments. Now England, like Israel of old, was in danger of suffering the wrath of God. Thus, Tyndale wrote,

> Gildas preached repentance unto the old Britains that inhabited England. They repented not, and therefore God sent in their enemies upon them . . . and destroyed them. . . . Wicliffe preached repentance unto our fathers not long since: they repented not for their hearts were indurate."

Then Tyndale made the point so crucial for us to grasp if we wish to understand why he so completely embraced the themes of chosen people and national covenant:

> And now Christ to preach repentance, is risen yet once again out of his sepulcher in which the pope had buried him and kept him down with his pillars and poleaxes and all disguisings of hypocrisy.

... And as I doubt not of the examples that are past, so am I sure that great wrath will follow, except repentance turn it back again, and cease it.[13]

Unlike the 1526 edition, Tyndale's 1534 New Testament received wide circulation in England, mainly because Henry VIII was preoccupied with his divorce from Catherine of Aragon, his marriage to Anne Boleyn, and his break from the Roman pope. Because the pope refused either to ratify his divorce from Catherine or to sanction his marriage to Anne, Henry essentially fired the pope and proclaimed himself supreme head of the church in England, thus creating the Church of England in lieu of the Roman Church.

Under these conditions, Tyndale's New Testament flourished and helped to shape the religious sentiments of his contemporaries. Indeed, that text did its work so well that for generations to come, English Protestants embraced the twin themes of chosen people and national covenant. In time, they would bring that very same vision to America.

Indeed, the themes of chosen people and national covenant were central to the Puritan imagination, especially for those Puritans who settled the American colonies. John Winthrop, the first governor of the Massachusetts Bay Colony, refused to allow the Puritans to set foot on American soil until he had first impressed on their minds his deep conviction that they were a latter-day chosen people, standing in covenant relationship with God.

Thus, he explained, they must not "think that the Lord will bear with such failings at our hands as he doth from those among whom we have lived [the English]." And why? Because "of the more near bond of marriage between Him and us, wherein He hath taken us to be His, after a most strict and peculiar manner, which will make Him the more jealous of our love and obedience. So he tells the people of Israel, you only have I known of all the families of the earth, therefore will I punish you for your transgressions." Winthrop concluded, "Thus stands the cause between God and us. We are entered into a Covenant with him for this work. . . . Now if the Lord shall please to hear us, and bring us in peace to the place we desire, then hath he ratified this Covenant and sealed our commission."[14]

Indeed, New England Puritans typically understood themselves as God's new Israel—a people God had chosen for Himself, had led out of Egyptian bondage (England), across the Red Sea (Atlantic

Ocean), and into the promised land (the American wilderness). Numerous Puritans rehearsed precisely that scenario as the cornerstone for their own self-understanding.

The theme of New England as God's chosen people dominated colonial life. During the Revolution, colonial preachers routinely compared New England to ancient Israel, suggesting that God had chosen the colonies for victory over Great Britain. Abraham Keteltas, for example, told his congregation that the colonial struggle was "God's own cause" and "a cause for which the Son of God came down from his celestial throne and expired on a cross." Other preachers like Nicholas Street appealed to the theme of covenant that was part and parcel of the chosen people motif. If the colonies were faithful to God, he said, God would be faithful to them and grant them victory. But if they behaved like the children of Israel who rebelled against God in the wilderness, God would punish them with defeat.[15]

Even the Founders embraced the myth that in some important sense, America was God's chosen people, a new Israel for these latter days. Thus, when Congress appointed Franklin, Jefferson, and Adams to design a seal for the United States, Franklin suggested a seal portraying "Moses lifting his hand and the Red Sea dividing, with Pharaoh in his chariot being overwhelmed by the waters, and with a motto . . . 'Rebellion to tyrants is obedience to God.'" Jefferson made a similar suggestion—"a representation of the children of Israel in the wilderness, led by a cloud by day and a pillar of fire by night."[16]

Twenty years after the Revolution, in 1796, John Cushing spoke at a Fourth of July celebration at Ashburnham, Massachusetts, and rehearsed the myth that now stood at the heart of the new nation's self-understanding: the myth of the chosen people. "In the history of the United States, particularly New England," Cushing proclaimed, "there is as great similarity perhaps in the conduct of Providence to that of the Israelites as is to be found in the history of any people."[17]

By 1850 the notion that the United States was God's chosen people—a new Israel for these latter days—was so pervasive that even Herman Melville, one of the great literary figures of his time, could pick up on this theme in his novel *White Jacket*. He wrote, "Escaped from the house of bondage, we Americans are the peculiar, chosen people—the Israel of our time; we bear the ark of the liberties of the world."[18]

The theme of the United States as God's chosen people, standing in a covenant relationship with the Almighty, persisted into the twentieth century and beyond. Billy Graham, for example, made the motif of national covenant a centerpiece of his preaching when, in the late 1940s and 1950s, he warned the nation of the danger of communism. "If we repent, if we believe, if we turn to Christ in faith and hope," he told a crowd assembled in Los Angeles in 1949, "the judgment of God can be stopped." At a later rally, he told the audience, "Only as millions of Americans turn to Jesus Christ at this hour and accept him as their Savior, can this nation possibly be spared the onslaught of a demon-possessed communism."[19]

By the early years of the twenty-first century, scores of fundamentalist and evangelical preachers—D. James Kennedy was an obvious example—persisted with the claim that America was both a chosen nation and a Christian nation, and that a strong connection tied these two themes together.

Assessing the Claim

The question we now must ask is this: How do these claims hold up in light of the one text that Christians value more than any other—the Bible?

In the first place, the Bible is clear—as we have seen—that God selected Israel as his chosen nation, but the Bible offers no evidence that God ever placed any other nation in that same category. This is precisely why Roger Williams, founder of Rhode Island, rejected the assumption so commonly made by his Puritan colleagues that God had selected New England as his chosen people for those latter days. New England, he argued, was not Israel and had no more warrant for thinking itself a chosen nation than any other nation on earth. Thus, he wrote, "The State of the land of Israel, the Kings and people thereof in Peace & War, is proved figurative and ceremonial, and no pattern nor precedent for any Kingdom or civil state in the world to follow."[20]

Second, note the circular reasoning that lies at the heart of the claim that America is a chosen nation. It begins with the premise, "Because America is a Christian nation," and concludes that America should emulate ancient Israel. And if America should emulate ancient Israel, it further concludes that America should be faithful to its role as a Christian nation. This circular reasoning is rooted in the assumption that the Bible is a flat and undifferentiated book that reflects no historical development. It therefore assumes there is no significant difference between the Hebrew Bible and the New Testament or between Judaism and Christianity. This conflated view of the Bible therefore sustains the notion of the United States as a chosen nation, just as it sustains the erroneous but common designation of the United States as a Judeo-Christian nation.

But if we take seriously the significant differences between the Hebrew Bible and the New Testament, then the Bible itself makes it difficult to argue for any link between the theme of chosen nation and the theme of Christian nation, since the chosen nation motif as it appears in the Hebrew Bible is foreign to the Christian faith. This is true for one simple reason: The chosen nation motif is obviously national in both scope and intent, while the Christian religion is transnational and universal in scope and intent.

Precisely for that reason, numerous New Testament writers redefined the meaning of "chosen" to point not to Israel alone, but to all in every nation—Jew or Gentile, slave or free, male or female— who place their trust in Jesus Christ. This attempt to redefine the meaning of "chosen" lies at the heart, in fact, of Paul's letter to the Romans, where he asked, for example, "Is God the God of Jews only? Is he not the God of Gentiles also? Yes, of Gentiles also, since God is one; and he will justify the circumcised [i.e., the Jews] on the ground of faith and the uncircumcised [i.e., the Gentiles] through that same faith" (Rom. 3:29–30). Later in Romans, Paul made the same point in a slightly different way. "For there is no distinction between Jew and Greek; the same Lord is Lord of all and is generous to all who call on him. For, 'Everyone who calls on the name of the Lord shall be saved'" (Rom. 10:12–13).

Other New Testament texts specifically refer to the entire Christian community—regardless of ethnicity or national origin— as "chosen." Thus, the author of I Peter began his epistle like this: "Peter, an apostle of Jesus Christ, to the exiles of the Dispersion in Pontus, Galatia, Cappadocia, Asia, and Bithynia, who have been chosen and destined by God the Father and sanctified by the Spirit to be obedient to Jesus Christ" (I Peter 1:1–2). The author of Colossians referred to the Christians at Colossae as "God's chosen ones, holy and beloved" (Col. 3:12). And Paul, in I Thessalonians, made one of the strongest possible statements about the new understanding of "chosenness" that now defined the Christian community. "For we know, brothers and sisters, beloved by God," Paul writes, "that he has chosen you, because our message of the gospel came to you not in word only, but also in power and in the Holy Spirit and with full conviction" (I Thess. 1:4–5).

Finally, precisely because the Hebrew notion of the chosen people was national—even tribal—in scope and intent, any attempt to appropriate that myth for national purposes today leads almost inevitably to behavior that is alien to the universal purposes of the Christian gospel—to wars, for example, to massacres, to ethnic cleansings, and to destruction of those who are different from the "chosen people."

Granted, God chose ancient Israel to serve—as Isaiah 42 puts it—"as . . . a light to the nations, to open the eyes that are blind, to bring out the prisoners from the dungeon, from the prison those who sit in darkness" (Isa. 42:6–7). But the author of that text wrote those words at a period quite late in Israel's history—likely the sixth century BCE—when the prophets were pushing Israel toward a far more universal understanding of its mission. Indeed, Isaiah 49:6 argued that Israel was a light to the nations specifically so that "my salvation may reach to the end of the earth" (Isa. 49:6).[21]

Earlier in its history the meaning of chosenness was exclusive, highly particularistic, and—as noted above—even tribal. The classic statement that "the LORD your God has chosen you out of all the peoples on earth to be his people, his treasured possession," stands at the end of a longer section calling for the complete and utter destruction of Israel's enemies. Here is the full text from Deuteronomy 7:1–6:

> When the LORD your God brings you into the land that you are about to enter and occupy, and he clears away many nations before you—the Hittites, the Girgashites, the Amorites, the Canaanites, the Perizzites, the Hivites, and the Jebusites, seven nations mightier and more numerous than you—and when the LORD your God gives them over to you and you defeat them, then you must utterly destroy them. Make no covenant with them and show them no mercy. Do not intermarry with them, giving your daughters to their sons or taking their daughters for your sons, for that would turn away your children from following me, to serve other gods. Then the anger of the LORD would be kindled against you, and he would destroy you quickly. But this is how you must deal with them: break down their altars, smash their pillars, hew down their sacred poles, and burn their idols with fire. For you are a people holy to the LORD your God; the LORD your God has chosen you out of all the peoples of the earth to be his people, his treasured possession.

A notable example of the destruction the Israelites wreaked on the Canaanite tribes when they entered the land God had promised them is the story of Israel's destruction of Jericho. According to the biblical account, God told Joshua, "See, I have handed Jericho over to you, along with its king and soldiers." Then, the soldiers of Israel marched around Jericho once a day for six days and seven times on the seventh day. When the priests of Israel blew on the ram's horn, the walls of Jericho fell, and the soldiers of Israel fell upon the city. The account concludes, "Then they devoted to destruction by the edge of the sword all in the city, both men and women, young and old, oxen, sheep, and donkeys" (Josh. 6:2–7:21).

Unfortunately, most of the modern nations that have appropriated the Hebrew metaphor of the chosen people have embraced the earlier tribal understanding, depicted in the Pentateuch (first five books of the Hebrew Bible), and have ignored the later, more universal understanding of chosenness that one finds in the Hebrew prophets, beginning with the eighth century BCE.

Thus, the New England Puritans embraced the myth of the chosen people—in large part because they imagined themselves so thoroughly Christian—and launched their wars of extermination against the Native Americans who resided in New England. Tellingly, the Puritans quite self-consciously re-enacted the early biblical saga, believing themselves the chosen people in a promised land, called to rid the land of its heathen tribes.

Later in the seventeenth century, a small group of Dutchmen—employees of the Dutch East India Company—settled on the southern tip of Africa and became the first of what would later become a sizable body of Afrikaners—Dutch, French, and Germans who made their home on the southernmost part of the African continent. Like the Puritans in New England, the Afrikaners were devoted to the Reformed expression of the Christian faith, a form of Christianity that can be traced to John Calvin in the sixteenth century. Like the Puritans, they also imagined themselves God's chosen people in a pagan land. And like the Puritans, they based their understanding of chosenness on the early Hebrew texts that exalted tribal domination. Armed with those understandings, they imposed on the native population a brutal system of apartheid and oppression. In a book he appropriately entitled *The Covenant*,[22] James Michener chronicled this saga, complete with its theological underpinnings in the early Hebrew myth of the chosen people.

In February 1899 the United States launched a war against the Philippines, a war designed to impose American domination over the Filipino people and American control over Filipino markets. By the time that war had ended, at least a quarter-million Filipino civilians were dead. In 1900—the year after the American invasion—Senator Albert Beveridge, a United States senator from Indiana and a man who considered himself a devout and serious Christian, explained to the Senate that the course on which the country had embarked was moral and right. After all, he said, God had "marked the American people as His chosen nation to finally lead in the redemption of the world." Here is a slightly fuller text of Beveridge's remarks on the floor of the United States Senate:

> God has not been preparing the English-speaking and Teutonic peoples for a thousand years for nothing but vain and idle self-contemplation and self-admiration. No. He made us master organizers of the world to establish system where chaos reigned. He has given us the spirit of progress to overwhelm the forces of reaction throughout the earth. He has made us adept in government that we may administer government among savage and senile peoples. Were it not for such a force as this the world would relapse into barbarism and night. And of all our race He has marked the American people as His chosen nation to finally lead in the redemption of the world.[23]

Some one hundred years later, some Christians made similar appeals in their defense of America's invasion of Iraq. In October 2004 the *Harrisburg Patriot News* (Pa.) published an editorial I wrote questioning why "so many evangelical Christians reject the killing of a fetus while, at the very same time, often give their complete support to the killing of adult human beings, so long as those killings are carried out in the name of the nation and inflicted on the nation's enemies."[24]

One respondent grounded her objection to my editorial squarely in her understanding of the metaphor of God's chosen people that dominates the Hebrew Bible. "You never mentioned the Old Testament," she complained, "where God led the Israelites into battle on many occasions. He wanted Israel to stamp out sin so it would not lead their sons and daughters astray. . . . When they obeyed Him in going to war, He always provided the victory." Based on that premise, she then presented the following picture of Jesus. "If you read the book of Revelation, you see an image of the godly Son of God (yes, the Lamb of God) ready to do vicious battle. He is not meek. He is not a pacifist. He is angry and powerful, and will wage war."[25] On that basis, she justified America's invasion and occupation of the sovereign nation of Iraq.

Chapter 2

THE WITNESS
of the Hebrew Bible

Americans can claim their country as a Christian nation if they wish, but to make that argument stick, they must somehow make it square with the Bible. For it makes no sense to hail the United States as a Christian nation while ignoring the only text that can ultimately define what "Christian" means.

As we have seen, only two biblical themes could conceivably support the notion of Christian America. One is the biblical vision of the chosen people—an idea we explored in the previous chapter. The other is the biblical vision of the kingdom of God. More than any other biblical concept, that is the theme by which we must measure the notion of Christian America.

In this chapter and the next, we will examine the biblical vision of the kingdom of God in great detail. We will discover that the kingdom of God motif is a powerful theme that appears virtually everywhere in Scripture— in the Hebrew Bible, especially the Hebrew prophets, as well as in every major section of the New Testament: the Gospels, the epistles of the apostle Paul, and even in the last book of the New Testament, the Apocalypse of John, often known as the Book of Revelation.

In this chapter, we will explore the vision of the kingdom or rule of God as it appears in the Hebrew

Bible. And in chapter 3, we will explore that theme as it appears in the New Testament.

As we make our journey through the Bible, those with eyes to see will quickly discern that the biblical vision of the kingdom of God stands in radical opposition to the traditional understanding of Christian America. I explained in the introductory chapter why that opposition is inevitable:

> The kingdom of God . . . and the nations of the earth . . . embody radically different values and reflect radically different orders of reality. The kingdom of God relies on the power of self-giving love while nations—even so-called "Christian" nations—rely on the power of coercion and the sword. For that reason, nations—even "Christian" nations—inevitably go to war against their enemies while the kingdom of God has no enemies at all. The kingdom of God is universal and those who promote that kingdom care deeply for every human being in every corner of the globe, regardless of race or nationality. But earthly nations—even so-called "Christian" nations—embrace values that are inevitably nationalistic and tribal, caring especially for the welfare of those within their borders. And while the kingdom of God exalts the poor, the disenfranchised, and the dispossessed, earthly nations inevitably exalt the rich and powerful and hold them up as models to be emulated. In fact, in the context of earthly nations—even so-called "Christian" nations—the poor seldom count for much at all.

We begin our discussion of the kingdom of God with a brief definition of that concept offered by the New Testament scholar John Dominic Crossan—a definition based on his reading of New Testament texts. Crossan writes that, according to the Bible,

> the kingdom of God was what this world would look like if and when God sat on Caesar's throne. . . . This is very clear in these parallel phrases of the Lord's Prayer in Matthew 6:10: "Your kingdom come. Your will be done, *on earth* as it is in heaven." The Kingdom of God is about the Will of God for this earth here below. . . . It is about the transformation of this world into holiness, not the evacuation of this world into heaven.[1]

Crossan's emphasis on the this-worldly dimension of the kingdom of God offers an important corrective for those Christians who denigrate this world and project the kingdom of God into an afterlife. Those who confine the kingdom of God to the afterlife base their understanding, to some degree at least, on the phrase, "kingdom of heaven"—a phrase that suggests to them that the kingdom of God is an otherworldly kingdom, virtually unrelated to the travails, the sorrows, and the politics of this earth.[2]

Regarding the phrase "kingdom of heaven," Crossan notes that, of the gospel writers, only Matthew employs that phrase and that, for him, "'Heaven' was simply a euphemism for 'God,' the Dwelling used interchangeably with the Dweller, as when we say, 'The White House announces' when we mean, 'The president announces.' In other words, 'Kingdom of Heaven' meant exactly the same as 'Kingdom of God.'"[3]

As we begin to examine the biblical concept of the kingdom of God, we shall see time and again that it heralds a world marked by two primary attributes: (1) equity and justice for all human beings, especially the poor, the marginalized, and the dispossessed, and (2) a world governed by peace and goodwill for all human beings. As Crossan has already told us, the kingdom of God is "what this world would look like if and when God sat on Caesar's throne."

But God does not sit on Caesar's throne and never has. Still, the Bible insists that the kingdom of God will one day triumph over all human governments, "the very best as well as the very worst," as the frontier preacher Alexander Campbell perceptively put it in 1830. Campbell simply meant that while the kingdom of God would subvert dictatorial nations and oppressive nations, it would also subvert democratic nations like the United States, for they also run on principles alien to the kingdom of God—violence, war, slavery, and economic injustice, for example.

Campbell's comment was radical in 1830 when many Americans, enamored as they were with American freedom and American potential, imagined that the United States was either the embodiment of the kingdom of God or would surely usher in the fullness of that kingdom in due time.[4] Campbell therefore reassured his patriotic American readers that they need not dread the kingdom's final triumph. "The admirers of American liberty and American institutions have no cause to regret such an event, nor cause to fear it," Campbell wrote. "It will be but the removing of a tent to build a temple—the falling of a cottage after the family are removed into a castle."[5]

Even though Campbell sought to reassure his American readers in the face of the coming kingdom, one fact remains, and that fact can hardly be reassuring to the nations of the world: The biblical vision of the kingdom of God is a subversive and countercultural vision, standing in radical opposition to empires, kingdoms, and nations that build their wealth and power on the backs of the poor and maintain their standing in the world through violence, war, injustice, and oppression. We will see exactly how radical that vision is when we begin to probe its most fundamental principles in the biblical text.

But before we do that, one more preliminary point remains. While the Bible presents the kingdom of God as (1) earthly, (2) concerned with peace and justice, and (3) future, it also presents that kingdom as partially present, even in the here and now. The kingdom is present wherever and whenever human beings carry out the mandates of God's rule. When human beings promote economic justice, especially for the poor, the kingdom of God is present. When human beings reject war and work for nonviolent solutions to national and tribal disputes, the kingdom of God is present. And when human beings work on behalf of policies that are favorable to the long-term health of this island planet, the kingdom of God is present, simply because the health of the planet is crucial for peace and justice among human beings. The following exploration of the kingdom of God in the biblical text will validate these claims.

The Kingdom of God in the Hebrew Bible

We want to begin our exploration of the kingdom of God by looking first at the Hebrew Bible, where the actual phrase "kingdom of God" never appears, but where the concept of the kingdom of God—that is, the rule of God—appears often.

One of the earliest and most important statements in the Hebrew Bible on the kingdom of God appears in I Samuel 8:4–22, where the elders of Israel pled with the prophet Samuel, "Appoint for us, then, a king to govern us, like other nations." When Samuel told the Lord about this request, the Lord told Samuel that the Israelites "have not rejected you, but they have rejected me from being king over them." God's statement in this text is terribly important, for it clearly indicates God's intention that the Hebrew nation would be, in fact, a "kingdom of God," ruled directly by God himself.

But what would that mean? How would a "kingdom of God" look different from the "other nations" upon whom Israel sought to pattern itself?

We get a clear indication of the contours of that kingdom when God had Samuel argue with Israel's elders by pointing out the inevitable outcomes of human rule: war, violence, and slavery. Thus, Samuel said:

> These will be the ways of the king who will rule over you: he
> will take your sons and appoint them to his chariots and to be his
> horsemen, and to run before his chariots; and he will appoint for
> himself commanders of thousands and commanders of fifties, and
> some to plow his ground and to reap his harvest, and to make his
> implements of war and the equipment of his chariots.

According to the text, "The people refused to listen to the voice of
Samuel; they said, 'No! but we are determined to have a king over
us, so that we also may be like other nations, and that our king
may govern us and go out before us and fight our battles.'" At that,
God gave in and said to Samuel, "Listen to their voice and set a
king over them."

In the context of the biblical vision of the kingdom of God, this
story is a crucially important metaphor, suggesting that the kingdom
of God would be both nonviolent and just, while human governments would inevitably practice both violence and oppression.

Under Solomon, Israel's third king, the truth of Samuel's words
became apparent, for Solomon controlled an empire that depended
on violence and oppression for its very existence. The text of I Kings
makes this clear:

> Solomon was sovereign over all the kingdoms from the Euphrates
> to the land of the Philistines, even to the border of Egypt; they
> brought tribute and served Solomon all the days of his life. Solo-
> mon's provision for one day was thirty cors of choice flour, and
> sixty cors of meal, ten fat oxen, and twenty pasture-fed cattle, one
> hundred sheep, besides deer, gazelles, roebucks, and fatted fowl.
> (4:21–23)

Of this stunning level of luxury that characterized the royal court,
Walter Brueggemann comments, "Then or now, eating that well
means food is being taken off the table of another."[6]

Further, "Solomon . . . had forty thousand stalls of horses for
his chariots" and conscripted twelve thousand horsemen to drive
his chariots of war (I Kings 4:26). And in order to build the temple
in Jerusalem, he "conscripted forced labor out of all Israel; the levy
numbered thirty thousand men" whom Solomon put to work in
Lebanon. (I Kings 5:13–14) But there was more:

> Solomon also had seventy thousand laborers and eighty thousand
> stonecutters in the hill country, besides Solomon's three thousand
> three hundred supervisors. . . . At the king's command, they quar-
> ried out great, costly stones in order to lay the foundation of the
> house with dressed stones. (I Kings 5:15–17)

Once again, Walter Brueggemann: "While the shift had no doubt begun and been encouraged by David, . . . the entire program of Solomon now appears to have been a self-serving achievement with its sole purpose the self-securing of king and dynasty."[7]

After Solomon, much of the history of Israel (the northern kingdom) and Judah (the southern kingdom)—according to the biblical text—is the history of wars those nations fought to maintain their imperial power, the oppression they levied against the poor to maintain the lifestyle of the ruling classes, and their misguided alliances with stronger kingdoms (e.g., Egypt and Assyria) as the Hebrew children slowly lost their dominance and vainly sought to defend themselves from slavery, death, and destruction.

In the eighth century BCE, a most remarkable development began to unfold. The Hebrew prophets from that time on increasingly returned to Samuel's vision of a kingdom ruled by God. These prophets raised serious questions about the viability, even the legitimacy, of waging war. They argued that neither violent warfare, nor military alliances, nor fortified cities had the power to save Israel and Judah from their enemies. They argued that only one path would save Israel from destruction, and that was the path of economic justice, especially for the poor who so often had been objects of abuse and exploitation.

When American Christians attempt to defend the United States as a latter-day chosen people, they typically ignore this prophetic literature and appeal instead to those sections of the Hebrew Bible that depict war, violence, and injustice—the very behavior the Hebrew prophets condemned. Because Israel and Judah waged war and killed and subjugated their enemies, they often argue, the Bible justifies this Christian nation—the United States—in doing the same.

But how would one know which of these two storylines should be taken as normative—the story of Israel the violent or the vision of Israel the just? This question can be especially acute for Christians who view the Bible as one-dimensional, flat, and entirely consistent with itself. But the Old Testament scholar Gordon Brubacher reminds us that "there is no such thing as *the* OT [Old Testament] witness." Brubacher elaborates as follows:

> The OT does not present a single, flat, monolithic "witness" to be extrapolated by balancing or synthesizing its various elements as found throughout. Instead, the OT presents an extended narrative journey, in which the destination is more important—more

authoritative and normative—than the beginning or the middle of that experience.[8]

And what particular books in the Hebrew Bible depict that destination? Again, Brubacher explains that the "new land, that destination for the journey, is proclaimed especially in a group of passages in Second Isaiah and in other, related, prophetic witness[es]." In other words, those sections of the Hebrew Bible that should carry especially normative weight for Christians are the Hebrew prophets, beginning in the eighth century BCE, for example, Isaiah, Jeremiah, Amos, Hosea, and Micah.

At this point, one more question begs for an answer: On what possible basis could we make the judgment that this late prophetic material should be more normative for Christians than, say, Leviticus or Deuteronomy? Once again, we turn to Brubacher who makes the logical assumption that the first and highest allegiance of Christians should be to Jesus. After all, Christians claim to be followers of Jesus, and have signified that allegiance by wearing his name. They call themselves *Christ*-ians.

The question, then, must be, to which sections of the Hebrew Bible did Jesus appeal as he sought to define his own ministry, identity, and sense of vocation? The answer, quite simply, is that Jesus appealed to those radical Hebrew prophets who rejected war and oppression and proclaimed, instead, nonviolence, peace, and justice. Not only did Jesus appeal to those prophets; he embodied their teachings in his own life and ministry. Brubacher thus concludes that Christians should "take Jesus as guide for deciding *which* stage of the OT journey constitutes the OT witness for the church today."[9]

John Dominic Crossan makes essentially the same point, though in a somewhat different way. Crossan vividly contrasts *human civilization*—which inevitably advocates peace through *victory*, on the one hand—with the *kingdom of God*, which always advocates peace through *justice*, on the other. He also points to the age-old struggle between the two.

It is striking, however, that Crossan wants us to see that this struggle between human civilization and the kingdom of God "is depicted *inside the Bible* itself." We witnessed that struggle, for example, when the Hebrews begged Samuel, "Appoint for us, then, a king to govern us, like other nations," and when God resisted but finally gave in to that request. Later in this chapter, we will witness that struggle again in the biblical texts that juxtapose just and peaceful Israel, on the one hand, with violent and oppressive Israel, on the other.

Crossan concludes, "The Christian Bible forces us to witness the struggle of these two transcendental visions *within its own pages* and to ask ourselves as Christians how we decide between them." Crossan's answer is essentially the same as Brubacher's: "My answer is that *we are bound to whichever of these visions was incarnated by and in the historical Jesus.*"[10]

The fact is, when Jesus defined his own mission, identity, and vocation, he never appealed to texts like the one in Deuteronomy 7 that commissioned Israel to "utterly destroy" the nations that lived in the land of Canaan. Nor did he appeal to texts like Joshua 6 that record how Israel "devoted to destruction by the edge of the sword all in the city [of Jericho], both men and women, young and old, oxen, sheep, and donkeys" (Josh. 6:21).

Instead, when Jesus sought to define his ministry, identity, and vocation, he used a text from Isaiah that reads as follows:

> The spirit of the Lord God is upon me, because the LORD has anointed me; he has sent me to bring good news to the oppressed, to bind up the brokenhearted, to proclaim liberty to the captives, and release to the prisoners; to proclaim the year of the LORD's favor, and the day of vengeance of our God; to comfort all who mourn. (Isa. 61:1–2)

Exactly how did Jesus use that passage? The Gospel of Luke records the following:

> When he [Jesus] came to Nazareth, where he had been brought up, he went to the synagogue on the Sabbath day, as was his custom. He stood up to read, and the scroll of the prophet Isaiah was given to him. He unrolled the scroll and found the place where it was written:
> The Spirit of the Lord is upon me,
> because he has anointed me to bring good news to the poor.
> He has sent me to proclaim release to the captives
> and recovery of sight to the blind,
> to let the oppressed go free,
> to proclaim the year of the Lord's favor.
> And he rolled up the scroll, gave it back to the attendant, and sat down. The eyes of all in the synagogue were fixed on him. Then he began to say to them, "Today this scripture has been fulfilled in your hearing." (Luke 4:16–21)

It is interesting that, while Jesus used Isaiah 61:1–2 as the basis for the proclamation of his vocation, he evidently declined to use one key phrase of that passage: "He has sent me . . . to proclaim . . . the day of vengeance of our God." Whatever else one might say about this omission, it is clear that Jesus focused this proclamation on issues of justice, not issues of vengeance.

The Gospels record only one other instance when Jesus defined the concerns that would characterize his mission, ministry, and vocation. Matthew reports that John the Baptist, languishing in prison, heard of the work Jesus was doing, and "sent word by his disciples and said to him, 'Are you the one who is to come, or are we to wait for another?'" Matthew further reports that Jesus replied, "Go and tell John what you hear and see: the blind receive their sight, the lame walk, the lepers are cleansed, the deaf hear, the dead are raised, and the poor have good news brought to them" (Matt. 11:2–5). In using these words, Jesus summarized another passage from Isaiah: "On that day the deaf shall hear the words of a scroll, and out of their gloom and darkness the eyes of the blind shall see. The meek shall obtain fresh joy in the LORD, and the neediest people shall exult in the Holy One of Israel" (29:18–19).

In proclaiming his mission, identity, and vocation in these ways, Jesus was lining out the contours of what he often called "the kingdom of God" or "the rule of God." But the Hebrew prophets who proclaimed the prophetic word beginning in the eighth century BCE had established the basic contours for that kingdom long before Jesus. Jesus' vision for the kingdom of God, therefore, was rooted and grounded in the prophetic imagination and stood squarely in the tradition of the Hebrew prophets.

We must now ask, how did the prophets understand the meaning of the kingdom of God? We mentioned earlier that two primary themes consistently define the kingdom of God in the biblical text, regardless of whether the kingdom vision appears in the Hebrew Bible, the Gospels of the New Testament, or the writings of the apostle Paul. Those two themes are peace and justice. And in the prophetic imagination, they often went hand in hand.

Justice As a Mark of the Kingdom of God

The Hebrew prophets who admonished Israel (the northern kingdom) and Judah (the southern kingdom) in the eighth and subsequent centuries BCE provide a graphic picture of the kingdom of

God through their vigorous demands for justice, especially for the poor, the widow, and the orphan.

In the entire Hebrew Bible, there is perhaps no more definitive statement on social justice than that of Amos who prophesied against Israel—the northern kingdom—during the eighth century BCE, most likely during the decade 760–750 BCE. His message was clear: because the ruling elites of Israel oppressed the poor and crushed the needy, the Assyrians would take Israel into captivity. That, of course, is exactly what happened in 721 BCE.

What follows are several passages that I have pulled together from chapters 3, 4, 5, and 6 of the book of Amos—passages that unambiguously demonstrate the depth of God's concern for the poor in any society. The combined text that follows is lengthy, but well worth reading in its entirety.

- They do not know how to do right, says the LORD, those who store up violence and robbery in their strongholds. Therefore thus says the Lord GOD: An adversary shall surround the land, and strip you of your defense; and your strongholds shall be plundered. (3:10–11)
- Hear this word, you cows of Bashan who are on Mount Samaria, who oppress the poor, who crush the needy, who say to their husbands, "Bring something to drink!" The Lord GOD has sworn by his holiness: The time is surely coming upon you, when they shall take you away with hooks, even the last of you with fishhooks. (4:1–2)
- Therefore because you trample on the poor and take from them levies of grain, you have built houses of hewn stone, but you shall not live in them; you have planted pleasant vineyards, but you shall not drink their wine. For I know how many are your transgressions, and how great are your sins— you who afflict the righteous, who take a bribe, and push aside the needy in the gate. (5:11–12)
- Alas for those who lie on beds of ivory, and lounge on their couches, and eat lambs from the flock, and calves from the stall; who sing idle songs to the sound of the harp, and like David improvise on instruments of music; who drink wine from bowls, and anoint themselves with the finest oils, but are not grieved over the ruin of Joseph! Therefore they shall now be the first to go into exile, and the revelry of the loungers shall pass away. (6:4–7)

Amos also argued that when people practice social injustice, their worship is an abomination to God. Thus, in Amos 5:21–23,

Amos records God speaking directly to Israel in these harsh and uncompromising words:

> I hate, I despise your festivals, and I take no delight in your solemn assemblies. Even though you offer me your burnt offerings and grain offerings, I will not accept them; and the offerings of well-being of your fatted animals I will not look upon. Take away from me the noise of your songs; I will not listen to the melody of your harps. But let justice roll down like waters, and righteousness like an ever-flowing stream.

Oracles from the book of Isaiah, reflecting the late sixth century BCE, picked up on this very same theme. Here, however, the prophet directed his critique not against the northern kingdom of Israel but against the southern kingdom of Judah. Like Amos, who claimed that fairness and equity were more important to God than worship and sacrifice, this text critiqued Judah's religious fasts, claiming that the fast God really desired was the fast of justice.

Especially pertinent for our purposes is the clear connection this text from Isaiah makes between social justice and national well-being. Judah had by then returned from Babylonian captivity, and Isaiah argued that if Judah would feed the hungry, care for the homeless, and clothe the naked, "Your ancient ruins shall be rebuilt; you shall raise up the foundations of many generations; you shall be called the repairer of the breach, the restorer of streets to live in." This passage, like the earlier text from Amos, is lengthy, but bears so directly on our topic that it deserves to be quoted in full:

> Is not this the fast that I choose; to loose the bonds of injustice, to undo the thongs of the yoke, to let the oppressed go free, and to break every yoke? Is it not to share your bread with the hungry, and bring the homeless poor into your house; when you see the naked, to cover them, and not to hide yourself from your own kin? Then your light shall break forth like the dawn, and your healing shall spring up quickly; your vindicator shall go before you, the glory of the LORD shall be your rear guard. . . . If you offer your food to the hungry and satisfy the needs of the afflicted, then your light shall rise in the darkness and your gloom be like the noonday. The LORD will guide you continually, and satisfy your needs in parched places, and make your bones strong; and you shall be like a watered garden, like a spring of water, whose waters never fail. Your ancient ruins shall be rebuilt; you shall raise up the foundations of many generations; you shall be called the repairer of the breach, the restorer of streets to live in. (Isa. 58:6–8, 10–12)

Another classic prophetic passage demanding social justice comes from Micah, who prophesied against the southern kingdom of Judah during the eighth century BCE when Judah faced the very real possibility of invasion by the Assyrian army and subsequent exile. Like Amos, Micah used strong and graphic words to condemn the way Judah's rulers and elites enriched themselves on the backs of the poor. In fact, he depicted Judah's rulers as cannibals who boiled the poor in cauldrons and then ate their flesh.

> And I said: Listen, you heads of Jacob and rulers of the house of Israel! Should you not know justice?—
> you who hate the good and love the evil, who tear the skin off my people, and flesh off their bones;
> who eat the flesh of my people, flay their skin off them, break their bones in pieces, and chop them up like meat in a kettle, like flesh in a cauldron. (3:1–3)

Precisely because Judah's rulers rejected justice for the sake of personal gain, Micah envisioned the day when the Assyrians would swarm over the land and destroy the nation.

> Hear this, you rulers of the house of Jacob and chiefs of the house of Israel, who abhor justice and pervert all equity, who build Zion with blood and Jerusalem with wrong!
> Therefore, because of you Zion shall be plowed as a field; Jerusalem shall become a heap of ruins. (3:9–10, 12)

These oracles typify the message preached by virtually all the Hebrew prophets who proclaimed God's will to the Hebrew people beginning in the eighth century BCE.

We now must ask, what do all these passages have to do with the kingdom of God? Two prophetic passages make that connection especially clear—one from Micah and one from Isaiah.

Though Micah railed against the injustices entrenched in Judah, he was not without hope, for he envisioned a whole new kingdom that he described as "the mountain of the Lord," clearly a synonym for the kingdom of God.

> In the days to come the mountain of the LORD's house shall be established as the highest of the mountains, and shall be raised up above the hills. Peoples shall stream to it, and many nations shall come and say: "Come, let us go up to the mountain of the LORD, to the house of the God of Jacob; that he may teach us his ways and that we may walk in his paths." (4:1–2)

According to Micah, two qualities would define the essence of that kingdom: peace and justice. Thus, he proclaimed:

> For out of Zion shall go forth instruction, and the word of the LORD from Jerusalem. He shall judge between many peoples, and shall arbitrate between strong nations far away; they shall beat their swords into plowshares, and their spears into pruning hooks; nation shall not lift up sword against nation, neither shall they learn war any more. (4:2–3)

Isaiah, too, made explicit the connection between social justice and the kingdom of God, for he envisioned a time when Judah would, in fact, become that kingdom—a kingdom defined not by ritual, but by justice, and a kingdom whose ruler would judge the poor and meek with equity and compassion. Further, Isaiah argued that justice embraced by that kingdom would bring peace to the earth. In the entire Bible, there is no more compelling description of the kingdom of God than this:

> A shoot shall come out from the stump of Jesse, and a branch shall grow out of his roots. The spirit of the LORD shall rest on him, the spirit of wisdom and understanding, the spirit of counsel and might, the spirit of knowledge and the fear of the LORD. His delight shall be in the fear of the LORD. He shall not judge by what his eyes see, or decide by what his ears hear; but with righteousness he shall judge the poor, and decide with equity for the meek of the earth; he shall strike the earth with the rod of his mouth, and with the breath of his lips he shall kill the wicked. Righteousness shall be the belt around his waist, and faithfulness the belt around his loins. The wolf shall live with the lamb, the leopard shall lie down with the kid, the calf and the lion and the fatling together, and a little child shall lead them. The cow and the bear shall graze, their young shall lie down together; and the lion shall eat straw like the ox. The nursing child shall play over the hole of the asp, and the weaned child shall put its hand on the adder's den. They will not hurt or destroy on all my holy mountain; for the earth will be full of the knowledge of the LORD as the water covers the sea. (11:1–9)

Many Christians take this powerful description of the coming kingdom of God as a prediction of the Messiah—the one they call Jesus the Christ. Whether they are correct in that claim is another question for another place and another time. But one thing is clear: If Christians believe this passage predicts their Messiah, then one would think they would read the entire Hebrew Bible through the lens of texts like this rather than texts that advocate violence, war, and the destruction of the enemies of the chosen people of God. In truth, the prophets portrayed a nonviolent kingdom, devoted to peace throughout all the earth, as we shall now discover.

Peace As a Mark of the Kingdom of God

When one moves from the Pentateuch to the prophetic literature of the eighth century BCE and later, one has come a very long way on the issue of war and peace. While the Pentateuch sanctioned violence, war, and death against Israel's enemies, the prophets proclaimed the way of peace. Already we have seen strong hints of this transition in Micah—"They shall beat their swords into plowshares, and their spears into pruning hooks; nation shall not lift up sword against nation, neither shall they learn war any more" (4:3)—and in Isaiah—"The wolf shall live with the lamb, the leopard shall lie down with the kid, the calf and the lion and the fatling together, and a little child shall lead them" (11:6).

The reason for this transition is not difficult to find: Violence and war simply did not work. As Gordon Brubacher notes,

> The military defense option . . . rarely worked despite the massive resources invested. A determined army usually succeeded in the end. The fact that even the powerfully fortified cities of the Northern and Southern Kingdoms fell to attack and thus failed in their purpose is a matter of record in the archaeological remains.[11]

Among the eighth-century prophets, none was more insistent that the way of war did not work than Hosea. But Hosea placed that argument in a much larger context. Hosea harked back to Samuel's dispute with the elders of Israel who demanded a human king and rejected the rule of God. As we recall, the elders told Samuel, "We are determined to have a king over us, so that we also may be like other nations, and that our king may govern us and go out before us and fight our battles" (I Sam. 8:19–20).

Now in the eighth century BCE, with the Assyrian threat looming large over the northern kingdom, Hosea tweaked the Israelites with these biting words: "I will destroy you, O Israel; who can help you? Where now is your king, that he may save you? Where in all your cities are your rulers, of whom you said, 'Give me a king and rulers'" (13:9–10)? Hosea, therefore, based his claim that war did not work on the supporting claim that long, long ago, Israel had exchanged the rule of God—that is, the kingdom of God—for a human kingdom and human rulers who placed their trust in war, violence, and military might. But, Hosea warned, naming an earthly king was counterproductive.

> Because you have trusted in your power and in the multitude of your warriors, therefore the tumult of war shall rise against your people, and all your fortresses shall be destroyed, as Shalman destroyed Beth-arbel on the day of battle when mothers were dashed in pieces with their children. (10:13–14)

Based on the premise that war does not work and that human kingdoms are deeply flawed, virtually all the later Hebrew prophets became proponents of peace, and they did so in the context of their vision of the coming kingdom of God.

Perhaps the best-known text that makes this point is Isaiah 9:6–7, another passage Christians like to claim as a prophecy of the coming Christ and the passage that inspired George Frideric Handel to compose the classic musical score "The Messiah" in 1741.

> For a child has been born for us, a son given to us; authority rests upon his shoulders; and he is named Wonderful Counselor, Mighty God, Everlasting Father, Prince of Peace. His authority shall grow continually, and there shall be endless peace for the throne of David and his kingdom. He will establish and uphold it with justice and with righteousness from this time onward and forevermore.

This passage is profoundly a rejection of war and an affirmation of peace and peacemaking in the context of a radically new kingdom with a new and different kind of ruler—a "Prince of Peace." Indeed, if we pick up the verse that immediately precedes the phrase, "For a child has been born to us," the passage reads:

> For all the boots of the tramping warriors and all the garments rolled in blood shall be burned as fuel for the fire. For a child has been born for us, a son given to us; authority rests upon his shoulders, and he is named Wonderful Counselor, Mighty God, Everlasting Father, Prince of Peace. (9:5–6)

Zechariah picked up this very same theme of a radically new kind of ruler but did so with fresh and fascinating imagery. This king would make his appearance not in a chariot of steel but on a donkey, and his power would lie not in military might but in humility. Indeed, this ruler would abolish war throughout the earth. Here is the actual text:

Rejoice greatly, O daughter Zion! Shout aloud, O daughter Jerusalem! Lo, your king comes to you; triumphant and victorious is
he, humble and riding on a donkey, on a colt, the foal of a donkey.
He will cut off the chariot from Ephraim and the war-horse from
Jerusalem; and the battle bow shall be cut off, and he shall command peace to the nations; his dominion shall be from sea to sea,
and from the River to the ends of the earth. (9:9–10)

Regarding this text, John Dominic Crossan has observed:

Like any city of the ancient world, Jerusalem knew that a conqueror entered it at best through opened gates and at worst through
shattered walls. In either case, he came on a battle chariot or war
horse. But [here] . . . the prophet imagines this anti-triumphal future entrance of the Messiah on a donkey.[12]

In the New Testament, Matthew made much of this passage,
interpreting Jesus as the radically new ruler who exchanged chariots
of war for a donkey. Thus,

Jesus sent two disciples, saying to them, "Go into the village
ahead of you, and immediately you will find a donkey tied, and a
colt with her; untie them and bring them to me. . . ." This took
place to fulfill what had been spoken through the prophet, saying,
"Tell the daughter of Zion, Look, your king is coming to you,
humble, and mounted on a donkey, and on a colt, the foal of a
donkey." The disciples went and did as Jesus had directed them;
they brought the donkey and the colt, and put their cloaks on them,
and he sat on them. A very large crowd spread their cloaks on the
road, and others cut branches from the trees and spread them on
the road. The crowds that went ahead of him and that followed
were shouting, "Hosanna to the Son of David! Blessed is the one
who comes in the name of the Lord." (21:1–9)

When one compares Zechariah's description of this new kind of
ruler—the coming "Prince of Peace"—with Samuel's description
of human rulers, we get an extraordinary glimpse into the radical
difference between human kingdoms and the kingdom of God. We
have already seen that when Israel pled for a king in order to be like
other nations, Samuel warned

These will be the ways of the king who will reign over you: he
will take your sons and appoint them to his chariots and to be his
horsemen, and to run before his chariots; and he will appoint for
himself commanders of thousands and commanders of fifties, and
some . . . to make his implements of war and the equipment of his
chariots. (I Sam. 8:11–12)

But the ruler whom Zechariah described would "cut off the chariot from Ephraim and the war-horse from Jerusalem; and the battle bow shall be cut off, and he shall command peace to the nations; his dominion shall be from sea to sea, and from the River to the ends of the earth."

Not only did the prophets of the eighth and subsequent centuries proclaim peace, they also proclaimed *peacemaking*, and they expected God's people—those who belonged to the kingdom of God—to serve as peacemakers. We find in the prophetic literature three ways in which peace should be pursued.

Over and again the prophets insisted that the first and most important tool for peacemaking was the pursuit of justice. Jeremiah, for example, wrote:

> Thus says the LORD: Act with justice and righteousness, and deliver from the hand of the oppressor anyone who has been robbed. And do no wrong or violence to the alien, the orphan, and the widow, or shed innocent blood in this place. For if you will indeed obey this word, then through the gates of this house shall enter kings who sit on the throne of David, riding in chariots and on horses, they and their servants, and their people. (Jer. 22:3–4)

On the other hand, Jeremiah warned, "If you will not heed these words, I swear by myself, says the LORD, that this house shall become a desolation" (22:5).

No single prophet made the point that the path of justice was the path of peace more clearly and succinctly than Isaiah: "The effect of righteousness [justice] will be peace, and the result of righteousness [justice], quietness and trust forever. My people will abide in a peaceful habitation, in secure dwellings, and in quiet resting places." (32:17–18)

Isaiah offered an extended commentary on this point in a passage we have already cited.

> Is not this the fast that I choose; to loose the bonds of injustice, to undo the thongs of the yoke, to let the oppressed go free, and to break every yoke? Is it not to share your bread with the hungry, and bring the homeless poor into your house; when you see the naked, to cover them, and not to hide yourself from your own kin? Then . . . your ancient ruins shall be rebuilt; you shall raise up the foundations of many generations; you shall be called the repairer of the breach, the restorer of streets to live in. (Isa. 58:6–7, 12)

The second path to peace is the most obvious path imaginable, though it is one that was seldom tried in ancient Israel and one that is seldom tried today: refuse to fight. Jeremiah made that option central to the message he proclaimed to the southern kingdom on the eve of the Babylonian invasion of Judah and subsequent exile of its people—developments that occurred in 586 BCE. Jeremiah claimed he was setting before the Hebrews "the way of life and the way of death." The way of death was military resistance; the way of life was surrender.

> Thus says the LORD: See, I am setting before you the way of life and the way of death. Those who stay in this city shall die by the sword, by famine, and by pestilence; but those who go out and surrender to the Chaldeans [Babylonians] who are besieging you shall have their lives as a prize of war. (21:8–9)

Jeremiah repeated the same message in a later chapter:

> Bring your necks under the yoke of the king of Babylon, and serve him and his people, and live. Why should you and your people die by the sword, by famine, and by pestilence, as the LORD has spoken concerning any nation that will not serve the king of Babylon? (27:12–13)

In the midst of that calamity, some self-styled prophets urged Judah to resist, but Jeremiah argued that Judah should reject those preachers as false prophets and preachers of death.

> Do not listen to the words of the prophets who are telling you not to serve the king of Babylon, for they are prophesying a lie to you. I have not sent them, says the LORD, but they are prophesying falsely in my name, with the result that I will drive you out and you will perish, you and the prophets who are prophesying to you. (27:14–15)

The context makes it clear that resisting Babylon was resisting God, since God had already decreed that Babylon would take Judah captive as a punishment for its sins against the powerless and the poor. But Gordon Brubacher notes that something else was at work here as well.

> The value here was on human life rather than on ego, or on some ephemeral appeal to "freedom." Also, by implication, the value was on re-allocating massive defense budgets and human resources from military use to the well-being of the general population. However, this option did not come naturally to people in power, for it had a certain cost in treasure, humility, and loss of face. Moreover, this response took no little faith or trust in God, no small commitment to obedience despite the cost. So it was easier said than

done and rarely tried at all, whether in the biblical world or in any other place or time.[13]

Finally, the prophets encouraged God's people to work for peace by praying for their enemies. Thus, Jeremiah encouraged the Jews to "seek the welfare of the [enemy] city where I have sent you into exile, and pray to the LORD on its behalf, for in its welfare you will find your welfare" (29:7)—a recommendation that points us in the direction of Jesus' advice, recorded in the Gospel of Matthew: "Love your enemies and pray for those who persecute you" (5:44).

The Hebrew prophets consistently portrayed the kingdom of God as a radical alternative to politics as usual—to peace and prosperity maintained through war, violence, and oppression. For the most part, they portrayed the kingdom of God as an alternative to conventional politics *within their own nation*.

By the second century BCE, the notion of the kingdom of God took on even more profoundly political overtones. Some in Israel now began to argue that the kingdom of God would transform not only the Jewish nation but would defeat all the empires of the earth and would nurture both peace and justice until the end of time.

The immediate context for this new understanding of the kingdom of God was the reign of Antiochus Epiphanes, a Syrian who ruled over Israel from 175 to 164 BCE. Antiochus Epiphanes sought to force Greek culture on the Jews, a move that stood squarely in the Hellenizing tradition of Alexander the Great. This man whose name, "Epiphanes," meant "God made manifest," forbade Jewish religious practice, dedicated the temple in Jerusalem to Zeus, erected in the temple an altar to Zeus, and defiled the temple in a variety of ways.

Against that backdrop, the book of Daniel appeared sometime between 167 and 164 BCE and used the metaphor of the kingdom of God to stand in judgment on the imperial politics of Antiochus Epiphanes. An example of apocalyptic literature—the only example in the Hebrew Bible—the book of Daniel employed human history not to report on facts, but to interpret current events.

In that context, it told a story about King Nebuchadnezzar, who ruled Babylon some 400 years before. In this story, the king dreamed of a great statue whose head was of gold, its chest and arms of silver, its middle and thighs of bronze, its legs of iron, and its feet partly of iron and partly of clay. Then, as the dream continued,

A stone was cut out, not by human hands, and it struck the statue on its feet of iron and clay and broke them in pieces. Then the iron, the clay, the bronze, the silver, and the gold, were all broken in pieces and became like the chaff of the summer threshing floors, and the wind carried them away, so that not a trace of them could be found. But the stone that struck the statue became a great mountain and filled the whole earth. (2:34–35)

Puzzled by this dream, Nebuchadnezzar sought an interpretation from Daniel who told the king that "you [and by extension, the Babylonian empire] are the head of gold," but that his kingdom would be followed by three others—one of silver, one of bronze, and one of iron. Finally, Daniel offered this interpretation:

The God of heaven will set up a kingdom that shall never be destroyed, nor shall this kingdom be left to another people. It shall crush all these kingdoms and bring them to an end, and it shall stand forever; just as you saw that a stone was cut from the mountain not by hands, and that it crushed the iron, the bronze, the clay, the silver, and the gold. (2:44–45)

If we keep in mind what we have learned about the kingdom of God to this point, we will be in a better position to understand Daniel's interpretation. As we have worked our way through the prophetic literature of the Hebrew Bible, we have learned that the kingdom of God is a kingdom of justice, especially for the powerless and the poor, and a kingdom that always trumps the violence of this earth with the peace of God. Daniel takes that vision to a new level and suggests that the kingdom of God will finally subvert the violent and oppressive empires of this earth and stand forever.

That understanding of the kingdom of God is precisely the vision at work in the Christian New Testament, for author after author and book after book employ the just and peaceful kingdom of God as a radical alternative to the violent and oppressive Roman Empire—a theme that will become apparent as we turn our attention first to the Gospels, then to the letters of the apostle Paul, and finally to the Apocalypse of John, otherwise known as the book of Revelation.

Chapter 3

THE WITNESS
of the New Testament

Of all the biblical concepts that advocates of Christian America fail to grasp, the most important is the biblical vision of the kingdom of God. If they had any comprehension of that notion at all, they would abandon their claim that America is a Christian nation.

The kingdom of God is one of the central themes in the New Testament text, and the phrases "kingdom of God" and "kingdom of heaven"—phrases that have the very same meaning, as we saw in the previous chapter—appear there some one hundred times. The mere frequency of those phrases suggests that it may well be impossible to grasp the overall message of the New Testament text unless one first comes to terms with the meaning of the kingdom of God.

The same two ideas that stood at the heart of the kingdom of God motif in the Hebrew Bible also stand at the heart of the kingdom of God ideal in the New Testament. Those two ideas, as we know by now, are the themes of peace and justice. The vision of peace looms large in the New Testament text, as when Jesus—for example—counsels his followers, "Blessed are the peacemakers, for they will be called children of God" (Matt. 5:9), or when he tells them, "Love your enemies and pray for those who persecute you" (Matt. 5:44), or when the apostle Paul writes, "Do not repay anyone evil for evil, but . . . live peaceably with all" (Rom. 12:17–18).

What must be said about the theme of social and economic justice in the New Testament's presentation of the kingdom of God is this: In almost every instance where the phrase "kingdom of God" appears in the New Testament, it is closely linked to concern for the poor, the dispossessed, those in prison, the maimed, the lame, the blind, and all those who suffer at the hands of the world's elites. In other words, the kingdom of God is where the powerless are empowered, where the hungry are fed, where the sick are healed, where the poor are sustained, and where those who find themselves marginalized by the rulers of this world are finally offered both equality and justice.

There is therefore great continuity between the vision of the kingdom of God in the Hebrew prophets and the vision of the kingdom of God in the New Testament. And Jesus—the founder of the Christian religion and the centerpiece of the New Testament text—stood squarely in that prophetic tradition.

But two additional ideas characterize the meaning of the kingdom of God in the New Testament text. Donald Kraybill put his finger on the first of those ideas—the paradoxical dimensions of the kingdom of God—in a book he entitled *The Upside-Down Kingdom*.[1] Simply put, the kingdom of God is that kingdom where the poor and the weak are exalted while the rich and the powerful are brought low; where one achieves greatness not by pursuing success, ambition, and self-interest, but by emptying one's self on behalf of others; where the wise are foolish and the foolish are wise; and where one preserves and enhances one's life not by pursuing health, wealth, and success, but by dying to self so that others might live.

Put another way, the kingdom of God requires what most human beings would never anticipate, what most would view as nonsense, and what most, therefore, would tend to resist. Thus, when we think success lies straight ahead, the kingdom of God takes us backward. When we think we need to go up, the kingdom of God takes us down. And when we think we can meet our goals by going in one direction, the kingdom of God takes us in quite another. This is why the kingdom of God is so fundamentally paradoxical.

In our analysis of the Hebrew Bible, we saw hints of this paradoxical dimension of the kingdom of God when, for example, Zechariah told of the king who would ride on the donkey. But in the New Testament, especially in the teachings of Jesus, the theme of paradox emerges full-blown.

The Kingdom of God and the (American) Empire

The fourth theme central to the New Testament's understanding of the kingdom of God is this: When the New Testament uses the phrase "kingdom of God," the context is almost always a struggle between the reign or rule of God on behalf of the poor and the dispossessed, on the one hand, and the empires of this world that serve powerful and privileged elites on the other. Indeed, the kingdom of God—as the New Testament presents that vision—offers a radical alternative to imperial regimes. This is why Donald Kraybill describes that alternative with the adjective *upside-down*, since the kingdom of God *always* exalts the *poor* at the expense of the rich, the *powerless* at the expense of the powerful, and the *weak* at the expense of the strong.[2]

The immediate context for what the New Testament says about the kingdom of God was the first-century world ruled by imperial Rome. In that world, there was no middle class, but only rich and poor, the elites and the dispossessed. The elites, who comprised only 3 percent of the population, aligned themselves with the imperial power, while everyone else fell in the remaining 97 percent. The world defined by imperial Rome, therefore, was a world that exalted the rich at the expense of the poor, the powerful at the expense of the powerless, and the strong at the expense of the weak.

Precisely for that reason, the New Testament consistently views the empire as the arch-villain in the biblical drama. After all, the empire consistently built its wealth and power on the backs of those for whom the New Testament expresses the greatest concern—the powerless and the poor. And then, in a perverse inversion of biblical values, the emperor—the one who sponsored the wars of oppression against the poor across the then-known world—claimed to be savior and god. These are the conclusions of some of the best and most recent New Testament scholarship—the work, for example, of Warren Carter, Richard Horsley, Neil Asher Silberman, Barbara Rossing, John Dominic Crossan, Jonathan L. Reed, and others.[3] Horsley and Silberman, for example, frame the issue like this:

> In Roman eyes, the emperor—as the object of elaborate ceremonies of public veneration and the subject of wondrous tales of miracu-

lous birth, charmed childhood, and divine ordination for imperial power—was the larger-than-life figure to whom all the empire's subjects were trained to look for guidance and to whom every knee was required to bend.

But "no believing Christian," these scholars point out, "could possibly accept any of this Augustan propaganda." As they explain,

> For them, Rome was the Beast, the Harlot, the Dragon, Babylon, the Great Satan. They knew that Rome's empire was made possible not by divine order but by the acquisition of vast territories through . . . deadly violence. . . . They knew that, step by step, the Romans had bullied, invaded, and eventually occupied all the lands around the Mediterranean, arrogantly assigning formerly independent peoples roles as clients or servants in their larger imperial schemes.

Against this backdrop, the Christian narrative, embodied in four versions—Matthew, Mark, Luke, and John—"described a different kind of Kingdom that would harbor no violence, inequality, or injustice—nor tolerate the arrogance of earthly emperors, rich men, and kings."[4] This is why Horsley writes:

> Trying to understand Jesus . . . without knowing how Roman imperialism determined the conditions of life in Galilee and Jerusalem would be like trying to understand Martin Luther King without knowing how slavery, reconstruction, and segregation determined the lives of African Americans in the United States.[5]

If we wish to consider the validity of the concept of Christian America, then, this struggle between empire and the kingdom of God—a struggle played out on the very pages of Christian scripture—is a crucial consideration, especially since the United States has now become an imperial power.

An American Empire?

I am aware that many Americans are reluctant to concede the imperial status of the United States, for after all, the United States is not an empire in any traditional sense. Unlike ancient Rome, it does not seek to rule the world by military occupation of all its client states. And unlike European empires of days gone by, it has no "colonies."

But there is another reason so many Americans are loath to admit to America's imperial status: The values for which this nation stands strike most Americans as universal "self-evident truths," to borrow a phrase from the Declaration of Independence. Most Americans, for example, imagine democracy to be a universal value, grounded in a grand design for the whole human race. In contrast, most Americans envision empires as sinister regimes that impose on other nations ideas, lifestyles, and systems of government that are *alien* to the subjugated countries.

Thus, when the United States seeks to export democracy, as it did during its occupation of Iraq, Americans are reluctant to discern—and eager to deny—any imperial designs on the part of their own nation. Instead, they widely regard such efforts as fundamentally benevolent. One of the classic statements of America as a benevolent empire appeared in Ronald Steel's book, *Pax Americana*, published in 1967, at the height of the Vietnam War. Steel acknowledged that the United States was an imperial power but insisted that America was "engaged in a kind of welfare imperialism, empire building for noble ends rather than for such base motives as profit and influence." Indeed, he argued, America intervenes in the world only with "the most noble motives and with the most generous impulses."[6]

That view has long been the norm for assessing the global power and influence of the United States. Thus, Ronald Reagan argued in 1983, "We're not in the business of imperialism, aggression, or conquest. We threaten no one."[7] More recently, neoconservatives Richard Perle and David Frum wrote of the war on terror and America's occupation of Iraq, "America's vocation is not an imperial vocation. Our vocation is to support justice with power." President George W. Bush concurred. In a speech delivered at West Point in June 2002, the president flatly declared, "We don't seek an empire." And to a foreign reporter who asked about American "empire-building," Secretary of Defense Donald Rumsfeld responded, "We don't seek empires. We're not imperialistic. We never have been. I can't imagine why you'd even ask the question."[8]

But benevolence is in the eye of the beholder. When the president of the United States declares, as he did in his Second Inaugural Address, that "the policy of the United States [is] to seek and support the growth of democratic movements and institutions *in every nation and culture* [italics mine],"[9] he thereby announces the nation's intent to bring the world under the sway of American ideals. Further, when the United States seeks to export democracy, it inevitably seeks to export a *particular vision* of reality, colored by American concerns and American presuppositions, which may be entirely foreign—and may even seem subversive—to other nations and other cultures in other parts of the world. At the very least, those nations rightly discern in such efforts what so many Americans fail to see, namely, a considerable degree of American self-interest.

Indeed, the United States has long sought to reshape the world into its own image. It has done so through military power, economic power, and cultural transformation. It has done so by propping up dictators friendly to American interests (e.g., Ngo Dinh Diem in South Vietnam). And it has done so by attempting to overthrow governments opposed to American interests (e.g., Jacobo Arbenz in Guatemala, Fidel Castro in Cuba, Salvador Allende in Chile, and the Sandinista government in Nicaragua).

But all those operations preceded the tragic events of September 11, 2001—events that prompted the United States to proclaim its right to engage in preemptive war. The Bush administration issued that proclamation in a historic document entitled "The National Security Strategy of the United States," released on September 20, 2002, roughly one year after the attacks of September 11, 2001. That document did not mince words: "While the United States will constantly strive to enlist the support of the international community, we will not hesitate to act alone, if necessary, to exercise our right of selfdefense [sic] by acting preemptively against such terrorists, to prevent them from doing harm against our people and our country."[10] In the view of former vice-president Al Gore, that proclamation included the "unilateral U.S. right to ignore international law wherever it wished to do so and [to] take military action against any nation, even in circumstances where there was no imminent threat."[11]

"The National Security Strategy of the United States" further argued that the United States must maintain global military dominance: "Our forces will be strong enough to dissuade potential adversaries from pursuing a military build-up in hopes of surpassing, or equaling, the power of the United States."[12] That aspiration rested, in turn, on the presupposition that the United States should deter "potential competitors from *even aspiring* [italics mine] to a larger regional or global role"—an objective spelled out in a document entitled "Defense Planning Guidance," written by Paul Wolfowitz and Dick Cheney in 1992, almost ten full years before the tragedy of 9/11.[13]

Cheney and Wolfowitz were key players in a neoconservative movement that emerged as the Cold War ended, leaving the United States as the world's lone superpower. Essentially, the neoconservatives argued that the United States should exploit its window of opportunity for the sake of global dominance. Charles Krautham-mer, for example, argued that the United States should lay down "the rules of world order" and "enforce them."[14] The alternative to American dominance, he thought, would be global "chaos."[15]

As David Ray Griffin points out, the first important document to attempt to transform that kind of neoconservative thinking into national policy was the Cheney-Wolfowitz document mentioned above: "Defense Planning Guidance."[16] Andrew Bacevich's seminal book, *American Empire*, called that document "a blueprint for per-manent American hegemony."[17] That blueprint was important since it provided the ideological foundation for the official document published by the Bush administration ten years later: "National Security Strategy of the United States."

In the late 1980s and early 1990s, few were willing to em-brace the neoconservatives' prescription for American global domi-nance. But as David Ray Griffin points out, many neoconservatives viewed the tragedy of 9/11 as a moment of opportunity.[18] For Donald Rumsfeld, 9/11 offered "the kind of opportunities that World War II offered, to refashion the world."[19] And, indeed, the language of opportunity runs throughout the "National Security Strategy of the United States." That document viewed the post-9/11 situation as "an historic opportunity to preserve the peace," "a moment of opportunity to extend the benefits of freedom across the globe," and "the opportunity to further freedom's triumph over all . . . [its] foes."[20] Above all, 9/11 offered neoconservatives the opportunity they needed to urge implementation of their recommendations for unrivaled American dominance in the world. That implementation began with the doctrine of preemptive war.

The proclamation on preemptive war that appeared in the "National Security Strategy of the United States" put the world on notice that the United States would deal swiftly and decisively with nations that challenged American interests and American security anywhere in the world. In this way, the United States erected an empire implemented not so much by occupation as by intimidation. Then, to put teeth into that threat, the United States did invade and occupy the sovereign nation of Iraq, a nation that— as the world now knows—posed no imminent threat to the United States whatsoever.

As the United States prepared to launch its preemptive strike against Iraq, foreign observers discerned what most Americans were not prepared to see, namely, that this country had, indeed, become an empire, comparable in certain ways to ancient Rome. Thus, the British newspaper the *Guardian* asked the rhetorical question "Is America the New Rome?"[21]

Some Americans discerned that point as well. Joseph Nye, Harvard professor and assistant secretary of defense under President Bill Clinton, observed in 2003, "Not since Rome has one nation loomed so large above the others. Indeed, the word 'empire' has come out of the closet. Respected analysts on both the left and the right are beginning to refer to 'American empire' approvingly as the dominant narrative of the 21st century."[22] Charles Krauthammer, who had long urged American dominion over the globe, now rejoiced that the United States was "the dominant power in the world, more dominant than any since Rome" and that Americans were the "undisputed masters of the world."[23] A few conservatives lamented this development. Andrew Bacevich, for example, faced the American imperial reality head-on and wrote, "Like it or not, America today *is* Rome, committed irreversibly to the maintenance and, where feasible, expansion of an empire. . . . This is hardly a matter for celebration; but neither is there any purpose served by denying the facts."

Indeed, Bacevich devoted his book, *American Empire*, to a detailed explanation of the realities of America's imperial policies and how those policies emerged, especially during the presidencies of George H. W. Bush and Bill Clinton.[24] In a more liberal genre, Gary Dorrien tracked the role of the neoconservative movement in the evolution of the American empire in his important book, *Imperial Designs*.[25]

America's imperial aspirations first emerged in its nineteenth-century doctrine of manifest destiny—a doctrine that encouraged one editor to write:

> We have a destiny to perform, a "manifest destiny" over all Mexico, over South America, over the West Indies and Canada. . . . The gates of the Chinese empire must be thrown down. . . . The eagle of the republic shall poise itself over the field of Waterloo . . . and a successor of Washington ascend the chair of universal empire![26]

We shall consider the doctrine of manifest destiny in substantially more detail in chapter 4.

More recently this country has sought to protect its economic interests abroad—coupled with its claim on the world's natural resources—with a vast military presence scattered across the globe. Indeed, the United States now maintains more than 700 military bases in foreign nations, with some 255,000 military personnel deployed in 156 countries. American military bases abroad sit on approximately 30 million acres of land, making the Pentagon one of the largest landholders in the world.[27] That fact alone should give pause to those Americans unwilling to admit to the imperial status of the United States.

In the early 1990s, Lee Camp, author of the book *Mere Discipleship: Radical Christianity in a Rebellious World*, visited Dyess Air Force Base near Abilene, Texas, and witnessed there a sign that symbolized in a powerful way the imperial dimensions—and the imperial ambitions—of the United States. Camp writes:

> While in seminary at Abilene Christian University in west Texas, I had several occasions to visit Dyess Air Force base, just outside the city limits. I was particularly struck by one of the very large hangars situated alongside the midpoint of the main runway—not because anything about the building itself was impressive, but because of the very large block letters, inordinately larger than any other sign on the base, [with] words in all caps . . . : GLOBAL POWER FOR AMERICA.[28]

For all the reasons we have discussed, few Air Force personnel stationed at that base would have seen in that proclamation a manifestation of American imperialism. But a proclamation like that would strike most men and women in other parts of the world as the essence of imperial thinking.

To return to our discussion of the contest between the kingdom of God and the imperial powers in the context of the New Testament—I want to look at three particular sections of that text. First, we will explore the kingdom of God motif in the Gospels, since there we find the record of the life and teachings of Jesus. Within the Gospels, we will focus especially on the Gospel of Luke and on the famous Sermon on the Mount as recorded in the Gospel of Matthew. Second, we will explore the kingdom of God as we find that kingdom discussed in the epistles of the apostle Paul. Third, we will explore the contest between the kingdom of God and the empires of the world as that contest plays itself out in the Book of Revelation. Finally, we will explore the implications this material holds for understanding Christian America today.

Luke's Understanding of the Kingdom of God

As the Gospel of Luke opens, four messengers—Mary, the mother of Jesus, an angel, John the Baptist, and Jesus himself—announce the emergence of the kingdom of God. Each announcement reinforces the conviction that the kingdom of God will lift up the poor, the downtrodden, and the dispossessed, turning the tables on the empire that exploits these people for imperial gain.

The first of these messengers, Mary made her announcement in chapter 1. When she learned she would give birth to Jesus, she burst out in song (Luke 1:46–55). Christians commonly refer to her song as "the Magnificat." While Mary nowhere mentioned the phrase "kingdom of God" in the Magnificat, she unmistakably spoke of the way this radically new order would reverse traditional social roles. After all, had not God selected her, a poor, humble Jewish woman from Galilee, to give birth to the long-expected Messiah? That realization prompted Mary to sing praises to God, "for he has regarded the low estate of his handmaiden." When Mary expanded on her vision, she described what this new social order would look like.

> He has shown strength with his arm;
> he has scattered the proud in the thoughts of their hearts.
> He has brought down the powerful from their thrones,
> and lifted up the lowly;
> he has filled the hungry with good things,
> and sent the rich away empty.

In the second chapter of Luke, an angel announced this new social order. Appearing to shepherds in the field, the angel told them, "Do not be afraid; for see—I am bringing you good news of great joy for all the people: to you is born this day in the city of David a Savior, who is the Messiah, *the Lord*" (Luke 2:10–11). I have italicized the phrase, "the Lord," since, in making this announcement, the angel clearly proclaimed a ruler. But in this upside-down kingdom, this ruler would be neither conventional royalty nor someone born to privilege. Rather, the angel said, "You will find a child wrapped in bands of cloth and lying in a manger." In the ancient world, a manger was nothing more than a feeding trough for farm animals— hardly a fitting place for the birth of a king.

Moreover, in the context of imperial Rome, the angel's announcement was both revolutionary and seditious, for its two key words—Savior and Lord—were titles routinely applied to the emperor Caesar Augustus. Indeed, Caesar's titles included "Divine," "Son of God," "God," "God from God," "Redeemer," "Liberator," "Lord," and "Savior of the World." "[Early] Christians must have understood," John Dominic Crossan concludes, "that to proclaim Jesus as Son of God was deliberately denying Caesar his highest title and that to announce Jesus as Lord and Savior was calculated treason."[29] If Rome could have found the angel and put him or her to death, it surely would have done so.

In the third chapter of Luke, John the Baptist offered the third announcement of the kingdom of God and contrasted that kingdom with the empire's all-pervasive power and splendor. Luke set up the contrast beautifully, referring first to the ruling elites of his day.

> In the fifteenth year of the reign of Emperor Tiberius, when Pontius Pilate was governor of Judea, and Herod was ruler of Galilee, and his brother Philip ruler of the region of Ituraea and Trachonitis, and Lysanias ruler of Abilene, during the high priesthood of Annas and Caiaphas, the word of God came . . . (3:1–2)

Came to whom? It came, Luke tells us, "to John son of Zechariah in the wilderness." Here Luke subtly contrasted the wilderness where John resided with the imperial courts of Tiberius Caesar, Herod, Philip, and Lysanias. Later in his Gospel, Luke was not so subtle, since he reports that Jesus himself contrasted John's poverty with the luxury of imperial power. "What then did you go out to see?" Jesus asked the people. "Someone dressed in soft robes? Look, those who put on fine clothing and live in luxury are in royal palaces. What then did you go out to see? A prophet? Yes, I tell you, and more than a prophet" (7:25).

Finally, what message did John preach? Did he preach the American gospel that "God helps those who help themselves"? Hardly. According to Luke, John preached a message of radical compassion for those in need. "And the crowds asked him, 'What then should we do?' In reply he said to them, 'Whoever has two coats must share with anyone who has none; and whoever has food must do likewise'" (3:10–11). According to Matthew, John's message of compassion for those in need was nothing more and nothing less than the proclamation of the kingdom of God or, in Matthew's words, the kingdom of heaven (3:2).

Moreover, John apparently used that message to stand in judgment on the empire, for Luke also wrote that John rebuked Herod "because of all the evil things that Herod had done." Little wonder that Herod "shut up John in prison" (3:20). For a while, Herod protected John from those who sought to kill him, "knowing that he was a righteous and holy man" (Mark 6:20). But this preacher of the kingdom of God finally fell victim to imperial decadence and imperial politics.

Indeed, it was Herod's birthday, and the king gave a banquet for the elites of the realm—"for his courtiers and officers and for the leaders of Galilee." When Herod's daughter Herodias danced for the imperial guests, her dance pleased the king and his guests so well that he told the girl, "Ask me for whatever you wish, and I will give it." Herodias's mother, who had a grudge against John the Baptist, advised the girl to ask for John's head on a platter (Mark 6:17–26). Mark reported the rest of the story: "Immediately the king sent a soldier of the guard with orders to bring John's head. He went and beheaded him in the prison, brought his head on a platter, and gave it to the girl. Then the girl gave it to her mother" (Mark 6:27–28). The biblical text could hardly be more graphic in the way it contrasts John's message of compassion for the dispossessed— his proclamation of the kingdom of God—with the brutality of an oppressive empire.

Jesus himself offered the fourth announcement of the kingdom or rule of God—an announcement that appears in Luke, chapter 4. We considered this passage earlier in this book in another context, but shall do so again here in an effort to complete our catalog of the four Lukan messengers who announced the kingdom of God. As we noted earlier, Jesus in this instance—quoting from Isaiah 61:1–2—defined the scope of his ministry and the nature of his ministry and vocation.

> When he came to Nazareth, where he had been brought up, he went to the synagogue on the Sabbath day, as was his custom. He stood up to read, and the scroll of the prophet Isaiah was given to him. He unrolled the scroll and found the place where it was written:
>> The Spirit of the Lord is upon me,
>> because he has anointed me to bring good news to the poor.
>> He has sent me to proclaim release to the captives
>> and recovery of sight to the blind,
>> to let the oppressed go free,
>> to proclaim the year of the Lord's favor.
> And he rolled up the scroll, gave it back to the attendant, and sat down. The eyes of all in the synagogue were fixed on him. Then

he began to say to them, "Today this scripture has been fulfilled in your hearing." (Luke 4:16–21)

In its remaining chapters, the Gospel of Luke continues to elaborate on the meaning of the kingdom of God. In that kingdom, those who are first (the rich and the powerful) will be last, while those who are last (the poor and the dispossessed) will be first (13:29–30). Only those who are humble like little children can enter the kingdom of God (18:16–17). And Luke reports Jesus' comment: "How hard it is for those who have wealth to enter the kingdom of God" (18:24)!

In other words, at every step of the way, Luke takes pains to contrast the reign of God with the empires of the world, whose values stand opposed to the values of the kingdom of God.

Matthew's Understanding of the Kingdom of God

Like Luke, Matthew's gospel goes out of its way to set up the contrast between the empires of the world and the kingdom or reign of God. His first four chapters provide both prelude and context for the Sermon on the Mount, and in those chapters Matthew tells four stories that illustrate this point.

First, Matthew explains in chapter 2 that Herod—technically the "king of the Jews," but in reality a puppet of the Roman Empire—"was frightened" when he learned of the birth of Jesus, since Jesus also had been announced as king of the Jews. And well he should have been, for as John Dominic Crossan points out, "A new and therefore a replacement King of the Jews had been appointed by God and not by Rome. . . . [We should] recognize that Matthew's first-century counter-story is [therefore] high treason, not just a cute Christmas carol whose historicity we can discuss once a year in our media."[30]

Herod, of course, got this point and made every attempt to have Jesus killed. To make certain he left no stone unturned, Herod even ordered the murder of every child two years old and younger in the entire region of Bethlehem. In reporting this story, Matthew embraces a purpose identical to that of Luke: to highlight the radical difference between empire—a regime that seeks to maintain its power by intimidation, violence, and murder—and the upside-down kingdom of God.

Following on the heels of this story, Matthew juxtaposes empire and the kingdom of God a second time. Mary and Joseph foiled Herod's attempt to murder their child, Matthew tells us, by fleeing to Egypt. Only when the parents learned that Herod had died did they consider returning to Israel. But when Joseph "heard that Archelaus was ruling over Judea in place of his father Herod, he was afraid to go there. And after being warned in a dream, he went away to the district of Galilee" (2:22).

Immediately after reporting that Archelaus bore all the imperial traits of his father Herod, Matthew tells us that "in those days John the Baptist appeared proclaiming," not in an imperial palace, but "in the wilderness of Judea." And what was John's message? "Repent, for the kingdom of heaven has come near." In keeping with the values of the kingdom of heaven—or the kingdom of God—Matthew wants us to know that John the Baptist was not clad in imperial regalia, but rather "wore clothing of camel's hair, and a leather belt around his waist; and his food was locusts and wild honey" (3:4). The contrast between John, on the one hand, and Herod and Archelaus on the other—and therefore between the kingdom of God and empire—could hardly be greater.

In chapter 4, verses 8–10, Matthew sets up the third contrast between empire and the kingdom of God. In that text, Matthew reports that "the devil took him [Jesus] to a very high mountain and showed him all the kingdoms of the world and their splendor; and he said to him, 'All these I will give you, if you will fall down and worship me.'" Here Matthew makes a point that is crucial for grasping the New Testament understanding of empire: in the present age, Satan rules all the empires and kingdoms of this world. For this reason, Jesus responds, "Away with you, Satan! For it is written, 'Worship the Lord your God, and serve only him.'" And then, in an effort to contrast empire and the kingdom of God once again, Matthew tells us, "From that time Jesus began to proclaim, 'Repent, for the kingdom of heaven has come near.'"

What should we make of these stories? And why would Matthew report that Jesus said, "Repent, for the kingdom of heaven has come near"? Matthew's point is simply this: Empires inevitably embrace greed, self-interest, and violence in order to maintain their power and privilege. But the kingdom of God lifts up those who suffer at the empire's hands. Jesus wants his hearers to know that a radically new kingdom—one that turns the empire's values upside down—has become a reality for them. For this reason, Jesus tells his audience, "Repent, for the kingdom of heaven has come near."

Matthew concludes chapter 4 by relating his fourth vignette, namely that Jesus preached "the good news of the kingdom." Tellingly, Matthew links the phrase "the good news of the kingdom," with Jesus' concern for those whom the Roman Empire had brushed aside. Central to the "good news of the kingdom," therefore, is Matthew's report that Jesus healed "every disease and every sickness among the people. . . . And they brought him all the sick, those who were afflicted with various diseases and pains, demoniacs, epileptics, and paralytics, and he cured them" (4:23–24). The gospel—the good news—of the kingdom, therefore, proclaims that while empires exalt the rich, the privileged, and the elite, the kingdom of God exalts the poor, the suffering, the sick, and those society has rejected.

A story that illustrates Matthew's message is one told by Eldridge Cleaver, one-time minister of information for the Black Panther Party, in his book, *Soul on Ice*. There Cleaver tells of Chris Lovdjieff, an extraordinary teacher who cared so deeply for the prisoners—those outcasts from American life—that he voluntarily taught at San Quentin federal penitentiary every day, from 8:00 a.m. until 10:00 p.m., except Sunday, when the prison officials deliberately kept him away. "Had they given him a cell," Cleaver reports, "he would have taken it." At 10:00 p.m., when the guards made him leave, "he'd go home to suffer in exile until school opened the next day."

Not only did Lovdjieff care more for prisoners than for those outside the prison's walls; within the prison he cared especially for those who were slow to learn. "He was drawn," Cleaver reports, "to those students who seemed impossible to teach—old men who had been illiterate all their lives and set in their ways." Then Cleaver adds:

> Lovdjieff didn't believe that anyone or anything in the universe was "set in its ways." Those students who were intelligent and quickest to learn he seemed reluctant to bother with, almost as if to say, pointing at the illiterates and speaking to the bright ones: "Go away. Leave me. You don't need me. These others do."[31]

This story of Lovdjieff—a man who committed himself to the poorest of the poor and those who were marginal even among the marginalized—illustrates almost perfectly Matthew's understanding of the kingdom of God as he presents that kingdom in chapters 1 through 4.

By the time Matthew relates Jesus' Sermon on the Mount,[32] beginning in chapter 5, he has already set up the context in which the sermon should be understood: the struggle between the empire, with its concern for wealth, power, and privilege, and the kingdom of God, with its concern for the poor, the downtrodden, and the dispossessed.

Warren Carter, whose superb scholarship on the book of Matthew has inspired my own understanding of that text, explains that Matthew's Sermon on the Mount is a "work of imagination" that enables "disciples to envision life shaped by God's reign/empire."[33] In other words, the Sermon on the Mount, and especially the Beatitudes with which that sermon begins, invite the dispossessed to *imagine* a life that is rich and abundant—a life that conforms to the reign of God as opposed to the reign of Caesar.

Matthew's invitation to imagination was itself a subversive act, for imagination is precisely what all imperial regimes seek to suppress. As Walter Brueggemann explains in his aptly titled book, *The Prophetic Imagination*, "The same royal consciousness that makes it possible to implement anything and everything is the one that shrinks imagination because imagination is a danger."[34] Indeed, Brueggemann notes that imperial regimes seek to thwart not only imagination but passion as well:

> Passion as the capacity and readiness to care, to suffer, to die, and to feel is the enemy of imperial reality. Imperial economics is designed to keep people satiated so that they do not notice. Its politics is intended to block out the cries of the denied ones. Its religion is to be an opiate so that no one discerns misery alive in the heart of God.[35]

This is why "the vocation of the prophet [is] to keep alive the ministry of imagination, to keep on conjuring and proposing alternative futures to the single one the king wants to urge as the only thinkable one."[36]

As we know, Jesus stood squarely in the prophetic tradition, and it should therefore come as no surprise to discover that the Beatitudes are, at heart, an invitation to imagine—to imagine a richer, fuller, more abundant life, though a life independent of the values of the empire. And for Jesus, abundant life is life defined by the kingdom of God.

As we begin to explore the Beatitudes, we should recognize that, like the kingdom of God to which they point, they too are concerned with two primary virtues: justice and peace. The first four Beatitudes address the subject of social justice, while the last five address the subject of peace and peacemaking.

The First Four Beatitudes:
Justice for the Poor and the Dispossessed

According to Matthew, Jesus begins his comments on social justice in the opening words of the Sermon on the Mount: "Blessed are the poor in spirit," Jesus says, "for theirs is the kingdom of heaven." As we noted earlier, Matthew is the only gospel writer to use the phrase "kingdom of heaven," and he means for that phrase to signify the kingdom of God. Further, the "poor in spirit" are the poor, those who comprise ninety-seven percent of the population of the Roman Empire. I base this interpretation on the Gospel of Luke whose rendition of the Sermon on the Plain has Jesus saying "Blessed are you who are poor, for yours is the kingdom of God" (6:20).

I am aware that some scholars understand the phrase "poor in spirit" to signify humility. But I find very compelling Warren Carter's view that these "are the literal, physical poor, the destitute, those who live in social and economic hardship, lacking adequate resources, exploited and oppressed by the powerful and despised by the elite." The notion that "poor in spirit" means "humility" runs counter, Carter argues, to the overarching theme in scripture that "God will save the poor."[37]

We must remember that both Matthew and Luke were composed during the last third of the first century. By then, the Christian movement had attracted numerous adherents, and those adherents were poor, indeed. Horsley and Silberman write that "'Christianity' in its early decades was a network of poor people and marginal communities in both cities and rural areas."[38] These were people, then, who would have found this Beatitude—"Blessed are the poor in spirit, for theirs is the kingdom of heaven"—enormously comforting. They knew full well what this Beatitude promised: justice in the face of injustice and redemption in the face of oppression.

But why would Matthew have Jesus describe these people as "the poor in spirit" instead of simply "the poor"? He does this because he knows that empire inevitably grinds the faces of the poor, crushes the human spirit, and leaves its victims with little hope, virtually no sense of worth, and minimal self-esteem. In this Beatitude, therefore, Jesus brings good news: Though the empire has rejected these people as completely worthless, the kingdom of God restores their dignity and views them as blessed and highly esteemed. In this way, the first Beatitude—"Blessed are the poor in spirit, for theirs is the kingdom of heaven"—challenged the empire's values with the values of the kingdom of God.

Each of the other Beatitudes picked up on this very same theme. For example, Jesus told those who mourned that they, too, would be blessed. "Blessed are those who mourn, for they will be comforted," Matthew reports that Jesus said (Matthew 5:4). In the empire they will find no comfort, but in the kingdom of God they will.

In the third Beatitude, Jesus told his hearers, "Blessed are the meek, for they will inherit the earth" (Matthew 5:5). In this Beatitude, Jesus picked up on Psalm 37:11—a passage that assured the meek that they "shall possess the land"—another way of saying that the meek would inherit the earth. Psalm 37 fit Jesus' concern precisely, for it turned the tables on those who aligned themselves with imperial values at the expense of the poor and the dispossessed:

> The meek shall inherit the land, and delight themselves in abundant prosperity.
> The wicked plot against the righteous, and gnash their teeth at them;
> but the LORD laughs at the wicked, for he sees that their day is coming.
> The wicked draw the sword and bend their bows to bring down the poor and needy, to kill those who walk uprightly;
> their sword shall enter their own heart, and their bows shall be broken. (11–15)

The fourth Beatitude pronounced a blessing on those "who hunger and thirst for righteousness, for they will be filled." Since the Greek language uses the very same word for "justice" as for "righteousness," it is safe to conclude that those who hunger and thirst for righteousness are those who hunger and thirst for justice. But the empire offered precious little justice for the poor and the dispossessed. Indeed, Horsley and Silberman report that early Christians "were rounded up, beaten up, and condemned to execution for atheism and treason—that is, failing to participate in the state-controlled cults of the gods of the Greco-Roman pantheon and abandoning honored family values of pagan society."[39] But Matthew's Sermon on the Mount assured the oppressed that the day would come when their longing for justice would be satisfied.

If the kingdom of God was that place or circumstance in which the poor and the disenfranchised would find justice, compassion, and mercy, Jesus also made it clear that no one could enter the kingdom of God without reaching out to the poor and the dispossessed in precisely those ways. For example, Luke reports that a ruler asked Jesus what he must do to inherit eternal life. Jesus told him to keep the commandments. That response obviously pleased the ruler who quickly replied, "I have kept all these since my youth." Then Luke adds:

> When Jesus heard this, he said to him, "There is still one thing lacking. Sell all that you own and distribute the money to the poor, and you will have treasure in heaven; then come, follow me." But when he heard this, he became sad; for he was very rich. Jesus looked at him and said, "How hard it is for those who have wealth to enter the kingdom of God!" (18:18–24)

Luke also reports that Jesus gave this advice to his followers:

> When you give a luncheon or a dinner, do not invite your friends or your brothers or your relatives or rich neighbors, in case they may invite you in return, and you would be repaid. But when you give a banquet, invite the poor, the crippled, the lame, and the blind. And you will be blessed, because they cannot repay you, for you will be repaid at the resurrection of the righteous. (14:12–14)

But there is no passage in the entirety of the New Testament that sets the terms for entry into the kingdom of God in such stark relief as does the description of the last judgment that appears in Matthew's gospel. That passage makes it clear that compassion for the dispossessed is the fundamental criterion for entry into the kingdom of God. This passage is lengthy, but it is so important for grasping the meaning of the phrase "kingdom of God" that it deserves to be quoted in its entirety:

> When the Son of Man comes in his glory, and all the angels with him, then he will sit on the throne of his glory. All the nations will be gathered before him, and he will separate people one from another as a shepherd separates the sheep from the goats, and he will put the sheep at his right hand and the goats at the left. Then the king will say to those at his right hand, "Come, you that are blessed by my Father, inherit the kingdom prepared for you from the foundation of the world; for I was hungry and you gave me food, I was thirsty and you gave me something to drink, I was a stranger and you welcomed me, I was naked and you gave me clothing, I was sick and you took care of me, I was in prison and you visited me." Then the righteous will answer him, "Lord, when was it that we saw you hungry and gave you food, or thirsty and gave you something to drink? And when was it that we saw you a stranger and welcomed you, or naked and gave you clothing? And when was it that we saw you sick or in prison and visited you?" And the king will answer them, "Truly I tell you, just as you did

it to one of the least of these who are members of my family, you did it to me." Then he will say to those at his left hand, "You that are accursed, depart from me into the eternal fire prepared for the devil and his angels; for I was hungry and you gave me no food, I was thirsty and you gave me nothing to drink, I was a stranger and you did not welcome me, naked and you did not give me clothing, sick and in prison and you did not visit me." Then they also will answer, "Lord, when was it that we saw you hungry or thirsty or a stranger or naked or sick or in prison, and did not take care of you?" Then he will answer them, "Truly I tell you, just as you did not do it to one of the least of these, you did not do it to me." And these will go away into eternal punishment, but the righteous into eternal life. (25:31–46)

To make certain that we understand this passage, it will be helpful to cite Michael Himes, who offers the following comments on this text from Matthew 25:

> To the best of my knowledge, this is the only passage in the whole of the collection of documents which we call the New Testament which describes the last judgment. . . . And notice what the only criterion of the last judgment is. There is not a word about whether you belonged to the church, not a word about whether you were baptized, not a syllable about whether you ever celebrated the eucharist, not a question about whether you prayed, nothing at all about what creed you professed or what you knew about doctrine or theology. Indeed, there is nothing specifically religious at all. Not one doctrine, not one specifically religious act of worship or ritual turns out to be relevant to the criterion for the last judgment. The only criterion for that final judgment according to Matthew 25, is how you treated your brothers and sisters.[40]

As a Roman Catholic priest, Himes was not willing to suggest that prayer, sacraments, and liturgy were unimportant. But he did want to suggest that without compassion for one's brothers and sisters—and especially for those Jesus called "the least of these"—religious ritual becomes essentially meaningless. That, of course, is the witness of the biblical text from start to finish. Some of the passages we have cited—and many we have not—make precisely that point. Recall, for example, these words from Amos that we considered earlier in this book:

> Take away from me the noise of your songs;
> I will not listen to the melody of your harps.
> But let justice roll down like waters,
> and righteousness like an ever-flowing stream! (5:23–24)

Or these words from Isaiah:

> Is not this the fast that I choose:
> to loose the bonds of injustice . . . ?
> Is it not to share your bread with the hungry . . .
> —when you see the naked, to cover them? (58:6–7)

Or these words from Hosea:

> I desire mercy, not sacrifice. (6:6)

Jesus himself quoted this passage from Hosea—"I desire mercy, not sacrifice"—when he sought to explain that justice and mercy always trump religious ritual (Matthew 12:7). And he told numerous stories that made this very same point. Especially well known is the story about the "good Samaritan" who helped a traveler whom robbers had beaten and left on the side of the road to die. But the Samaritan did so only after religious professionals, eager to tend to their ceremonial duties in the temple, ignored the traveler and passed him by on the far side of the road. Then Jesus asked:

> "Which of these three, do you think, was a neighbor to the man who fell into the hands of the robbers?" [The lawyer] said, "The one who showed him mercy." Jesus said to him, "Go and do likewise." (Luke 10:36–37)

In his book *A Man without a Country*, Kurt Vonnegut told a story that captures the compelling power of Jesus' teachings—especially his teachings in the Sermon on the Mount—about the vulnerable and the poor. Vonnegut's story also explains why those who have embraced the values of empire find Jesus' teachings so puzzling.

Reflecting on the fact that so many socialists aided the poor in the early years of the twentieth century, Vonnegut told of one of those socialists with whom he was personally acquainted—Powers Hapgood, a Hoosier from Indianapolis. Hapgood was reared in a middle-class home and earned a degree from Harvard but decided to devote his life to tireless labor on behalf of the poor. After graduating from Harvard, he took a job as a coal miner and, as Vonnegut put it, urged "his working-class brothers to organize in order to get better pay and safer working conditions." When the state of Massachusetts executed anarchists Nicola Sacco and Bartolomeo Vanzetti in 1927, Hapgood was there, protesting their execution. Having sketched out this background, Vonnegut then recalled that:

We met in Indianapolis after the end of the Second World War. He had become an official in the CIO. There had been some sort of dust-up on a picket line, and he was testifying about it in court, and the judge stops everything and asks him, "Mr. Hapgood, here you are, you're a graduate of Harvard. Why would anyone with your advantages choose to live as you have?" Hapgood answered the judge: "Why, because of the Sermon on the Mount, sir."[41]

What more can one say?

The Last Five Beatitudes: Jesus' Teachings on Peacemaking, Suffering, and Nonviolence

The fifth through ninth Beatitudes are all closely related, since they counsel mercy, peacemaking, and nonviolence. "Blessed are the merciful," Jesus says in the fifth of these statements, "for they will receive mercy." And then in the seventh, "Blessed are the peacemakers, for they will be called children of God."

When Jesus says that peacemakers will be called "children of God," he rejected the values of the empire in two respects. First, as we have seen, "Son of God" was one of the titles the emperor ascribed to himself. And second, the word used here for "peacemaker"— *eirenepoios* in Greek—was inscribed on imperial coins during Jesus' own time, thereby suggesting that the emperor—that imperial "son of God"—was himself a peacemaker.[42] And indeed he was. But the emperor made peace by force of arms, thereby sustaining the *Pax Romana* (the peace of Rome), while the peacemakers Jesus commends made peace through kindness, forgiveness, and patience. Indeed, they made peace by showing mercy. In this way they resisted the empire's values and embraced instead the values of the kingdom of God. Jesus' blessing on these peacemakers—and his affirmation that they would be called the "children of God"—was itself an act of subversion.

Both mercy and peacemaking are essentially foreign to the imperial vision and those who support it, both then and now. This truth helps explain why so many Americans were shocked when the Amish refused to take vengeance against the killer of their children—or against the killer's family—but forgave instead. It also explains why the United States responded to the tragedy of September 11, 2001, with vengeance and retribution. In other words, the American response to 9/11 reflected the way empires inevitably behave. But in these two Beatitudes, Jesus counsels values that are foreign to any empire but central to the kingdom of God: mercy and peacemaking.

The sixth, eighth, and ninth Beatitudes continue the themes of peacemaking and nonviolence, since they pronounce blessings both on the pure in heart and on those who suffer persecution for righteousness' sake. Here is the way those Beatitudes read:

> Blessed are the pure in heart, for they will see God. (5:8)
>
> Blessed are those who are persecuted for righteousness' sake, for theirs is the kingdom of heaven. (5:10)
>
> Blessed are you when people revile you and persecute you and utter all kinds of evil against you falsely on my account. Rejoice and be glad, for your reward is great in heaven, for in the same way they persecuted the prophets who were before you. (5:11–12)

Why do I suggest that these three Beatitudes go together? Because those who are pure in heart are those who reject the impulse to hate when faced with oppression and persecution. And in the context of the Roman Empire, the poor were faced with oppression every day.

Later in the Sermon on the Mount, in his most explicit and radical teaching on peacemaking and nonviolence, Jesus enlarged on the Beatitudes that focused on these themes when he counseled love for one's enemies. Here is the way Matthew reports that teaching.

> You have heard that it was said, "An eye for an eye and a tooth for a tooth." But I say to you, Do not resist an evildoer. But if any one strikes you on the right cheek, turn the other also; and if any one wants to sue you and take your coat, give your cloak as well; and if any one forces you to go one mile, go also the second mile. Give to everyone who begs from you, and do not refuse anyone who wants to borrow from you.
>
> You have heard that it was said, "You shall love your neighbor and hate your enemy." But I say to you, Love your enemies and pray for those who persecute you, so that you may be children of your Father in heaven. (5:38–45)

It is difficult for Americans, so accustomed to violence and retribution, to imagine that Jesus could possibly have meant these teachings in any literal sense. Yet the emphasis on peacemaking and nonviolence is constant throughout the Christians' New Testament. In fact, there is no theme more central to what Christians call their "gospel" (good news), since the gospel focuses on the Christian claim that Jesus refused to resist those who sought to kill him but instead gave his life for the sake of others.

According to Matthew, just hours before he was crucified, one of his disciples, in an obvious attempt to defend Jesus, drew a sword and "struck the slave of the high priest, cutting off his ear." But Matthew reports that Jesus said to his disciples:

> Put your sword back into its place; for all who take the sword will perish by the sword. Do you think that I cannot appeal to my Father, and he will at once send me more than twelve legions of angels? (26:51–53)

John's gospel reports that during the course of his trial, Jesus said to Pilate, "My kingdom is not from this world. If my kingdom were from this world, my followers would be fighting to keep me from being handed over to the Jews. But as it is, my kingdom is not from here." Indeed, it was not, for Jesus consistently claimed that he represented an altogether different kingdom that he called "the kingdom of God." And this kingdom was one of peacemaking and nonviolence.

Paul's Understanding of the Kingdom of God

Second only to Jesus, the apostle Paul stands at the heart of the New Testament text. Scholars have credited Paul with writing between seven and thirteen of the twenty-two New Testament epistles. And Luke's history of the earliest Christians—a book called the Acts of the Apostles—devotes an extraordinary amount of time, space, and attention to Paul's work as a missionary to the Gentile world. Because Paul plays such an integral role in the New Testament, it is important to ask how he understood the meaning of the kingdom of God.

Before addressing that question, we need to address two preliminary issues. First we must acknowledge that many Christians over the past five hundred years, at least in Protestant circles, have been slow to discern Paul's theology of the kingdom of God. This theological blind spot is largely due to Martin Luther. In 1517 Luther discovered the theme of justification by grace through faith—surely one of the central themes in Paul's thought—and built the Reformation around it.

In elaborating the notion of justification by grace through faith, Paul argues that the human condition is so compromised that no person can possibly win God's favor—that is, God's love and forgiveness—by performing good works. Rather, God bestows his favor freely, by *grace*. That is such an incredible proposition,

Paul argues, that it makes no sense to human reason. The gospel therefore asks men and women to accept God's grace through *faith*. Ever since Luther, Christians have used a shorthand description for this rather elaborate theology, and that shorthand is the simple phrase *justification by grace through faith*.

There is no question that justification by grace through faith is a central theme in Paul's theology. The passage that first alerted Luther to the prominence of that motif is Romans 1:16–17: "For I am not ashamed of the gospel [good news]; it is the power of God for salvation to everyone who has faith, to the Jew first and also to the Greek. For . . . 'The one who is righteous will live by faith.'" In time, Luther found that theme throughout Paul's writings. For example, Paul writes in Galatians, "We ourselves are Jews by birth and not Gentile sinners; yet we know that a person is justified not by works of the law but through faith in Jesus Christ" (2:15–16). The most pointed statement on justification by grace through faith appears in Ephesians 2:8: "For by grace you have been saved through faith, and this is not your own doing; it is the gift of God—not the result of works, so that no one may boast."

Many Christians have supposed that justification by grace through faith precludes a robust theology of the kingdom of God, simply because kingdom theology entails ethics and behavior— what some Christians regard as *works*. As we have seen, Paul clearly warned that no good works of any kind, whether moral or ceremonial, can possibly secure one's salvation. But in Paul's theology, justification by grace through faith by no means precludes the theme of the kingdom of God, as we shall shortly see. In fact, these two themes are closely related to each other, tied together by the centerpiece of Paul's theology, namely, Jesus the Christ.

The second preliminary issue concerns the extent to which Paul may have built his understanding of the kingdom of God on the Hebrew prophets and on the teachings of Jesus. In the context of that question, the fact that Paul was martyred in Rome sometime between 62 and 67 BCE is a crucial consideration. Since all the Gospels—Matthew, Mark, Luke, and John—appeared during the last third of the first century BCE, Paul's epistles obviously precede the Gospel accounts of the life and teachings of Jesus. At the same time, Paul must have known the oral tradition of Jesus' understanding of the kingdom of God. And as a learned Jew who studied at the rabbinical school of Gamaliel, he clearly was familiar with the Hebrew prophets who preached to Israel and Judah during the eighth century BCE and afterward.

Paul seldom uses the actual phrase, "kingdom of God." If, however, we allow Jesus and the prophets to define the meaning of the kingdom of God, then it is clear that Paul employs the *concept* of the kingdom of God with great regularity. In fact, it is safe to say that the notion of the kingdom of God—that is, God's rule, dominion, and authority over all the earth—is among the most important motifs in Pauline thought, for Paul returns time and again to the two principal characteristics of that kingdom—peace and justice.

But what sets Paul apart from the prophets, on the one hand, and Jesus, on the other, is the way he grounds his vision of the kingdom of God in his conviction that Jesus Christ is Lord. Of course, one finds the claim that Jesus is Lord in the Gospels as well—a point we emphasized in a previous discussion. The angel, for example, announced to the shepherds, "To you is born this day . . . a Savior, who is the Messiah, the Lord" (Luke 2:11). But Paul turns that confession into an elaborate theological framework that undergirds everything he says about peace and justice in the kingdom of God.

Paul's starting point for understanding the kingdom of God is a notion we encountered in the gospels and the notion Donald Kraybill has described as "the upside-down kingdom." In other words, Paul begins with a paradox, and the heart of that paradox is this: Because Jesus emptied himself, took on the form of common humanity, and finally succumbed to the most disgraceful form of death in the ancient world—death by crucifixion—he has become Lord of the universe. It would be difficult to find a more striking paradox than this, for by the standards of the Roman Empire, this assertion was simply absurd.

Paul makes this argument often, but he never makes it more forcefully than he does in Philippians 2:5–8:

> Let the same mind be in you that was in Christ Jesus, who, though he was in the form of God, did not regard equality with God as something to be exploited, but emptied himself, taking the form of a slave, being born in human likeness. And being found in human form, he humbled himself and became obedient to the point of death—even death on a cross. Therefore God also highly exalted him and gave him the name that is above every name, so that at the name of Jesus every knee should bend, in heaven and on earth and under the earth, and every tongue should confess that Jesus Christ is Lord, to the glory of God the Father.

Three features of this passage deserve special comment, and these three features are, in fact, the defining elements of Paul's understanding of the kingdom of God. First, in this text Paul clearly—

and no doubt deliberately and self-consciously—rejects the Roman Empire's claim of supremacy and the emperor's claim of divinity. In fact, since the proclamation that "Jesus is Lord" was treason against the empire, one would be hard-pressed to find a more treasonous statement than this in the entire New Testament. For Paul here not only claims that Jesus is Lord. He also claims that the day will come when, at the name of Jesus, *every* knee will bend and *every* tongue will confess that Jesus is Lord. Further, one would be hard-pressed to find anywhere in the biblical text a more definitive description of the kingdom of God—the rule of Christ over all the earth.

We begin to realize how radical Paul's assertions in this text really are when we realize that he wrote these words from an imperial prison, and that from that prison he could claim that "our citizenship is in heaven [i.e., in God's kingdom], and it is from there [and not from the empire] that we are expecting a Savior, the Lord Jesus Christ" (Phil. 3:20). Both here and in his other letters, Paul hammers on this anti-imperial theme time and again. For example, in I Corinthians 15:24–25, he writes that when the end finally comes, Christ will "hand over the kingdom to God the Father, after he has destroyed every ruler and every authority and power. For he must reign until he has put all his enemies under his feet." It is important to note that Paul in this text classifies "*every* ruler and *every* authority and power" as among God's "enemies" whom Christ will place "under his feet."

Second, Paul portrays Jesus as one who "emptied himself," "humbled himself," and "became obedient to the point of death." In other words, by accepting persecution and death on behalf of others, Jesus modeled self-giving and self-abasing love. That kind of love, Paul writes, is essentially unknown: "Rarely will anyone die for a righteous person—though perhaps for a good person someone might actually dare to die. But God proves his love for us in that while we still were sinners Christ died for us" (Rom. 5:7–8).

In Paul's judgment, that sort of radical, self-giving love is utterly foreign to the empires and rulers of this world and beyond their comprehension. For them, therefore, the story of Jesus is utter foolishness. "For the message about the cross is foolishness to those who are perishing," he writes in I Corinthians 1:19. And that assertion becomes the basis for an extended contrast Paul makes between the "wisdom of God" that is foolishness to this world, and the "wisdom of this world" that, in the grand scheme of things, is utter foolishness, at least if judged by what we know about God

(I Cor. 1:18–2:8). In drawing that contrast, Paul once again revels in paradox—this time the paradox of the upside-down-ness of the kingdom of God.

Indeed, Paul uses the term *God's wisdom* to describe radical, self-giving love, and the term *human wisdom* to describe the depths of self-interest, violence, and greed that always characterize the imperial powers. The "wisdom" that characterized his preaching, he claims, was "not a wisdom of this age or of the rulers of this age, who are doomed to perish. But we speak God's wisdom" (I Cor. 2:6–7). Further, "none of the rulers of this age understood this; for if they had, they would not have crucified the Lord of glory" (I Cor. 2:8). John Dominic Crossan and Jonathan Reed are exactly right when they note that "the rulers of this age are, proximately, the Roman authorities who executed Jesus, but they are, ultimately, the cosmic powers that make imperial violence and human injustice the normalcy of human history and the permanent patina of civilization."[43] This means that Paul's judgment on the Roman Empire is equally a judgment on the American empire, for both are rooted in what Paul calls the "wisdom of this age."

Third, based on this Christ who "empties" and "humbles" himself, Paul develops his understanding of social ethics—the way those who belong to the kingdom of God must behave. And the heart of Paul's social ethic appears in the very first line of our paradigmatic passage: "Let the same mind be in you that was in Christ Jesus" (Phil. 2:5). And as we have seen, the mind that was in Christ Jesus was a mind of humility, compassion, and self-giving love.

Based on that "mind of Christ" and that "wisdom of God," Paul places two themes at the heart of his social ethic—an ethic that reflected his view of the kingdom of God. Those two themes are justice, on the one hand, and peace and peacemaking, on the other. As we have seen, these are the same two themes that defined the kingdom of God in both the preaching of the Hebrew prophets and the teachings of Jesus.

Paul's Theology of Justice

Paul's theology of social justice revolves around one core conviction: equality in Christ. Outside Christ, people were bound by the social hierarchies that defined the Roman Empire: Masters controlled slaves, men controlled women, and the poor were subject to oppression and exploitation by the rich. But in the kingdom of God, all that had changed. Indeed, in his great declaration of Christian equality (Gal. 3:27–28), Paul exulted that "as many of you as were baptized into Christ have clothed yourselves with Christ. There is no longer Jew or Greek, there is no longer slave or free, there is no longer male and female; for all of you are one in Christ Jesus."

Paul applied that principle to numerous social relationships in the context of the kingdom of God. In his letter to the Roman Christians, he argued at length that Gentiles were equal to Jews. "For there is no distinction," he wrote, "between Jew and Greek; the same Lord is Lord of all and is generous to all who call on him" (Rom. 10:12). In his first letter to the Corinthian Christians, he applied the principle of equality to the male-female relationship. Thus, "the husband should give to his wife her conjugal rights, and likewise the wife to her husband. For the wife does not have authority over her own body, but the husband does; likewise the husband does not have authority over his own body, but the wife does" (I Cor. 7:3–4). For Paul, life in Christ transformed all human relationships so that equality displaced hierarchy and justice displaced injustice in the context of the kingdom of God.

Critics will be quick to object that a passage in I Timothy—a letter that begins, "Paul, an apostle of Christ Jesus . . . to Timothy"— admonishes women to be in subjection to men and to keep quiet. The text reads like this: "Let a woman learn in silence with full submission. I permit no woman to teach or to have authority over a man; she is to keep silent" (I Tim. 2:11–12). This passage is fundamentally out of step with everything we know about Paul's theology of social justice. While this passage no doubt reflects a Pauline context, some scholars conclude that one of Paul's disciples wrote these words in the apostle's name, and others suggest that it reflects a particular circumstance and was never intended as a universal rule of faith.

Be that as it may, it is precisely here that John Dominic Crossan's observation still rings true, namely, that the struggle between the principles of the kingdom of God and the principles of human civilization "is depicted *inside the Bible* itself." Thus Crossan writes, "The Christian Bible forces us to witness the struggle of these two transcendental visions *within its own pages* and to ask ourselves as Christians how we decide between them." And his answer is this: "We *are bound to whichever of these visions was incarnated by and in the historical Jesus.*"[44] In other words, when the New Testament offers a choice between gender equality, on the one hand, and subjugation of women, on the other, the choice is no choice at all, at least for people who take seriously the biblical vision of the kingdom of God. For in the context of that vision, the decision has already been made: in Jesus Christ, equality always trumps subjugation and hierarchy.

Much the same can be said regarding Paul's treatment of slaves and masters. We have already noted that Paul includes the slave-master relationship in his declaration of Christian equality. "There is no longer slave or free," he wrote in his letter to the Galatians, "for all of you are one in Christ Jesus" (3:28). Paul had the chance to live that principle out in a bold and decisive way when he encountered a slave named Onesimus who had run away from his master, Philemon. In the Roman Empire, slaves had no rights, and the penalty for running away from one's master could be severe and could even include execution. So Paul was now faced with a very delicate problem.

He converted Onesimus to Christ, then sent him back to Philemon with a letter addressed to Philemon and to "the church in your house." In that letter, he wrote

> Perhaps this is the reason he [Onesimus] was separated from you for a while, so that you might have him back forever, no longer as a slave but more than a slave, a beloved brother—especially to me but how much more to you, both in the flesh and in the Lord. So if you consider me your partner, welcome him as you would welcome me. If he has wronged you in any way, or owes you anything, charge that to my account. I, Paul, am writing this with my own hand: I will repay it. (Phlm. 15–19)

It is clear from the key phrases in this letter that Paul believed—and believed very deeply—that Philemon should free his slave, since Paul had already laid down the principle "There is no longer slave or free . . ., for all of you are one in Christ Jesus." For Paul, it was inconceivable that one Christian man could keep another Christian man in physical bondage. So Paul wrote that Philemon should take "him [Onesimus] back forever, no longer as a slave but more than a slave, a beloved brother." Further, "If you consider me your partner, welcome him as you would welcome me."

Clearly, Paul was not seeking to overthrow the Roman institution of slavery. That would have been impossible in any event. But he could certainly attempt to abolish a single instance of slavery in the context of a Christian relationship, and that is exactly what he did.

Once again we encounter the problem that other letters—also purporting to be from the hand of Paul but whose authorship is routinely debated by scholars—dealt with the slave-master relationship but in a very different way. Indeed, Colossians, Ephesians, and Titus offered slaves the same kind of advice that slaveholders in the American South offered their slaves on a regular basis: don't talk back, don't pilfer, obey your masters with fear and trembling, since God will reward you at the end of time. Indeed, American slaveholders used these very arguments and appealed to these very texts as a means of keeping their slaves in subjection.

Colossians 3:22–24, for example, advised slaves to "obey your earthly masters in everything . . . since you know that from the Lord you will receive the inheritance as your reward." At least this text did offer some balance, since it also admonished masters to "treat your slaves justly and fairly" (4:1). But it stopped far short of the kind of advice that Paul gave to Philemon that he should take "him [Onesimus] back forever, no longer as a slave but more than a slave, a beloved brother." Another text that offered balance but stopped short of Paul's advice to Philemon is Ephesians 6:5–9, a text that advised slaves to "obey your earthly masters with fear and trembling," but also commanded masters to "stop threatening them."

Very likely we should understand both these texts in light of the rigidly hierarchical household codes that governed social relationships in the Roman Empire. The fact that these codes governed every relationship within a household explains why both these texts, in their larger contexts, offered advice not just to slaves but to others in the household as well—wives, children, fathers, and masters. Indeed, the Roman household was a microcosm of the empire itself, with the head of the household representing the emperor within his own walls.[45] Slaves, women, and children, therefore, were to remain in strict subjection to the ruler of the house.

The household codes that determined these relationships were so entrenched that virtually no one imagined they could be changed from the outside. The author(s) of Ephesians and Colossians, therefore, implicitly acknowledged the impregnable nature of that reality. But if one could never hope to change those social realities by external pressure, persuasion, or force, one could at least subvert them spiritually. And the authors of both Colossians and Ephesians attempt to do precisely that.

Accordingly, the author of Colossians prefaces his letter with a strong affirmation that Jesus is Lord, even over the rulers of the earth, and that all powers and authorities on earth are ultimately dependent on Jesus for their very existence. The text in question reads like this:

> In him [Jesus] all things in heaven and on earth were created, things visible and invisible, whether thrones or dominions or rulers or powers—all things have been created through him and for him. . . . He himself is before all things, and in him all things hold together. He is the head of the body, the church; he is the beginning, the firstborn from the dead, so that he might come to have first place in everything. (Col. 1:16–18)

When Colossians urges slaves, therefore, to "obey your earthly masters in everything . . . since you know that from the Lord you will receive the inheritance as your reward," the larger context suggests that they should always bear in mind that Jesus is Lord and that he, not the master, should "have first place in everything." Indeed, Colossians 3:24 reminds slaves that "you serve the Lord Christ." In their book on Colossians, Brian Walsh and Sylvia Keesmaat suggest that with this phrase, the author of Colossians "completely strips earthly masters of their ultimate sovereignty over their slaves."[46]

Likewise, the author of Ephesians, immediately after his lengthy treatment of the household codes, reminded his readers that these codes were born of Satan, not of Christ. They represented "the rulers," "the authorities," and "the cosmic powers of this present darkness" (Eph. 6:12), not the kingdom of God. He therefore called on Christians to resist and struggle against the spiritual oppression this system represented, even while conforming to the outward requirements of the household codes themselves. Put another way, he counseled the Ephesian Christians to conform, even as they practiced spiritual subversion. Here are his words:

> Finally, be strong in the Lord and in the strength of his power. Put on the whole armor of God, so that you may be able to stand against the wiles of the devil. For our struggle is not against enemies of blood and flesh, but against the rulers, against the authorities, against the cosmic powers of this present darkness, against the spiritual forces of evil in the heavenly places. Therefore take up the whole armor of God, so that you may be able to withstand on that evil day, and having done everything to stand firm. (Gal. 6:10–13)

Scholars debate the authorship of both Colossians and Ephesians, but one thing can be said with certainty: both passages quoted here clearly reflect Pauline theology, especially insofar as they counsel implicit resistance to the empire.

The letter to Titus offers advice to slaves as well and reflects this same concern with household codes. But it also reflects a concern that disobedient slaves might open the church to scathing criticism, and especially to the charge that the church was out of step with Roman custom and was therefore subversive. Because the writer of Titus wants the behavior of slaves to be "an ornament to the doctrine of God our Savior" (Titus 2:10), this text advises slaves "to be submissive to their masters and to give satisfaction in every respect; they are not to talk back, not to pilfer, but to show complete and perfect fidelity" (2:9–10). This text is obviously more conservative than Paul's letter to Philemon and more conservative even than the epistles to the Colossians and the Ephesians.

But this letter to Titus is more conservative in other ways as well, for while it requires "complete and perfect fidelity" on the part of slaves (2:9), it says nothing at all about the way masters should treat their servants. That is a startling omission in light of Paul's concern for mutual brotherhood and in light of the concern expressed even in Colossians and Ephesians for master-slave reciprocity.

It must be obvious that the advice offered to slaves in Titus—and to some extent, the advice offered to slaves in Colossians and Ephesians—is out of line with the passionate concern for social justice that dominates the biblical vision of the kingdom of God, whether we find that vision in the Hebrew prophets, in the Gospels, or in Paul's epistles. Whether one wants to argue that these are not authentically Pauline texts is really beside the point in this context.

What matters is the issue to which John Dominic Crossan has already called our attention, namely, that even in the Bible itself, we find a striking contest between the principles of the kingdom of God that promise to subvert the imperial powers, on the one hand, and the principles of civilization that promise to sustain them, on the other. When Titus requires slaves "to be submissive to their masters" with "complete and perfect fidelity," or when Colossians and Ephesians counsel Christians to conform to the empire's household codes, they implicitly encourage Christians to conform to the principles of civilization, notwithstanding the fact that these two letters counsel *spiritual* resistance.

The truth is, one can find in the Bible not only support for liberating slaves and women, but also support for keeping both slaves and women in bondage. One is in keeping with the kingdom of God;

the other is not. The fact that so many American Christians fail to make this distinction is a failure that is potentially catastrophic for the church, the nation, and the world. The problem is that many American Christians view the Bible as a perfectly flat text. Each biblical statement, injunction, or admonition becomes equally authoritative with every other statement, injunction, or admonition. They are all normative.

Thus, some Christians can—and do—find biblical authority for keeping women in subjection, just as slaveholders in the American South found biblical authority for slavery. Some Christians find biblical support for killing, violence, and war—even for a final Armageddon that will destroy the earth and every living thing upon it. And other Christians use the Bible as an excuse for ignoring global warming, since, as a student once told me, God will rapture the Christians away from the earth in any event, leaving the ungodly to suffer the effects of global warming.

Because the Bible bears witness to the principles of the kingdom of God, on the one hand, and the principles of civilization, on the other, Christians finally must choose: Will they pledge their allegiance to the Bible, the whole Bible, and nothing but the Bible, or will they pledge their allegiance to the principles of the kingdom of God? Will they pledge their allegiance to the Bible, the whole Bible, and nothing but the Bible, or will they pledge their allegiance to the radical teachings of Jesus?

That decision is up to them. But one thing is certain. Those Christians who read the Bible in a flat, uncritical fashion risk placing the Bible above the biblical vision of the kingdom of God, above the teachings of Jesus, and even above God himself. In this way, the Bible becomes the idol that sustains injustice, violence, and war. And in an ironic sort of way, the Bible becomes the text that can also sustain the traditional vision of Christian America.

Paul's Theology of Peacemaking

Alongside social justice, Paul viewed peacemaking as the second key component of the kingdom of God. In this way, he perpetuated a long and venerable tradition that reached back to Jesus and the Hebrew prophets.

One who reads the apostle Paul in any depth at all will quickly discover how much this man prized peace and a gentle spirit. To the church at Philippi he writes, "Let your gentleness be known to everyone" (4:5), and he reminds the Thessalonian Christians, "We were gentle among you, like a nurse tenderly caring for her own children" (I Thess. 2:7). In the church at Rome, dissension had emerged over the question of Jewish dietary regulations. In that context, Paul literally defined the kingdom of God as a kingdom of peace. "For the kingdom of God is not food and drink but righteousness and peace and joy in the Holy Spirit. . . . Let us then pursue what makes for peace and for mutual upbuilding" (Rom. 14:17, 19).

To that same church, he offered this additional advice: "We who are strong ought to put up with the failings of the weak, and not to please ourselves. Each of us must please our neighbor for the good purpose of building up the neighbor. For Christ did not please himself. . . . Welcome one another, therefore, just as Christ has welcomed you" (Rom. 15:1–3, 7).

Paul not only valued peace and a gentle spirit; he also rejected violence and war. Thus, to the church in Corinth he wrote that Christians wage war not with chariots and weapons of steel, but with the grace and wisdom of God: "We live as human beings, but we do not wage war according to human standards; for the weapons of our warfare are not merely human, but they have divine power to destroy strongholds" (II Cor. 10:3–4).

Strongholds, indeed! As we saw in the previous section, the author of Ephesians—either Paul or a disciple of Paul—suggests exactly what those strongholds were: "the rulers, . . . the authorities, . . . the cosmic powers of this present darkness, . . . [and] the spiritual forces of evil in the heavenly places" (6:12)—in other words, those spiritual powers that sustain war, injustice, and oppression. To counter those powers, this author insists that "God . . . raised him [Jesus] from the dead and seated him at his right hand in the heavenly places, far above all rule and authority and power and dominion, and above every name that is named, not only in this age but also in the age to come" (1:20–21). In writing words like these, this author stands in the long tradition of treason against Rome—a tradition we first encountered when the angel announced to the shepherds the birth of a child who was both Savior and Lord.

Because his struggle, and that of the Christians to whom he wrote, was "not against enemies of blood and flesh, but against . . . the cosmic powers of this present darkness," the author of Ephesians commended what he called "the whole armor of God"—an armor that includes a breastplate of justice and shoes of peace:

Therefore take up the whole armor of God. .... Stand therefore, and fasten the belt of truth around your waist, and put on the breastplate of righteousness [justice]. As shoes for your feet put on whatever will make you ready to proclaim the gospel of peace. With all of these, take the shield of faith, with which you will be able to quench all the flaming arrows of the evil one. Take the helmet of salvation, and the sword of the Spirit, which is the word of God. (6:13–17)

Perhaps the most important thing we could say about Paul in the context of peacemaking is this: he fully embraced Jesus' radical counsel of love for enemies. We recall that Jesus said in the Sermon on the Mount, "You have heard that it was said, 'You shall love your neighbor and hate your enemy.' But I say to you, Love your enemies and pray for those who persecute you" (Matt. 5:43–44). By any measure, that statement is the gold standard for peacemaking.

In the letter to the Romans, Paul offered a statement that sounds remarkably like Jesus' counsel in the Sermon on the Mount, though with considerably more amplification:

Bless those who persecute you; bless and do not curse them. ....
Do not repay anyone evil for evil, but take thought for what is noble in the sight of all. If it is possible, so far as it depends on you, live peaceably with all. Beloved, never avenge yourselves, but leave room for the wrath of God; for it is written, "Vengeance is mine, I will repay, says the Lord." No, "if your enemies are hungry, feed them; if they are thirsty, give them something to drink; for by doing this you will heap burning coals on their heads." Do not be overcome by evil, but overcome evil with good. (12:14–21)

This passage is especially remarkable when one considers that Paul had every reason to embrace hatred, vengeance, and a spirit of violence—if not violence itself—against those from whom he suffered so much. Both Jews and Gentiles harassed and persecuted the apostle, often in unspeakable ways, and in his various epistles, Paul describes his sufferings in graphic detail. For example, in II Corinthians, Paul mentions his sufferings time and again, as in 1:8–9: "We do not want you to be unaware, brothers and sisters, of the affliction we experienced in Asia; for we were so utterly, unbearably crushed that we despaired of life itself. Indeed, we felt that we had received the sentence of death." In 6:4–5, he returns to that theme: "As servants of God we have commended ourselves in every way: through great endurance, in afflictions, hardships, calamities, beatings, imprisonments, riots, labors, sleepless nights, hunger."

But nowhere does he catalog his sufferings more fully than he does in II Corinthians 11:23–27, where he makes suffering the measure of his ministry. Other apostles, he says, may be far more eloquent than he, but the measure of a true servant of Christ is not eloquence, but suffering:

> Are they ministers of Christ? . . . I am a better one: with far greater labors, far more imprisonments, with countless floggings, and often near death. Five times I have received from the Jews the forty lashes minus one. Three times I was beaten with rods. Once I received a stoning. Three times I was shipwrecked; for a night and a day I was adrift at sea; on frequent journeys, in danger from rivers, danger from bandits, danger from my own people, danger from Gentiles, danger in the city, danger in the wilderness, danger at sea, danger from false brothers and sisters; in toil and hardship, through many a sleepless night, hungry and thirsty, often without food, cold and naked.

The striking thing about Paul is that he responded to those who caused his suffering with a genuine spirit of patience, forbearance, and non-violence, and he did so, as he put it, "for the sake of Christ." Thus, he writes in II Corinthians 12:10, "I am content with weaknesses, insults, hardships, persecutions, and calamities for the sake of Christ; for whenever I am weak, then I am strong."

When Paul employs the phrase "for the sake of Christ," he doubtless means that he seeks to imitate Christ. For Paul was convinced that when he accepted in a nonviolent manner the persecution that came his way, he thereby reflected the life, teachings, and example of Jesus. He makes this point clear in II Corinthians 4:8–12:

> We are afflicted in every way, but not crushed; perplexed, but not driven to despair; persecuted, but not forsaken; struck down, but not destroyed; always carrying in the body the death of Jesus, so that the life of Jesus may also be made visible in our bodies. For while we live, we are always being given up to death for Jesus' sake, so that the life of Jesus may be made visible in our mortal flesh.

Not only did Paul refuse to resist his persecutors, either with a violent spirit or with violence itself. He also followed the counsel he himself had given the Roman Christians: "Bless those who per-

secute you; bless and do not curse them." Thus, in his first letter
to the Corinthians, he wrote, "To the present hour we are hungry
and thirsty, we are poorly clothed and beaten and homeless, and
we grow weary from the work of our own hands. When reviled,
we bless; when persecuted, we endure; when slandered, we speak
kindly. We have become like the rubbish of the world, the dregs of
all things, to this very day" (I Cor. 4:11–13). Then he counseled his
readers, "I appeal to you, then, be imitators of me" (I Cor. 4:16).

What could possibly have prompted such extraordinary behavior on Paul's part? Already we have noted that Paul embraced
nonviolence in his attempt to imitate Christ. But there is more,
for Paul uses two short words to explain the ultimate motivation
for the love he sought to extend even to his enemies: "God's love."
Thus, in Romans he writes that "we also boast in our sufferings,
knowing that suffering produces endurance, and endurance produces character, and character produces hope, and hope does not
disappoint us, because God's love has been poured into our hearts
through the Holy Spirit that has been given to us" (5:3–5).

God's love was not for Paul a mere fact of life. It was a constant source of amazement. After all, only a few years before, Paul
had viciously persecuted the earliest Christians, but in spite of
these crimes, Paul had become a recipient of God's grace. One can
almost feel, therefore, the sense of incredulity that gave birth to
these words: "For while we were still weak, at the right time Christ
died for the ungodly. Indeed, rarely will anyone die for a righteous
person—though perhaps for a good person someone might actually
dare to die. But God proves his love for us in that while we were still
sinners Christ died for us" (Rom. 5:6–8). In truth, Paul embodied
in his own life the essence of the Christian gospel: because God
had extended such unmerited love to him, he had no choice but to
extend that same unmerited love to others, including those who
made his life miserable through abuse and persecution.

This backdrop gives a whole new meaning to the well-known
hymn to love that Paul composed in his first letter to the Corinthians which appears in our English Bibles in chapter 13. Every
first-year Greek student knows that the Greeks had three words
for love. *Eros* meant physical love, as in our English word, erotic.
Phileo meant brotherly love. And *agape* meant self-giving, self-
effacing, and self-emptying love. It is significant that when Paul
writes of love in I Corinthians 13, he uses the word *agape* for that

is how he experienced the love of Christ, and that is how he sought to respond even to those who sought his life. Thus, he writes in the famous Corinthian passage:

> Love is patient; love is kind; love is not envious or boastful or arrogant or rude. It does not insist on its own way; it is not irritable or resentful; it does not rejoice in wrongdoing, but rejoices in the truth. It bears all things, believes all things, hopes all things, endures all things. Love never ends. (I Cor. 13:4–8)

Finally, armed with this kind of love, Paul turned the tables not only on his Jewish and Gentile opponents, but even on the Roman Empire itself. While the empire imagined itself the greatest conqueror of all time, Paul believed that he and his brothers and sisters were "more than conquerors through him who loved us" (Rom. 8:37). There is a sense, then—a very profound sense, in fact—in which Paul's remarkable statement in Romans 8 can be read as one more rebuke against the pretensions of the Roman Empire.

> If God is for us, who is against us? . . . Who will separate us from the love of Christ? Will hardship, or distress, or persecution, or famine, or nakedness, or peril, or sword? As it is written,
> "For your sake we are being killed all day long;
> we are accounted as sheep to be slaughtered."
> No, in all these things, we are more than conquerors through him who loved us. For I am convinced that neither death, nor life, nor angels, nor rulers, nor things present, nor things to come, nor powers, nor height, nor depth, nor anything else in all creation, will be able to separate us from the love of God in Christ Jesus our Lord. (Rom. 8:31, 35–39)

Nonviolence and the Early Church

For the most part, Christians for the first three hundred years of the Christian movement conformed their lives to the teachings of Jesus and Paul on peacemaking and nonviolence. I say "for the most part" because there are no references in Christian literature during this period that approve of Christian involvement in war and violence, but many references that denounce it. That said, it is also true that some of the earliest Christians did serve in the army. The most obvious example is Cornelius, the officer in the Roman military whose conversion to Christ is recorded in the tenth chapter of the book of Acts. But Luke tells the story of Cornelius to make the point that Gentiles were welcome in the Christian movement, not to make a point about military service. Whether Cornelius eventually abandoned the army must remain a matter of conjecture.

Still, it is clear that the tradition of nonresistance commended by Jesus and Paul dominated the witness of the early church. In fact, until the decade 170–80 C.E., we find precious little evidence of Christians serving in the armed forces. Even then, military involvement was a minority report, a fact noted by Celsus, the second-century pagan critic of the Christian movement. "If all were to do the same as you," Celsus charged, "there would be nothing to prevent [the emperor] being left in utter solitude and desertion, and the affairs of the earth would fall into the hands of the wildest and most lawless barbarians."[47] As Roland Bainton writes, "Such words are so explicit as to warrant the assumption that Celsus knew of no Christians who would accept military service." Yet, as Bainton points out, Celsus's assessment was not altogether correct, for in 173 C.E. we find evidence of Christians serving in Emperor Marcus Aurelius's Thundering Legion. From that time on, evidence for Christians in the military begins to mount.[48]

Still, the witness of the early Christian movement on behalf of nonresistance is overwhelming. The testimony from two Christian leaders during the late second and early third centuries must suffice. Tertullian (c. 155–230 C.E.) claimed that Jesus' command to love one's enemies is the "principal precept" of the Christian religion. In that light, he asked, "If we are enjoined to love our enemies, whom have we to hate? If injured we are forbidden to retaliate. Who then can suffer injury at our hands?" And Cyprian (c. 200–258 C.E.) summarized the heart of the Christian faith like this:

> That you should not curse; that you should not seek again your goods when taken from you; when buffeted you should turn the other cheek; and forgive not seven times but seventy times seven. . . . That you should love your enemies and pray for your adversaries and persecutors."[49]

If the rejection of vengeance and the commitment to peacemaking and nonviolence was such a central part of the Christian religion for its first three hundred years, it's fair to ask, what happened? Why do most American Christians—and most Christians around the world, for that matter—view Jesus' teachings on nonviolence as noble ideals but finally unrealistic and unworkable? To make this question even more pointed, why is the United States, widely recognized as the most Christian country in the world, so accepting of violence, especially state-sponsored violence? And to make this question more pointed still, why do Christians so seldom question the conventional American wisdom regarding the necessity for war?[50]

There are doubtless many answers to those questions, but any answer would have to begin with the radical changes that transformed the Christian religion in the fourth century, first under the Roman Emperor Constantine (272–337 C.E.) and then under the Emperor Theodosius the Great (347–395 C.E.). Before Constantine, Rome had officially outlawed the Christian religion, and for one to convert to the Christian faith might well cost one's life. In 313 C.E. Constantine legalized Christianity for the first time in its history. Then, in 391 C.E., Theodosius made Christianity the only legal religion in the Roman Empire. Historians and social scientists describe this kind of state-supported Christianity as a "Christian establishment."

These decisions were both momentous and far-reaching, for they created for the first time in Christian history the marriage of church and state, an arrangement that persists in Europe to this day. That marriage meant that the state would protect and honor the church, while the church was expected to honor the state and its rulers by encouraging the faithful to conform to the rulers' decrees. Inevitably, those decrees included the command to participate in the empire's wars.

Before Constantine, Christians most often resisted that command and refused to wage war on behalf of the empire. But after the empire had bestowed great favor on the Christian religion, it expected compliance in return. It is not surprising that Christian theologians now began to find ways for Christians to serve the empire by taking up the empire's sword.

The first Christian theologian to work out a systematic justification for this radical change was Augustine (354–430 C.E.) in his just war theory. In the thirteenth century, another Christian theologian—Thomas Aquinas (1225–74 C.E.)—both confirmed and elaborated on that theory. Basically, the theory stated that Christians could participate in warfare—and Christian emperors could declare and wage war—but only if that war was a defensive war, was fought for a just cause, was declared by a lawful authority, was fought with good intentions, was waged as a last resort, had a reasonable chance of success, had as its ultimate goal the reestablishment of peace, avoided the killing of noncombatants, and only used a level of force appropriate to achieve its objectives.

From the time of Augustine until the present, Christians have launched innumerable wars against their enemies. Based on just war theory, some of those wars may indeed have been "just." But if we take seriously Chris Hedges's description of modern industrial warfare as "impersonal slaughter," it is difficult to imagine any modern war conforming to just war theory.[51] As a foreign correspondent for the *New York Times*, Hedges covered many of America's wars—in the Balkans, the Middle East, and Central America. In that capacity, he witnessed modern warfare as few can unless they, themselves, are in the fight.

Among his many observations, Hedges noted that "modern war is directed primarily against civilians." Indeed, he reported that "in the wars of the twentieth century not less than 62 million civilians have perished, nearly 20 million more than the 43 million military personnel killed."[52] So much for one of the principal requirements of just war theory. Be that as it may, one thing is clear: as useful as just war theory may have been in certain circumstances, it is a radical departure from the teachings of Jesus and a radical departure from the dominant witness of the Christian community for its first three hundred years.[53]

The point, by now, must be clear. According to the Christians' own New Testament text, the values of the kingdom of God stand diametrically opposed to the values of empire. According to the New Testament, empires seek greater and greater power over others and more and more wealth for the elites who reside within the empire's boundaries. They achieve that expansion on the backs of the poor and the dispossessed, whether the poor reside within the empire or in other nations. And when their own self-interests are threatened, empires embrace violence and wars of vengeance or retribution—even wars of preemption—against their enemies. If the empire imagines itself a Christian empire—as so many Americans think of the United States—then it seeks to justify its wars with some version of Augustine's just war theory.

On the other hand, the Christians' New Testament tells us that the kingdom of God rejects self-interest, urges mercy instead of violence, promotes peacemaking instead of war, counsels love for one's enemies, and exalts the poor, the dispossessed, and the powerless—those whom the empire so often exploits.

The Kingdom of God in the Book of Revelation

We turn now to the last book of the New Testament—the Apocalypse of John, otherwise known as the book of Revelation. Scholars debate whether this book was written by John the apostle or by another John, sometimes known as John of Patmos. They also debate whether the book was written near the end of the reign of the Roman Emperor Nero, in the late 60s C.E., or near the end of the reign of Emperor Domitian in 95 or 96 C.E.

Either way, we can be confident of at least one of the book's central themes: the conviction that the kingdom of God will finally triumph over the oppressive, imperial power that was the Roman Empire. And we can be confident that the backdrop to this book was imperial persecution of the Christian movement. Revelation reflects these persecutions in several passages, but especially chapter 20, verse 4:

> I also saw the souls of those who had been beheaded for their testimony to Jesus and for the word of God. They had not worshiped the beast [read: empire or emperor] or its image and had not received its mark on their foreheads or their hands.

In the face of harassment and persecution, therefore, John counsels Christians to refuse allegiance to the empire but to remain faithful to the values of the kingdom of God, even unto death. In this way, the book of Revelation simply continues a theme that is prominent throughout the New Testament: the struggle between empire and the kingdom of God. One verse in Revelation captures this message nicely:

> Do not fear what you are about to suffer. Behold, the devil is about to throw some of you into prison so that you may be tested, and for ten days you will have affliction. Be faithful unto death, and I will give you the crown of life. (2:10)

The metaphor for empire in this particular text is Babylon. Since Babylon had long since vanished from the earth, it seems clear that Babylon is a symbol for Rome and its dominance over the ancient world. Indeed, John presents Rome as a violent and licentious empire that has corrupted the earth with its lust for power and wealth, defiled the nations with its greed, built its empire by oppressing the poor, and persecuted those who pledged allegiance to Jesus and refused allegiance to the state. John therefore writes to assure the Christian community that, even though Babylon seems all-powerful now, the day will come when Babylon will fall and the kingdom of God will emerge victorious. Thus, he writes:

> Fallen, fallen is Babylon the great!
> It has become a dwelling place of demons. . . .
> For all the nations have drunk of the wine of the wrath of her fornication,
> and the kings of the earth have committed fornication with her,
> and the merchants of the earth have grown rich from the power of her luxury. (18:2–3)

Further, the merchants of Babylon (read Rome)—the elites of the earth—had built their fortunes on the blood of the marginalized and the dispossessed. Reflecting on that fact, John continues:

> For your merchants were the magnates of the earth,
> and all nations were deceived by your sorcery.
> And in you was found the blood of prophets and of saints,
> and of all who have been slaughtered on earth. (18:23–24)

When Babylon falls—and fall she will—the kings and merchants of the earth will find themselves in despair, since the source of their own ill-gotten gain will be no more. John therefore offers this vision:

> The kings of the earth, who committed fornication and lived in luxury with her, will weep and wail over her when they see the smoke of her burning; they will stand far off, in fear of her torment, and say,
> "Alas, alas, the great city,
> Babylon, the mighty city!
> For in one hour your judgment has come. . . ." (18:9–10)
> [And] the merchants . . . who gained wealth from her, will stand far off, in fear of her torment, weeping and mourning aloud,
> "Alas, alas, the great city
> clothed in fine linen, in purple and scarlet,
> adorned with gold, with jewels, and with pearls!
> For in one hour all this wealth has been laid waste." (18:15–17)

Even the sailors from neighboring nations will weep and mourn, for they understood all too well that Babylon's destruction would put an end to their profit-taking.

> And all shipmasters and seafarers, sailors and all whose trade is on the sea, stood far off, and cried out as they saw the smoke of her burning,

> "What city was like the great city?"
> And they threw dust on their heads, as they wept and mourned, crying out,
>> "Alas, alas, the great city,
>> where all who had ships at sea
>> grew rich by her wealth!
>> For in one hour she has been laid waste." (18:17–19)

According to Revelation, what allowed Babylon to commit such extraordinary crimes was the fact that Babylon arrogated to itself qualities that belong only to God. Indeed, the text says that Babylon "glorified herself" (18:7). Through her extraordinary wealth and power, she sought to determine the course of human history. She denied she committed evil deeds and claimed for herself a radical sense of innocence. Though she herself was demonic, she confused herself with the holy city, Jerusalem. For all these reasons, she imagined that she was eternal and would have no end. Thus, she said, "I rule as a queen; I am no widow, and I will never see grief" (18:7).

What an extraordinary description of the Roman Empire this was! Domitian, who may have ruled when John wrote this book, required his subjects to address him as "*dominus et deus*," that is, "Lord and God," and worship his image. In truth, Rome imagined that she was the very "kingdom of God," though in point of fact, she opposed the kingdom of God at every step along the way.

The book of Revelation insists that glory and honor belong not to Babylon, but to God. John therefore exults over the destruction of Babylon in the following words:

> After this I heard what seemed to be the loud voice of a great multitude in heaven, saying,
>> "Hallelujah! Salvation and glory and power to our God,
>> for his judgments are true and just;
>> he has judged the great whore who corrupted the earth with her fornication,
>> and he has avenged on her the blood of his servants." (19:1–2)

Finally, John draws the contrast between Babylon, filled with brutality and debauchery, and the gentle kingdom of God:

> And I saw the holy city, the new Jerusalem, coming down out of heaven from God, prepared as a bride adorned for her husband. And I heard a loud voice from the throne saying,
>> "See, the home of God is among mortals.

He will dwell with them;
they will be his peoples, and God himself will be with them;
he will wipe every tear from their eyes.
Death will be no more;
mourning and crying and pain will be no more,
for the first things have passed away." (21:2–4)

Upon reading this passage, one can hardly help but recall the Beatitudes in Matthew's rendition of the Sermon on the Mount. In both texts, the kingdom of God will bring peace, mercy, justice, and comfort to those who have suffered and endured the twisted values of a brutal empire. Throughout the New Testament, this is the fundamental meaning—and the fundamental promise—of the kingdom of God.

Still, we must admit that in its portrayal of the kingdom of God, Revelation is a highly ambiguous text. It clearly depicts the triumph of the kingdom of God over the brutal, self-serving nations of the earth. But unlike other New Testament texts that argue that the kingdom of God will triumph not by might nor by power but, instead, by humility, patience, and love—even love for one's enemies—Revelation argues that the kingdom of God will triumph over the imperial powers through violent destruction. Put another way, while other New Testament texts present the paradoxical dimension of the kingdom of God—one lives by dying to self, one wins by losing, one becomes first by putting one's self last, and so on—one finds in Revelation no hint of paradox at all.

Indeed, Revelation 18:6–7 has an angel from heaven passing judgment on the Roman Empire, metaphorically depicted here as Babylon:

Render to her as she herself has rendered,
and repay her double for her deeds;
mix a double draught for her in the cup she mixed.
As she glorified herself and lived luxuriously,
so give her a like measure of torment and grief.

This judgment can only be described as "an eye for an eye and a tooth for a tooth" carried to an extreme, for the admonition is clear: "repay her double"—an ethic utterly foreign to the vision of the kingdom of God depicted in the rest of the New Testament text. After this portrayal of Babylon's utter destruction, this book offers a picture of the heavenly host rejoicing that God "has avenged on her [Babylon] the blood of his servants" (19:2).

After working one's way through the entire New Testament and growing accustomed to the standard picture of the kingdom of God—that is, "Blessed are those who are persecuted for righteousness' sake, for theirs is the kingdom of heaven"—one can only be startled by Revelation's portrayal of divine vengeance. But one is startled even further when one discovers that the purveyor of this violence is none other than Jesus, the Prince of Peace! Thus, according to Revelation 19:11–16,

> I saw heaven opened, and there was a white horse! Its rider is called Faithful and True, and in righteousness he judges and makes war. His eyes are like a flame of fire, and on his head are many diadems; and he has a name inscribed that no one knows but himself. He is clothed in a robe dipped in blood, and his name is called The Word of God. And the armies of heaven, wearing fine linen, white and pure, were following him on white horses. From his mouth comes a sharp sword with which to strike down the nations, and he will rule them with a rod of iron; he will tread the wine press of the fury of the wrath of God the Almighty. On his robe and on his thigh he has a name inscribed, "King of kings and Lord of lords." (19:11–16)

On the other hand, some have argued that the violent aspects of this book are metaphorical, not literal, since by its very nature, apocalyptic literature is highly symbolic. Certain aspects of this text seem to confirm that interpretation. Thus, the sword Jesus wields is not held in his hand but comes from his mouth, suggesting "the sword of the Spirit, which is the word of God" (Eph. 6:17). Likewise, some have argued that the "robe dipped in blood" is dipped in the blood of Jesus himself, not in the blood of his enemies.[54]

Be that as it may, this single text has encouraged endless appeals to violence and retribution on the part of Christians who support the imperial powers. For example, the reader will recall the woman referenced in chapter 1 who responded to an editorial I had written for the *Harrisburg Patriot-News*. When I wondered why so many evangelical Christians take a pro-life position but seem never to question the legitimacy of war, this woman wrote, "If you read the book of Revelation, you see an image of the godly Son of God (yes, the Lamb of God) ready to do vicious battle. He is not meek. He is not a pacifist. He is angry and powerful, and will wage war."[55] Her reading of that text assured her that America's invasion and occupation of Iraq was fully consistent with Christian ideals.

Julia Ward Howe, who celebrated the victories of the Union Army in her "Battle Hymn of the Republic," took inspiration from this very same passage. When Howe wrote the line that is so familiar to virtually every American—"Mine eyes have seen the glory of the coming of the Lord, He is trampling out the vintage where the grapes of wrath are stored"—she clearly found her source in Revelation 19:15: "He will tread the wine press of the fury of the wrath of God the Almighty."

Revelation's picture of Jesus, whose robe is "dipped in blood" and who will "strike down the nations" and "rule them with a rod of iron," also inspires many contemporary fundamentalists—those Christians who see the United States as God's chosen agent in the final Battle of Armageddon, and who sanction nuclear weapons as the means by which God will finally destroy his opponents—a chilling scenario we shall explore in chapter 5.

When one considers that Revelation's portrayal of divinely sponsored vengeance, violence, and retribution is so out of line with the dominant picture of the kingdom of God that we find elsewhere in the New Testament, one is forced to return again to John Dominic Crossan's observation that the struggle between human civilization, on the one hand, and the kingdom of God, on the other, "is depicted *inside the Bible* itself. . . . The Christian Bible forces us to witness the struggle of these two transcendental visions *within its own pages* and to ask ourselves as Christians how *we* decide between them." Crossan's conclusion bears repeating: "*We are bound to whichever of these visions was incarnated by and in the historical Jesus.*"[56]

On that basis, Crossan rejects the picture of violence presented in Revelation as completely out of keeping with the picture of the kingdom of God incarnate in the historical Jesus. "In the last century alone," he writes,

> we humans have done worse things to one another on this earth and to the earth itself than anything imagined even in that terrible vision of the Warrior Christ or in any of the other visions of the Great Apocalypse. And we may yet destroy our species or our earth. But how do we dare say that God plans and wants it or that Jesus leads and effects it? For me as a Christian, that seems to be *the* crime against divinity, *the* sin against the Holy Spirit.[57]

And yet the overall message of Revelation remains enormously instructive, namely, that the kingdom of God will finally triumph over the oppressive nations and empires of the earth.

The Kingdom of God in Scripture and Its Meaning
for the United States

From our brief review of the book of Revelation, we understand how its central theme simply extends and elaborates a motif that dominates the entire New Testament—the struggle between empire and the kingdom of God, waged on behalf of the poor and oppressed of every nation and every age.

At this point we must ask, what implications does this vision hold for the United States of America? Already we have seen that some use this text to justify righteous violence on the part of so-called Christian nations. But is it possible that that interpretation misses the fundamental point of this text?

For another interpretation, we turn to William Stringfellow—an activist, war resister, and lay theologian during the 1960s and 1970s. In his important book, *An Ethic for Christians and Other Aliens in a Strange Land*, Stringfellow specifically sought to understand America through the lens of the book of Revelation. He had no interest in using Revelation as a tool for justifying American violence against nations some American Christians might view as connected to the Antichrist. Nor did he wish to use that book as a tool to predict the future, as so many Christians use that book today. Nor, in his view, was Revelation helpful for understanding when Jesus might return and the end times might begin, or for exploring such fanciful notions as the rapture or the tribulation.

Rather, Stringfellow viewed Revelation as a paradigm for "ethics and political tactics" in our world today. Indeed, the first principle Stringfellow wishes his readers to understand is this: "The biblical topic is politics."[58]

And indeed it is. The Bible offers no counsel on how one should vote or whether Republicans or Democrats or some other political party should control the reins of power in the United States. But the Bible is a profoundly political book in this fundamental sense: It describes a struggle between two kingdoms, the kingdom of God on the one hand and the nations on the other. If that struggle is merely poetic, hypothetical, or esoteric, then biblical politics finally make no difference in the real world. But Revelation presents that contest as a struggle for life and death and a struggle in which the kingdom of God finally triumphs over the nations of this world.

Stringfellow felt called to join that struggle in a very concrete way, so he practiced law in Harlem, not on behalf of wealthy and privileged elites, but on behalf of the marginalized and the poor. For him, therefore, the struggle between the kingdom of God, on the one hand, and imperial values, on the other, was a real and tangible struggle that consumed his energies on a daily basis.

Then, in the early 1960s, the United States became involved in a long and deadly war in Vietnam. That war became the immediate context for his book, *An Ethic for Christians and Other Aliens in a Strange Land*, published in 1973, just after the last American troops had left that Southeast Asian country. From Stringfellow's perspective, one fact dominated that conflict: The United States had been responsible for the deaths of millions of Vietnamese peasants in order to satisfy its own imperial interests.

Among Christians, Stringfellow was not alone in that assessment. Martin Luther King Jr., for example, in his famous sermon at New York's Riverside Church, lamented the fact that the peasants of South Vietnam

> languish under our bombs and consider us—not their fellow Vietnamese—the real enemy. They move sadly and apathetically as we herd them off the land of their fathers into concentration camps where minimal social needs are rarely met. They know they must move or be destroyed by our bombs. So they go—primarily women and children and the aged. They watch as we poison their water, as we kill a million acres of their crops. They must weep as the bulldozers roar through their areas preparing to destroy their precious trees. They wander into the hospitals, with at least twenty casualties from American firepower for one "Vietcong"-inflicted injury. So far we may have killed a million of them—mostly children.[59]

King's description explains precisely why Stringfellow claimed that during the Vietnam War

> Americans have been successively induced to squander life on a scale so prodigious it appalls imagination and defies calculation for the sake of stopping the alleged threat of Communist China or of securing "self-determination" for the Vietnamese or of hindering the so-called domino theory or of vindicating American "honor" or of serving the "national security" interests.[60]

The Vietnam War, therefore, was the single factor that prompted Stringfellow to explore the book of Revelation in an effort to understand his own nation. In the process, he discovered several characteristics of Babylon that he found in his own nation at that time.

First, he concluded that Babylon is a symbol for any and every nation that seeks to usurp the role and power of God and, in that way, seeks to determine who shall live and who shall die, and for what reasons. Those nations, he wrote, seek to deceive their subjects "into thinking and acting as if the moral worth or justification of human beings is defined and determined by commitment or surrender—literally, sacrifice—of human life to the survival, interest, grandeur, and vanity" of the nation.[61] He added:

> The moral pretenses of Imperial Rome, the millennial claims of Nazism, the arrogance of Marxist dogma, the anxious insistence that America be "number one" among nations are all versions of Babylon's idolatry. All share in this grandiose view of the nation by which the principality assumes the place of God in the world.[62]

Second, he argued that Babylon symbolizes nations that imagine that they alone control the course of human history. Thus, he wrote,

> This is the vanity of every principality—and notably for a nation— that the principality is sovereign in history; which is to say, that it presumes it is the power in relation to which the moral significance of everything and everyone else is determined.[63]

It was this very moral arrogance that Stringfellow felt he had witnessed in the United States during the course of the Vietnam War.

His reading of the book of Revelation, along with his judgment that the United States had "squander[ed] life on a scale so prodigious it appalls imagination and defies calculation," led Stringfellow to identify a third characteristic of Babylon—a characteristic very much related to and dependent on the others. Babylon, Stringfellow concluded, is a symbol for any and every nation that is captive to the power of death. In the book of Revelation, he observed, the metaphor of Babylon pointed squarely to the Roman Empire, which routinely squandered human life to achieve its own imperial purposes. During the war in Vietnam, he had witnessed his own nation succumb to the power of death in the very same way.

Finally, Stringfellow found that the practice of deceit was central to the metaphor of Babylon. In this regard he argued that:

> A rudimentary claim with which the principalities confront and subvert persons is that truth in the sense of eventful and factual matter does not exist. In the place of truth and appropriating the name of truth are data engineered and manufactured, programmed and propagated by the principality. The truth is usurped

and displaced by a self-serving version of events or facts, with whatever selectivity, distortion, falsehood, manipulation, exaggeration, evasion, [or] concoction necessary to maintain the image or enhance the survival or multiply the coercive capacities of the principality.

Stringfellow found examples of this principle in both the Nixon and Johnson administrations, especially their

wide-ranging and systematic attack upon the media, upon newsmen, and upon citizens as auditors of news. In both of these administrations, the government's propaganda efforts have been especially concentrated upon selling a prevalent line about the Southeast Asian war.[64]

Stringfellow also found the principle of deceit in the wide-ranging "doublespeak" that characterized the American government during that war:

Doublespeak has been solemnly pronounced to deceive citizens, not to mention the Congress, about every escalation, every corruption, every wasted appropriation, every casualty report, every abdication of command responsibility and every insubordination, every atrocity of the war. For example, the cliché "winding down the war" has concealed the most deadly acceleration of firepower and destructive capability in the entire history of warfare on this planet. Again, in 1972, when the United Nations Secretary General verified American bombings of North Vietnamese dams and dikes, potentially jeopardizing as many as five million civilians, the response of the American authorities was classic doublespeak, to wit: "The dikes are not targeted." Or again, at the outset of the American combat involvement in Vietnam, doublespeak propagated the false conception that the U.S. intervention in Indochina with a handful of heavily subsidized mercenaries was an extension of the grand alliance of World War II.[65]

Relying, then, on the picture of Babylon presented in the text of Revelation, chapter 18, Stringfellow concluded that the Babylon metaphor points to any nation that seeks to usurp the role and power of God, that imagines it controls the course of human history, that allies itself with the power of death, and that justifies its actions with doublespeak and deceit.

Numerous nations have conformed to those criteria and have exemplified Babylon throughout human history, Stringfellow argued. The most obvious was ancient Rome, the very nation to which the metaphor of Babylon points in the text of John's Revelation. But there have been other nations in other periods that have conformed to the image of Babylon fully as much as ancient Rome.

"The spectacular example, in the earlier part of the twentieth century, of a nation and society and its majority classes and its leaders existing in precisely this condition," Stringfellow wrote, "is, of course, Nazi Germany." Then he added, "The extraordinary instance in the present time of the same situation is the United States of America."[66]

Many Americans may find shocking Stringfellow's attempt to link the moral purposes of the United States during the period of the Vietnam War with the moral purposes of Nazi Germany during World War II. But Stringfellow did not argue that the United States and Nazi Germany were in some final sense identical. Indeed, he readily admitted that there were fundamental differences between the two. But those differences, he argued, should not obscure the fact that both nations, in terms of their moral identity, reflected the essentially demonic dimensions of Babylon as portrayed in the book of Revelation.

By reflecting in this way on the meaning of the book of Revelation, William Stringfellow posed a direct and frontal challenge to the notion of Christian America. From his perspective, the United States—at least during the period of the Vietnam War—had taken on demonic proportions that linked it with Babylon and Rome and, at least in certain key respects, with Nazi Germany. In his view, America stood in resolute opposition to the principles of the kingdom of God that we considered earlier in this chapter.

But was Stringfellow right? And even if he was right about the United States during the period of the Vietnam War, could we possibly construe his argument as correct today? We will speak to those questions in the final chapter of this book.

A Postscript

In the meantime, we must address one final dimension of the kingdom of God as presented in the biblical text. We have seen how the kingdom of God places heavy emphasis on concern for the poor and for those on the margins of mainstream society. That emphasis is surely a central dimension of the Christian gospel. But there is another, equally important dimension of the Christian gospel, and that is the theme of forgiveness. The New Testament describes that theme with the word *grace*.

Grace is important, for who is capable of completely fulfilling the requirements of the kingdom of God? Who is capable of serving the poor and the dispossessed in such radically selfless ways as the New Testament seems to require? The theme of grace, therefore, suggests that God extends forgiveness to those who are able to admit their failures and imperfections.

Without this characteristic—without this willingness to admit one's failures and imperfections—one is hardly in a position to receive forgiveness. That is why humility and a rejection of claims to innocence constitute another fundamental dimension of the kingdom of God.

In Luke 18:10–14, Jesus told a story about two men who went to the temple to pray. One was a Pharisee. The other was a tax collector. In Jesus' day, Pharisees were widely regarded as self-righteous and unwilling to admit their failures and mistakes. That is why we often use the word *pharisaical* as synonymous with *hypocritical*.

On the other hand, Jews in first-century Palestine typically held tax collectors in utter contempt, first because they were servants of Rome, and second because they so often collected more taxes than Rome required and pocketed the difference.

In the story Jesus told,

The Pharisee, standing by himself, was praying thus, "God, I thank you that I am not like other people: thieves, rogues, adulterers, or even like this tax collector. I fast twice a week; I give a tenth of all my income." But the tax collector, standing far off, would not even look up to heaven, but was beating his breast and saying, "God, be merciful to me, a sinner!" (Luke 18:11–13)

Then Jesus drew the conclusion:

I tell you, this man went down to his home justified rather than the other; for all who exalt themselves will be humbled, but all who humble themselves will be exalted. (Luke 18:14)

To say that the tax collector went home justified was another way of saying that he had entered into the kingdom of God. He had entered the kingdom because he had humbled himself and acknowledged his significant wrongdoings. This is precisely why Jesus said to another group of religious leaders, "Truly I tell you, the tax collectors and the prostitutes are going into the kingdom of God ahead of you" (Mt. 21:31).

This is also why Jesus held up little children as exemplary of the kingdom of God. In Mark 9:35–37, Jesus said to his disciples, "Whoever wants to be first must be last of all and servant of all." Then, according to Mark, he took a child in his arms and said, "Whoever welcomes one such child in my name welcomes me." Only a few verses later (Mark 10:14–15), Jesus spoke of the children once again. "Let the little children come to me; do not stop them; for it is to such as these that the kingdom of God belongs. Truly I tell you, whoever does not receive the kingdom of God as a little child will never enter it."

But compare this emphasis on humility—a central feature of the kingdom of God—with the central characteristic the book of Revelation attributes to Babylon: "She [Babylon] glorified herself." And compare the humility that is so central to the kingdom of God with William Stringfellow's understanding of Babylon and those nations Babylon symbolizes. All those nations, Stringfellow argued, "share in this grandiose view of the nation by which the principality assumes the place of God in the world."[67]

In other words, in the kingdom of God there are no illusions of innocence. But claims of innocence are common among the empires of the world, a point that will become more apparent in the following chapters.

For now, we must ask two questions: How and why did the notion of Christian America emerge in the first place? And how has that notion functioned in the course of American history? We turn to those two questions in the following chapter.

Chapter 4

WHY DO WE THINK OF
America as a Christian Nation?

As we have made our way through earlier chapters of
this book, it has become increasingly clear that the idea
of Christian America is an oxymoron. But if that is true,
how and why did the notion of Christian America de-
velop in the first place? How and why have Christians
sought to promote that notion? What purpose did that
understanding serve? And how have Christians sought
to link the nation with the biblical vision of the kingdom of God? Answers to these questions, which we
explore in this chapter, inevitably lead us to periods
and events in western history that predate the birth of
the United States.

The Constantinian/Theodosian Settlement

We explored the first historical antecedent to the notion of Christian America in chapter 3 when we alluded
to the story of Constantine, who legalized Christianity
in 313 C.E. But Constantine was hardly the only actor
in that story. In 391 C.E. Theodosius the Great declared
Christianity *the only* legal religion of the empire. If in
earlier days the empire had launched sporadic persecutions against the church, now the empire persecuted
those who *refused to convert* to the Christian faith.

In time, emperors such as Justinian I in the sixth century would proclaim themselves both "priest and king"—the supreme head not only of the state but also of the church. These decisions required that the church would serve the state, even as the state protected the church—but only so long as the church was faithful to the imperial agenda.

Those developments created a type of Christianity that grew increasingly formal and ceremonial. After all, a church that rejected warfare and violence could hardly be useful to an empire. And a church whose chief concern was to care for the poor and the marginalized would be of no use at all to an empire committed to enlarging its power and wealth at the expense of the poor and the dispossessed.

It is hardly any wonder, then, that in this new imperial climate, ceremonial forms and liturgical rites increasingly displaced the ethical rigor of Jesus and the early church. What mattered now was not that one cared for the poor or the suffering or the dispossessed, but that one belonged to the church. What mattered now was not that one rejected violence, but that one participated in the Eucharist on a regular basis. What mattered now was not that one practiced the ethics of the kingdom of God, but that one confessed one's sins to an institutional priest in the context of an imperial church. The empire, in fact, hastened these transitions by constructing throughout its territories ornate and lavish buildings in which liturgy and ceremony could thrive.

These developments help explain the rise of the monastic movement in which monks and nuns sought solitude in places like the Egyptian desert. There, they believed, they could practice an austere and rigorous kind of Christianity that seemed so lacking in the context of the imperial church. In time, everyone understood that those who practiced such a radical form of the Christian life answered to a higher calling that never came to ordinary men and women. In this way, the empire largely succeeded in banishing from ordinary life the ethical norms associated with the biblical vision of the kingdom of God.

To make these observations is not to suggest that ceremonial forms and liturgical rites were either useless or irrelevant to the life of the church. Nor do I wish to suggest that liturgy and ceremony, on the one hand, and ethical rigor, on the other, are mutually exclusive. One need only recall the ethical witness of the Roman Catholic tradition for most of its history or, in recent times, the ethical witness of Christians like Dorothy Day, Oscar Romero, and Dietrich Bonhoeffer—to name but a few—to know that liturgy and ethics can reinforce one another. Still and all, the trend in the fourth- and fifth-century imperial church was toward the enhancement of ceremony at the expense of the ethical life—a fact to which the early monks and nuns bear witness.

And yet, the empire—at least after Constantine and Theodosius the Great—was a Christian empire. Everyone understood that fact. But the kind of Christianity that characterized this Christian empire had been severely compromised.

Our question now is this: What does this history of the ancient and medieval world have to do with the United States? There are at least two answers to that question.

First, if the United States is a Christian nation, it resembles in striking ways the sort of Christianized culture that thrived in medieval and Reformation Europe.

There are significant differences, of course. Every American schoolchild understands that the United States is the first nation in the history of the world to embrace the separation of church and state. Accordingly, the United States has never adopted the Christian religion in any official sense or mandated the Christian faith by force of law. Christianity in the United States is therefore voluntary, not coerced.

Yet to the extent that America is a Christian nation, it conforms to the imperial pattern of a Christian nation in this crucial regard: It routinely drives out the ethical and moral rigor the New Testament associates with the kingdom of God. If ecclesiastical ceremonies and liturgical rites supplanted the kingdom of God in the state-church arrangement of Europe, churchgoing and personal piety supplant that vision in the United States today. In many instances, therefore, Christianity in the United States has conformed to the mandates of the culture and the prerogatives of the state—patterns we shall trace in substantial detail in the following chapter.

The Calvinist Concern for the Sovereignty of God

The other answer to the question—what does the history of ancient, medieval, and Reformation Christianity have to do with the United States?—comes in two parts.

First, Europeans who settled the original thirteen colonies all arrived from nations that maintained state-church establishments.

Since that was the only arrangement they knew—and the only way a nation could be Christian, as far as they were concerned—they quite naturally expected the same kind of arrangement to prevail in their new home across the seas.

There were exceptions to this pattern, of course. Dissidents and dissenters—Quakers and Baptists, for example—routinely rejected both the moral failures and the religious tyranny that accompanied an established church. But many colonial Christians promoted the state-church relationship with as much rigor as if they had lived in tenth-century Europe.

And second, the majority of the early colonists in both New England and the Middle Colonies were Calvinists, informed not only by the long history of European Christianity, but also by the theology of their mentor, John Calvin.

Calvin was one of two preeminent Protestant reformers during the early sixteenth century. The other was Martin Luther. Calvin never questioned the assumption that church and state should be yoked together in a common enterprise. But he did seek to reverse the nature of the church-state relationship. In the Constantinian vision, the church served the purposes of the state, but Calvin determined that the state would serve the purposes of the church. And while the Constantinian settlement mandated that the values of the state would shape the values of the church, thereby transforming the church into the image of the state, Calvin moved in just the opposite direction. Calvin insisted that the church should shape the values of the state, thereby transforming both state and culture into the image of the kingdom of God.

And so it was that when Calvin arrived in Geneva, Switzerland, in 1536, he announced the vision that would drive his reform: He would seek in every way possible to transform Geneva into a model city of God. Put another way, Calvin sought to superimpose the values of the kingdom of God—as he understood the kingdom of God—on every dimension of Genevan life—its art, music, education, family life, and politics. It is true that Calvin sought to achieve these objectives not so much through external coercion as through careful teaching and preaching. Nonetheless, Calvin's Geneva became a model theocracy—a state in which the rule of God was both thorough and complete.

Calvin is significant for our story for a reason we have already stated: The majority of Europeans who settled the eastern seaboard of what would become the United States were Calvinists. Many of them brought to this brave new world Calvin's assumptions about transforming both state and culture into the image of the kingdom of God. In this way, they reinforced their culturally pragmatic allegiance to an established church with a powerful theological understanding of the sovereignty of God over all the earth.

The earliest Calvinists to settle North American shores were the Puritans who came first to Plymouth in 1620 and then, in 1630, to Massachusetts Bay. These two settlements differed in significant ways, but like Calvin before them, both sought to create a culture and a state modeled in every way on biblical norms and precedents.[1]

If measured by the external rules and regulations they erected, and even if measured by the pattern of the primitive church that they sought to restore, they succeeded remarkably well. But their failure to recreate the essence of the kingdom of God becomes apparent in their expulsion of dissenters, sometimes after excruciating torture; their practice of executing dissenters who proved especially recalcitrant; and their brutal treatment of Native Americans, whom they routinely viewed as children of the devil. The irony lay in this—that in their zeal to recreate the kingdom of God on earth, the Puritans of New England stand at the fountainhead of what would become the greatest shame of the American nation: the destruction of native populations.

If Puritans dominated New England, other branches of Calvinism—especially the Presbyterians from Scotland and Northern Ireland—sought to impose the sovereignty of God over colonial life in the Middle Colonies. As it turned out, many in the Middle Colonies resisted Calvinist domination and those colonies became, in some respects at least, a model for religious pluralism.

In the South, while Anglicans (members of the Church of England) controlled both wealth and land, ordinary people of the South allied themselves in extraordinary numbers with another wing of Calvinism—the Baptists. The Baptists differed in significant ways from their northern counterparts. While they maintained their allegiance to some of Calvin's doctrines, they vehemently rejected the union of church and state. In time, the Baptists would ally themselves with America's founders to overthrow religious establishments of every kind.

The Role of the American Founders

Even as that alliance was forming, the Founders of the United States resisted the mainstream Calvinists' vision for a thoroughly

Christianized culture. They also resisted the Calvinists' objective of bringing the nation under the sovereign sway of the Christian God. Some of the Founders were Christians, to be sure, but their great hope was for a nation whose citizens would be freed from religious constraints, not for a nation dominated by any one religion.[2]

The Calvinists' dreams for a Christianized American culture hit a roadblock, therefore, in the form of two seminal documents: the Declaration of Independence and the Constitution of the United States. We need now to explore both those documents and the implications each held for the possible creation of a Christian America.

THE DECLARATION OF INDEPENDENCE

Thomas Jefferson, the principal author of the Declaration, understood full well how divisive the Christian faith had been in Europe. Indeed, seventeenth-century Europe had witnessed numerous religious wars, fought between adherents of competing factions of the Christian religion. Since those wars had erupted only a century before, how—asked Jefferson—could leaders of the new American nation prevent similar wars from ripping the republic apart a century later?

This question was all the more pressing by the late eighteenth century since, alongside the varieties of Calvinists (Puritans in New England, Presbyterians in the Middle Colonies, and Baptists in the South), Catholics, Anglicans, Quakers, Anabaptists, and a variety of other denominations were emerging—and sometimes flourishing—on America's religious landscape. How could Jefferson and other national leaders prevent these sects from repeating on these shores the religious wars of the seventeenth century?

Jefferson answered that question by attempting to ground the nation's Declaration of Independence in religion, but not in traditional Christianity. Instead, Jefferson rooted the Declaration in Deism—a rational form of religion that jettisoned the Trinity, denied the deity of Christ, and rejected miracles along with most other claims for supernatural intervention. In their place, Deism substituted a sturdy belief in one God, often understood as benevolent providence; a firm conviction in an overarching moral order that governed the universe; and the belief that the best part of religion consisted in the good one might do for one's sisters or brothers.

In a letter to Benjamin Waterhouse, Jefferson summarized those truths like this:

1. That there is one only God, and he all perfect.
2. That there is a future state of rewards and punishments [reflecting the moral order of the universe].
3. That to love God with all thy heart and thy neighbor as thyself is the sum of religion.[3]

Deism also scuttled the Bible. It did so for four reasons. First, while Christians and Jews revered the Bible, most others in the human race did not. In the Deists' view, therefore, the Bible lacked universality.

Second, the Bible was a complex book, susceptible to a host of divergent interpretations. It lent itself, therefore, to religious divisions and potentially even to religious warfare. While wars inspired by religion had visited Europe in the seventeenth century, the Deists were determined that they would never plague this new nation.

Third, the Deists believed that because of its great complexity, the Bible was fundamentally unnecessary. However, they also believed that God had written a second book, the Book of Nature, that taught the core doctrines—those simple and universal truths— that were central to every religion.

And fourth, the Deists held suspect any supposed truth of revelation that failed to square with what might be known by reason. Thus, in an 1813 letter addressed to Thomas Jefferson, John Adams wrote,

> We can never be so certain of any Prophecy, or the fulfillment of any Prophecy; or of any miracle, or the design of any miracle as We are, from the revelation of nature i.e. nature's God that two and two are equal to four. Miracles or Prophecies might frighten Us out of our Witts; might scare us to death; might induce Us to lie; to say that We believe that 2 and 2 make 5. But We should not believe it. We should know the contrary.[4]

Benjamin Franklin illustrates well the skepticism many Founders held about the truth claims of the Christian faith, including the claims for the divinity of Jesus. "I have," he wrote,

> with most of the Dissenters in England, some Doubts as to his Divinity; tho' it is a question I do not dogmatize upon, having never studied it, and think it needless to busy myself with it now, when I expect soon an Opportunity of knowing the Truth with less Trouble. I see no harm, however, in its being believed, if that Belief has the good Consequence, as probably it has, or making his Doctrines more respected and better observed; especially as I do

not perceive, that the Supreme takes it amiss, by distinguishing the Unbelievers in his Government of the World with any peculiar Marks of his Displeasure.[5]

Other Founders expressed hostility toward the corruptions of organized Christianity. Thus John Adams, commenting on the creation of the American Bible Society in the early nineteenth century, complained to Jefferson that

> We have now, it seems, a National Bible Society, to propagate [the] King James' Bible, through all Nations. Would it not be better, to apply these pious Subscriptions, to purify Christendom from the Corruptions of Christianity; than to propagate their Corruptions in Europe, Asia, Africa, and America?[6]

Though many of the Founders questioned the divinity of Jesus, Jefferson believed that Deism represented the heart of Jesus' teachings. He claimed that orthodox Christianity—including many of the biblical writers—had warped those teachings beyond recognition. Indeed, he described the teachings of traditional, orthodox Christianity as "metaphysical insanities . . ., mere relapses into polytheism, differing from paganism only by being more unintelligible."[7]

Throughout his life Jefferson embraced some of Jesus' most basic teachings on how we should treat our sisters and our brothers. In a letter to Miles King, he wrote, "I must ever believe that religion substantially good which produces an honest life." He made it clear that he had little time for doctrinal disputes or denominational differences. In his view, "Our particular principles of religion are a subject of accountability to our God alone. I inquire after no man's and trouble none with mine." He believed there was "not a Quaker, or a Baptist, or a Presbyterian or an Episcopalian, a Catholic or a Protestant in heaven; that on entering that gate, we leave those badges behind, and find ourselves united in those principles only in which God has united us all."[8]

The principles in which God has united us all, Jefferson believed, were the principles of Deism—a belief in God, an affirmation that a moral order governs the universe, and a commitment to love God and neighbor. Because these principles struck Jefferson as supremely rational—and because he believed in their unifying power—he firmly believed "that the present generation will see Unitarianism (the institutional embodiment of Deism) become the general religion of the United States."[9] For all these reasons,

Jefferson grounded the Declaration of Independence in the tenets of the Deist faith.

Accordingly, Jefferson's Declaration appeals not once, but several times, to God. But nowhere in the Declaration does Jefferson refer to the "God of our Lord and Savior Jesus Christ" or the "God of Abraham, Isaac, and Jacob" or even to the "God we know in the Bible." Instead, Jefferson grounds the political principles of the Declaration in "the Laws of Nature and of Nature's God." Thus, the first paragraph of the Declaration reads like this:

> When in the Course of human events, it becomes necessary for one people to dissolve the political bands which have connected them with another, and to assume among the Powers of the earth, the separate and equal station to which *the Laws of Nature and of Nature's God* entitle them, a decent respect to the opinions of mankind requires that they should declare the causes which impel them to the separation [italics mine].

One finds, therefore, in the Declaration the very first principle of the Deist creed—an appeal to one God, knowable not from Scripture but from God's second book, the Book of Nature. This appeal was not a particular appeal that only Christians could understand and appreciate, but a universal appeal that could be understood by all humankind.

The second principle of the Deist creed—an affirmation of the moral order that governs the universe—found its way into the second paragraph of the Declaration where Jefferson wrote these words:

> We hold these truths to be self-evident, that all men are created equal, that they are endowed by their Creator with certain unalienable Rights, that among these are Life, Liberty and the pursuit of Happiness.

These truths, Jefferson believed, were self-evident, precisely because they were grounded in the very "Laws of Nature and of Nature's God." And nature, for Jefferson, was a far stronger guarantor of moral truths than all the texts of all the world's scriptures combined.

In the very words of the Declaration, therefore, Jefferson demonstrated that he had no interest in superimposing on the nation a Christian vision of the kingdom of God. Because in 1776, however, virtually everyone in the nation supported the cause of independence and freedom, it took some time for the Calvinists—and other orthodox Christians as well—to discern the fundamental differences between themselves and the author of the Declaration. But when they did, they were none too happy with Jefferson's adamant refusal to support their Christian agenda for the nation.

The gulf between Jefferson and the orthodox Christians widened over the years so that when Jefferson ran for the presidency of the United States in 1800, some Christians attacked him unmercifully. Though Jefferson was profoundly religious and believed strongly in the existence and providence of God, he rejected an exclusively Christian understanding of that God. Some Christians accused him, therefore, of rank infidelity and saddled him with the label "infidel." One clergyman even argued that Jefferson had preached both "atheism" and "the morality of devils."[10] But those events transpired in the earliest years of the nineteenth century. In a short time, the gulf between Jefferson and the Christian community would grow into a much wider gulf between evangelical Christians and the Deist founders, a point amply documented by Sidney E. Mead and Martin E. Marty.[11]

But the realization on the part of some Christians that Thomas Jefferson and his Declaration of Independence had betrayed their cause was but a prelude to a far greater disaster for orthodox, establishment-oriented Christians in the United States—their realization that the Constitution had done the very same thing.

THE CONSTITUTION

The Constitution betrayed the agenda that many Christians promoted for one simple reason: It failed to create a Christian establishment. Put another way, it failed to require by law that Christianity would become the official religion of the United States of America.

For many Christians, that failure was catastrophic, since—as we have seen already—the only way they knew to create a Christian nation was to create a Christian establishment. In addition, many Calvinists still nurtured dreams of transforming the United States into a model kingdom of God. But how could they achieve that objective if the Constitution outlawed the creation of a Christian establishment?

Yet in the first ten words of Article I of the Bill of Rights, that is precisely what the Constitution did: "Congress shall make no law respecting an establishment of religion." And then, in the next six words, the Constitution denied to government the right to prohibit the free exercise of religion on the part of any citizen. Clearly, the

Constitution had rendered null and void any hopes anyone might have had for a Christian nation enforced by law.

Compounding the dilemma of these establishment-oriented Christians, Article VI of the Constitution stipulated that "no religious Test shall ever be required as a Qualification to any Office or public Trust under the United States." But perhaps even more detrimental to the agenda many Christians embraced was the fact that the Constitution never once mentioned God. According to one report, when Alexander Hamilton was confronted with that omission, he responded, "We forgot."[12]

WHAT ABOUT THE FOUNDERS?

The Constitution, in a word, is a fundamentally secular document. But that fact has not prevented Christians in later years from claiming that the Founders were just like them—orthodox, Bible-believing Christians whose real intent was to create a Christian nation.

Accordingly, Pat Robertson, head of the Christian Coalition, complained in 1991 about the "emergence of a New Age world religion" that, in his judgment, aimed to replace the "biblically based" "Christian order" authored by America's founders.[13]

In 1989 David Barton founded WallBuilders, an organization dedicated to rebuilding America on what Barton viewed as its original Christian foundation. Indeed, his 1989 book, *The Myth of Separation*, flatly rejected the doctrine of the separation of church and state as a fraud, designed to undermine the nation's Christian origins.[14] The Texas Republican Party elected Barton as its vice chairman in 1997, and as we saw on the first page of this book, the 2004 platform of the Texas GOP also rejected church-state separation and affirmed the United States as a Christian nation. Texas Governor Rick Perry praised Barton in 2005 as "a truly national treasure" who "understands that America was founded on our Christian faith."[15] Over the years, Barton's influence has extended far beyond Texas. Salaried for a time by the Republican National Committee, Barton has drawn praise from evangelists Pat Robertson, Jerry Falwell, and James Kennedy, among others, and even from the former speaker of the House of Representatives, Newt Gingrich. His materials have been used by a variety of ministries across the country.[16]

Kennedy—prior to his death in 2007—shared with Robertson and Barton the standard view that the Founders intended the United States as a Christian nation. In a book published in 2003 with the

intriguing title *What If America Were a Christian Nation Again?*
Kennedy made the uncompromising claim that "America was a
nation founded upon Christ and His Word."[17]

If Robertson, Kennedy, Barton, and others who have carried
the banner of Christian America meant to suggest that the Founders were Christians, they were partly right. Some were Christians,
though the most influential among the Founders were Deists. And
even the Deists thought themselves committed to the core principles of Jesus Christ, as the case of Thomas Jefferson demonstrates.
Indeed, American Deism is incomprehensible apart from its Christian and Jewish roots.

But as Nathan Hatch, Mark Noll, and George Marsden have
demonstrated, even for those Founders who embraced the Christian
faith, that embrace sometimes made very little difference in the way
they envisioned the religious life of the nation. John Witherspoon
is a case in point.

Witherspoon, a Presbyterian, was the president of the College of
New Jersey—the forerunner of Princeton University—and perhaps
the best-known clergyman during the revolutionary generation.
While still in his native Scotland, he defended orthodox Christian
theology against its Enlightenment detractors and was a principal
leader in the evangelical party of the Presbyterian Church. Hatch,
Noll, and Marsden describe Witherspoon as "the most self-consciously evangelical of the founding fathers."

Strangely, once he arrived in the American colonies, Witherspoon failed to translate his Christian convictions into political
theory. Like the Deists who were his peers, he argued that reason
and experience should guide politics, not revelation. Witherspoon
was not alone. Though many of the Founders read the Bible, they
rarely brought biblical texts into political debates.[18]

On the other hand, James Wilson—one of only six Founders to
sign both the Declaration and the Constitution—relied quite specifically on the Christian natural law tradition to shape his political
philosophy. Wilson, like Witherspoon, also had a background in the
Scottish Presbyterian tradition and became an active Episcopalian
later in life.[19]

The point is this: The Founders occupied a continuum that ran
from orthodox Christianity to radical Deism. All of them—even
the most radical of the Deists—were children of biblical faith, since
American Deism is incomprehensible apart from biblical teachings
about God. But many of the Founders—and especially the most

influential of that group—also embraced, to one degree or another, a Deist perspective, and that is the difference that made all the difference. For Deism was not Christianity by any stretch of the imagination.

Regardless of their religious dispositions, the Founders' ultimate concern was for religious freedom, not to create a Christian America. Hatch, Noll, and Marsden's study of the Founders' religious beliefs bears out this conclusion when they write "No matter how favorable toward Christianity some of the founders may have been, their goal was pluralism, rather than the preferment of one religion to all others. . . . So long as religion supported political harmony, few of them were all that concerned with *what* a person believed."[20]

Finally, we must address one other aspect of the way some Christians in later years—especially since the 1970s—have interpreted the Founders. Those who argue that the Founders sought to create a Christian nation often base that claim on the simple fact that the Founders were religious and believed in God. But there are many varieties of religion, and almost all religions advocate belief in a deity. Put another way, the fact that one may believe in God—or may advocate belief in God—hardly makes one a Christian.

An example of the way many apologists for Christian America nonetheless confuse the broad category of religion with a particular religious tradition—the Christian faith—can be found in an American history text published in 1989 and designed for home schooling or for use in Christian schools. That text claims that when the Founders used the term "religion," they really "meant Christianity." When they spoke of morality, they really "meant Christian character." And when they referred to knowledge, they really "meant a Biblical worldview."[21]

This sort of claim reminds one of Henry Fielding's Parson Thwackum, who boldly declared, "When I mention religion I mean the Christian religion; and not only the Christian religion, but the Protestant religion; and not only the Protestant religion, but the Church of England."[22]

Regardless of the claims Christians have made for over two hundred years that the Founders sought to create a Christian nation, the Constitution stands as the supreme rebuttal to that contention. Indeed, the Constitution stands as written. It makes no mention of God, it prohibits the creation of a religious establishment, and it outlaws any religious test for public office. No matter how orthodox and devout certain Founders may have been in their personal religious beliefs, they refused to translate those beliefs into even the mildest constitutional requirement that the nation embrace the Christian faith.

The Battle for Christian America

In spite of the Constitution and the Founders' intentions, there have always been Christians who have sought to transform the nation into a Christian republic. While their work has been constant and unremitting over the course of the nation's history, two great movements have defined the battle for Christian America. One took place in the opening years of the nineteenth century; the other occurred in the opening years of the twentieth.

The first of those movements was the Second Great Awakening—a determined effort by Protestants in the United States to Christianize the republic and transform the nation into their own Protestant version of the kingdom of God. That revival lasted for some thirty years—from roughly 1800 to approximately 1830—and was so successful that historians often refer to the entire nineteenth century as the Christian century.

We will give considerable attention to the Second Great Awakening later in this chapter, since its influence extended throughout the nineteenth century and beyond. It shaped the nation's character so fully that Americans in the years after that revival tended to identify the United States as a Christian nation—even a Protestant nation—without regard to the nation's behavior. Many seemed to think that since the nation was Christian by definition, whatever the nation did was by definition a Christian work. In this way, the Second Great Awakening provided nurture and support both for the doctrine of manifest destiny (1845–1902) and for the gospel of wealth (1865–1900), as alien as those two movements were to the principles of the kingdom of God. We will explore both those movements in more detail later in this chapter.

If the Second Great Awakening defined the battle for Christian America in the nineteenth century, the fundamentalist movement defined that battle in the twentieth. Fundamentalists in the early twentieth century responded in a very negative way to pluralism, biblical criticism, and the assumptions of modern science, especially the notion of evolution, since—from their perspective—those ideas threatened to undermine and destabilize the Christianized culture the Second Great Awakening had produced. In effect, fundamentalism was an effort to rescue the nation from the jaws of modernism and reclaim the United States as a Christian nation once again.

While the Second Great Awakening and the fundamentalist movement shared in common the goal of Christianizing the nation, there were significant differences. The Second Great Awakening followed hard on the heels of the nation's birth. Leaders of that movement knew they had an opportunity to create something fresh and new. For that reason, the Second Great Awakening was a creative movement, optimistic, forward looking, and always on the offensive. Leaders of that movement waged their battles, to be sure—against Deism and skepticism, for example—but on the whole, that revival spread like a mighty torrent that baptized the youthful nation into Protestant versions of morality and righteousness.

On the other hand, when the fundamentalist movement emerged in the early twentieth century, its task was not to create something new and fresh and vibrant. Instead, its task was to defend the gains of the past against the onslaughts of modernism.

That difference is crucial, for if the Second Great Awakening had been forward-looking, the fundamentalist movement consistently looked backward—backward to a nineteenth-century golden age when the nation seemed so thoroughly Christian. If the Second Great Awakening had been optimistic about the future, leaders of the fundamentalist movement were often pessimistic. And well they should have been, for pluralism, on the one hand, and scientific assumptions inimical to their understanding of Christian America, on the other, now swept the nation. And if the Second Great Awakening consistently assumed an offensive posture, leaders of the fundamentalist movement almost always found themselves on the defense. They had enemies on every hand, and their enemies helped define the very nature of their movement. Indeed, one might well argue that apart from its enemies, fundamentalism could not exist.

In the following chapter, we will explore the leading characteristics of the fundamentalist movement and how a fundamentalist perspective helped to shape American culture, American politics, and American foreign policy in the twenty-first century, especially during the administration of George W. Bush. But for now, we turn our attention to the Second Great Awakening and the work it did to Christianize the republic in the nineteenth century.

The Second Great Awakening

Periodically, great Christian revivals have erupted in the United States, transforming America's cultural landscape in significant ways. We know the first of those revivals as the Great Awakening—a religious conflagration that swept up and down the eastern seaboard from 1734 to 1743, transforming the colonies into Christian centers of piety, zeal, and learning.

The Great Awakening also paved the way for the American Revolution inasmuch as it united thirteen very independent colonies into a common self-understanding that was, for all intents and purposes, a Christian self-understanding. No one contributed to that self-understanding more than Jonathan Edwards, one of the principal leaders of the revival. In 1742 Edwards claimed that the Great Awakening would usher in the final reign of God over all the earth. In fact, Edwards believed that "this new world is probably now discovered, that the new and most glorious state of God's church on earth might commence there."[23]

By the time the Revolution began in 1776, understandings like these allowed many colonists to interpret the Revolution as a Christian undertaking and political freedom as a Christian virtue. We have already mentioned the New England preacher Abraham Keteltas, who argued that the Revolution was the "cause for which the Son of God came down from his celestial throne and expired on a cross."[24] Another clergyman, Samuel Sherwood, viewed the Revolution both as a Christian undertaking and as an event that would usher in the rule of the kingdom of God. Sherwood was among the first to link the new nation to the kingdom of God, but he would by no means be the last. In any event, it is revealing to compare the militaristic and nationalistic content of Sherwood's statement with the biblical vision of the kingdom of God that we rehearsed in chapters 2 and 3. According to Sherwood,

> God almighty, with all the powers of heaven, is on our side. Great numbers of angels, no doubt, are encamping round our coast for our defense and protection. Michael stands ready, with all the artillery of heaven, to encounter the dragon, and to vanquish this black host. . . . It will soon be said and acknowledged that the Kingdoms of this world are become the Kingdoms of our Lord and of his Christ.[25]

The effects of the Great Awakening were short-lived, since after the Revolution the Christian faith fell on hard times. Martin E.

Marty has suggested that at no time in American history "were religious institutions so weak as they were in the first quarter-century after independence." Marty adds: "It is difficult to establish reliable statistics, but the best guesses suggest that from four to seven percent of the people were formally church members."[26] Add to that estimate the growing popularity of Deism, rationalism, and skepticism, and one has some measure of the crisis that faced American churches in the aftermath of the Revolution.

That crisis suggests that the Christian golden age of the American founding—the age to which Christian America advocates wish the nation to return—simply never existed. It also helps to explain the rise of the Second Great Awakening in approximately 1801.

The Second Great Awakening emerged, at least in part, in response to the lifeless nature of American Christianity in the post-Revolutionary period. But it also emerged in response to the Constitution's rejection of a legally established church.

As we have seen, many American Christians of that time were Calvinists who longed to bring the nation under the sovereign control of Almighty God. And almost all Christians of that time, whether Calvinist or not, knew only one way to infuse the culture with Christian influence and morals—through the power of an established church. And now that option was gone. Their only hope, therefore, for creating a Christian culture was through the power of persuasion, and the only way to persuade significant numbers of people was through a massive revival.

Stirrings of what would become the Second Great Awakening occurred as early as the 1790s, but historians generally date its birth at 1801. In that year, significant revivals began in opposite ends of the country.

A revival at Cane Ridge, Kentucky, attracted thousands to an ecumenical, backwoods, spiritual extravaganza where sinners were slain in the spirit, danced, barked, jerked, and fell to the ground under the influence of the Holy Ghost.

Also in 1801—this time in Connecticut—an altogether different sort of revival broke out among students at Yale University in response to the preaching of Yale's president, Timothy Dwight. Dwight lamented the Deism—he called it "infidelity"—that had become so popular in the nation, largely through the influence of American Founders like Jefferson. And he determined to do something about it.

A sampling of one of Dwight's sermons offers insight into the issues he believed were at stake:

What part hath he that believeth with an Infidel? . . . What will you
not lose? Their neighbourhood is contagious; . . . their communion
is death. . . . Will you enthrone a Goddess of Reason before the
table of Christ? Will you burn your Bibles? Will you crucify anew
your Redeemer? Will you deny your God?[27]

Though the Second Great Awakening grew from relatively
small beginnings at opposite ends of the country, it quickly cascaded
into a national revival that lasted some thirty years. The revival
did not rely upon preaching alone. Revivalists sought to ban the
Sunday delivery of mails and restrict the consumption of liquor.
They launched innumerable efforts to evangelize both the nation
and the larger world. They created the American Bible Society to
distribute Bibles, the American Tract Society to distribute Christian
literature, and the American Education Society to promote Christian education at the outposts of the American frontier. Indeed,
they established church-related colleges throughout the nation at
such a rapid pace that, by 1860, the number of these colleges had
reached 173, up from only 9 in 1780.[28]

For much of the Second Great Awakening, the man who coor-
dinated that revival and kept it alive was Charles G. Finney. Finney
traveled from town to town and city to city all over the United
States, proclaiming the good news of salvation, but also proclaiming
that America could and should become an outpost of the kingdom
of God.

Finney's work represented an entirely different side of the Second Great Awakening—and an entirely different vision of the kingdom of God—than that promoted by many other revival preachers.
Finney was far less concerned that Christianity dominate American
culture and far more concerned to bring his program into line with
the *biblical vision* of the kingdom of God. Finney understood that
vision as well as any preacher in American history. He knew what
Jesus had said about Himself—that He had come to liberate prisoners, heal the sick, and bring sight to the blind.

So Finney sought to translate that vision into categories appropriate for his day and age. He told his converts—and they were
many—that they must seek to transform society in some meaningful way. He urged some to take up prison reform and others the
banner of temperance. But most of all, he encouraged his converts
to do all in their power to abolish the evil of slavery.

Harriet Beecher Stowe and her antislavery novel, *Uncle Tom's
Cabin*, stand as a prime example of the kind of work the Second

Great Awakening promoted on behalf of slaves and their liberation. That work was extensive and involved the efforts of thousands of Christians. Indeed, apart from the Second Great Awakening, slavery might not have ended when it did.

Finally, we should note that the Second Great Awakening pursued one objective in addition to those already mentioned: The Great Awakening was in many respects an attempt to save the nation from the threat Protestants perceived in the rapid growth of Roman Catholicism on America's shores. By the beginning of the nineteenth century, Catholics had grown from some 20,000 during the colonial period to 40,000, and by 1850, that number had swelled to 1,606,000.[29] Because Protestants felt that the Catholic Church was, in principle, inimical to the cause of liberty, the Second Great Awakening was not so much an effort to Christianize the nation as to Protestantize the nation.

All in all, the Second Great Awakening combined radically different activities and motivations. Some, like Finney, used that revival to liberate slaves, to enhance the condition of prisoners, and to make other important gains in the arena of social reform. Some, on the other hand, used the Second Great Awakening to wed the nation more closely to the Christian faith, to impose a Christian vision on the larger culture, and to transform the United States into a Christian nation, if not in terms of national behavior, at least in a formal and ceremonial sense.

By the time the revival had run its course, the United States had become, in many respects, a Christian nation—even a Protestant nation. It was neither Protestant nor Christian in any legal sense, however. Nor was it Christian in a biblical sense. But it was profoundly Christian insofar as many Americans now employed Christian categories to describe and interpret the cultural life of the nation.

In his book *Righteous Empire*, Martin Marty reported that numerous "geographies, spellers, and readers from 1804, 1806, 1817, 1835, and 1846 included charts delineating the religions of the nations of the world. The United States was always listed as Protestant." But Marty puzzled over that fact. Only a minority of Americans belonged to Protestant churches, and the government was officially neutral toward religion. Still, Americans "had come to call their territory Protestant."[30]

Francis Wayland—preacher, economist, and president of Brown University from 1827 to 1855—made the point well. "Popular institutions," he wrote, "are inseparably connected with Protestant Christianity." Many other observers, both American and European, shared Wayland's perspective. Philip Schaff, the historian of Christianity from Mercersburg, Pennsylvania, commented in 1855, "I doubt whether the moral influence of Christianity and of Protestantism has more deeply and widely affected any nation, than it has the Anglo-Saxon." And the great French observer Alexis de Tocqueville thought "there was no country in the world where the Christian religion retained a greater influence over the souls of men than in America."[31]

From the Second Great Awakening to Manifest Destiny

As we have seen, many who participated in the Second Great Awakening sought to transform the United States into a more thoroughly Christian nation. On the other hand, the astounding success of that revival led many others to assume that the nation was Christian virtually by definition. Working from that assumption, they found little need to challenge the evils in American society. Many, for example, thought slavery thoroughly compatible with a thoroughly Christianized nation and fought to retain it.

Legions of blacks discerned this irony and rejected the myth of Christian America. A free black man named David Walker, for example, asked the simple but telling questions, "Have not the Americans the Bible in their hands? Do they believe it? Surely they do not." Walker could hardly believe that a religion that sanctioned slavery throughout the nation was "that which was preached by our Lord Jesus Christ from Heaven."[32] And the great black abolitionist Frederick Douglass pointed squarely to the tension between slavery, on the one hand, and the claim that the United States was a Christian nation, on the other. "I can see no reason, but the most deceitful one," he said, "for calling the religion of this land Christianity."[33] In this way, Walker, Douglas, and scores of other blacks showed how the Second Great Awakening had obscured the biblical vision that stood at its root.

The Second Great Awakening devoured that vision in other ways as well, for what began as a revival soon evolved into visions of Christian imperialism worldwide. The Baptist minister William R. Williams suggested in 1836, for example, that "the evangelical character of our land is to tell upon the plans and destinies of other nations."[34] Such sentiments were partly responsible for the doctrine of manifest destiny that emerged in the United States in the 1840s—a doctrine responsible for Indian removal and extermination and, by the end of the nineteenth century, American imperialism in both Cuba and the Philippines.

But manifest destiny owed its vitality to other American myths as well. The common belief that American core values reflected the natural order of things—that they were grounded in "self-evident truths"—surely reinforced that doctrine in powerful ways. So did the notion, rooted in Puritan thought, that God had chosen the United States—as a kind of "new Israel"—for a special mission in the world. And so did the millennial notion that in the last days the United States would transform the entire world into the kingdom of God—a vision we encountered earlier in the thought of Jonathan Edwards.[35]

Quite apart from these various American myths, the Second Great Awakening contributed significantly to the doctrine of manifest destiny. John L. O'Sullivan, the newspaperman who first articulated that doctrine, grounded it squarely in the very will of God. It was America's "manifest destiny," he wrote,

> to overspread and to possess the whole of the continent *which Providence has given us* for the development of the great experiment of liberty and federative self-government entrusted to us [italics mine].[36]

Another newspaperman, Horace Greeley, concurred. Speaking of the Delaware and Potawatomi people, whom the United States government had removed from other parts of the nation to Kansas, he wrote, "These people must die out—there is no help for them. God has given this earth to those who will subdue and cultivate it, and it is vain to struggle against His righteous decree."[37]

Christian America, however, set its designs on lands far beyond those owned by Native Americans. Regarding the Oregon Territory, a possession of Great Britain, O'Sullivan wrote,

> The God of nature and of nations has marked it for our own, and with His blessings we will firmly maintain the incontestable rights He has given, and fearlessly perform the high duties He has imposed.[38]

Indeed, most who argued on behalf of manifest destiny justified that doctrine in similarly religious terms. A case in point is the high religious rhetoric that surrounded the Mexican War.

In 1846 the United States, lusting for Mexican lands, tricked Mexican units into attacking American troops stationed along the Rio Grande River. President James K. Polk then used that attack as a pretext for declaring war against Mexico. At the war's conclusion, the Treaty of Guadalupe Hidalgo forced Mexico to recognize the annexation of Texas, which the United States had added to its territory in 1845. In addition, the treaty required Mexico to cede the entire southwest—what is now California, Nevada, and Utah and sizable portions of Colorado, Arizona, New Mexico, and Wyoming—to the United States.

Senator H. V. Johnson, a confessing Baptist from Georgia, offered the following justification for that war and for the doctrine of manifest destiny:

> If war is forced upon us, as this has been, . . . we should be recreant to our noble mission, if we refused acquiescence in the high purposes of a wise Providence. War has its evils. In all ages it has been the minister of wholesale death and appalling desolation; but however inscrutable to us, it has also been made, by the Allwise Dispenser of events, the instrumentality of accomplishing the great end of human elevation and human happiness. . . . It is in this view, that I subscribe to the doctrine of "manifest destiny."[39]

And so it went, with some Christians justifying war, genocide, and theft of land, all in the name of God and the Christian nation.

The United States played out the final phase of the doctrine of manifest destiny in the waning years of the nineteenth century. European Americans had pushed across the continent to the Pacific Ocean and now turned their eyes toward Southeast Asia. The United States invaded the Philippines in 1899 and occupied that nation until 1902. The president and Congress hoped thereby to extend American power and influence in that part of the world.

Although Emilio Aguinaldo, a Filipino freedom fighter, led his people in a popular revolution against American domination of his country, it never occurred to William McKinley, president during that period, that the Filipinos might not welcome the influence of the United States. Indeed, McKinley asked, "Did we need their consent to perform a great act for humanity? We had it in every aspiration of their minds, in every hope of their hearts."[40]

What is important for our purposes is the support that many Christians—and even churches in their formal pronouncements—lent to the American invasion and occupation of the Philippines.

The ground for this support had been well prepared by the widespread confusion of Christian faith with American culture in the years since the Second Great Awakening.

In 1885 Americans began to read the enormously popular book by Josiah Strong entitled *Our Country*. There Strong praised the Anglo-Saxon race—and by implication, the United States—as "the representative . . . of the purest Christianity." Its Christian character coupled with its love for liberty, he believed, had uniquely equipped this nation "to impress its institutions upon mankind . . . [and] spread itself over the earth." The Anglo-Saxon race, he argued, "is destined to dispossess many weaker races, assimilate others, and mold the remainder, until in a very true and important sense it has Anglo-Saxonized mankind."[41]

Two years earlier, Strong had cast his argument in the context of the familiar notion of the kingdom of God. World dominance by the Anglo-Saxon race and Anglo-Saxon principles, he suggested, would lead to "the kingdom of heaven fully come on earth." A Southern Baptist newspaper based in Atlanta, Georgia, repeated that same theme in 1890: "Oh, let the stars and stripes, intertwined with the flag of old England, wave o'er the continents and islands of earth, and through the instrumentality of the Anglo-Saxon race, the kingdoms of this world shall become the kingdoms of our Lord and His Christ."[42]

In 1887 James H. King, a Methodist minister from New York, picked up on the arguments Strong had made in *Our Country*. "God is using the Anglo-Saxon," he proclaimed, "to conquer the world for Christ by dispossessing feeble races, and assimilating and molding others."[43] And in 1890 Lewis French Stearns, a professor of Christian theology in Bangor Theological Seminary, proclaimed,

> Today Christianity is the power which is moulding the destinies of the world. The Christian nations are in the ascendant. Just in proportion to the purity of Christianity as it exists in the various nations of Christendom is the influence they are exerting upon the world's destiny. The future of the world seems to be in the hands of the three great Protestant powers—England, Germany, and the United States. The old promise is being fulfilled; the followers of the true God are inheriting the world.[44]

In 1897—on the eve of America's invasion of the Philippines—a missionary of the American Board of Foreign Missions named Sidney E. Gulick argued that "no peoples have been so controlled by the religion of Jesus Christ as the Anglo-American." As a consequence, he reasoned,

> God means that the type of religion and civilisation attained by the Anglo-Saxon race shall have, for the present at least, the predominating influence in moulding the civilization of the world. And everything points to the growing predominance of the Christian religion and Christian civilisation.[45]

And in 1901, even as American forces were subduing the Filipino population at the cost of thousands of civilian lives, the bishops of the United Brethren in Christ Church could observe that

> If we take the map of the globe and mark off the possessions and spheres of influence of the Christian powers, there will be little or nothing left to the independent control of nonChristian governments. The islands of the sea are all appropriated; the Western Continent is wholly under Christian rule; the partition of Africa among the Christian nations of Europe is well-nigh complete; Asia is slowly coming under the control of Christian nations.[46]

The United States finally achieved its objective in the Philippines, but at the cost of *at least* a quarter-million Filipino lives. But President McKinley persisted in justifying the American occupation of the Philippines as a Christian work.

In fact, McKinley told a group of ministers who visited the White House that he "did not know what to do with" the Philippines once they "dropped into our lap." As a result, "I went down on my knees and prayed Almighty God for light and guidance more than one night." When that guidance finally came, he suddenly knew "that there was nothing left for us to do but to take them all, and to educate the Filipinos, and uplift and civilize and Christian-ize them, and by God's grace do the very best for them, as our fellow-men for whom Christ also died." Then, he reported, he "went to bed and went to sleep, and slept soundly, and the next morning I sent for the chief engineer of the War Department (our map-maker), and told him to put the Philippines on the map of the United States."[47]

Even after that colossal abuse of the vision of the kingdom of God, most Americans still viewed the United States as a Christian nation. The irony that this altogether Christian nation could slaughter a quarter-million people simply to open commercial markets and impose its will in another part of the world escaped most Americans—including most American Christians. Only a few grasped the awful truth that Senator James Henderson Berry expressed when he told the United States Senate that America had occupied the Philippines "on the pretense, it may be, of humanity and Christianity, but behind it all . . . is the desire for trade and commerce."[48]

The Gospel of Wealth

The Second Great Awakening clearly did not inspire the gospel of wealth. No historian would make that claim. But the Second Great Awakening helped create the widespread assumption that American culture was Christian by definition—an assumption we have witnessed in the Christian support for the doctrine of manifest destiny. Apart from that assumption, it is difficult to explain how otherwise intelligent and well-meaning Christians could have promoted the agenda of the gospel of wealth—an agenda altogether alien to the biblical vision of the kingdom of God—and claim it was Christian in any sense at all.

What was the gospel of wealth? When the Civil War had ended, the northern section of the United States entered the period we know as the Gilded Age (1865–1900)—a period defined by unbridled greed and unprecedented wealth on the part of those men we call the "barons of industry." But the Gilded Age was also defined by grinding poverty, long working hours, and terrible working conditions on the part of the millions of working poor. Typically, the barons of industry and other wealthy Americans exploited the poor and built their fortunes on the backs of their labor.

Ironically, many Christians in the northern states praised America's wealthy entrepreneurs for their diligence, their honesty, and their Christlike character. On the other hand, they damned the poor and ascribed their poverty to laziness, drunkenness, and immorality. With the great opportunities America provided, they argued, anyone who remained in poverty had only himself or herself to blame. This mentality stood at the heart of the gospel of wealth.

A religious factor that helped to sustain the gospel of wealth was the assumption some Calvinists made that God blesses His elect with prosperity and curses the damned with poverty. But one might think that the biblical vision of the kingdom of God, coupled with the shocking disparity between rich and poor that characterized the Gilded Age, might have disabused even the most ardent Calvinist of the legitimacy of those assumptions.

The gospel of wealth never took root in the South in any substantial way, since the Civil War had so completely undermined the economic fabric of that region. But in the North where it flourished, its proponents routinely portrayed it as a Christian undertaking. They could do so for one fundamental reason: America, *by definition*, was a Christian nation. Of that, they were certain, thanks to the enduring influence of the Second Great Awakening. Any initiative proclaimed so widely by the churches of this Christian land must, therefore, be "Christian" as well. In my book, *Myths America Lives By*, I explore the ways that additional American myths sustained the gospel of wealth, but there is no need to repeat that analysis here.

Andrew Carnegie, one of the barons of industry who made his vast fortune in the steel industry, defined the principles of the Gilded Age—and the principles of the gospel of wealth—in an article he wrote for the *North American Review* in 1889—an article he entitled simply "Wealth." In it Carnegie affirmed that

> It is . . . essential for the progress of the race, that the houses of some should be homes for all that is highest and best in literature and the arts, and for the refinements of civilization, rather than that none should be so. . . .
> While the law [of competition] may be sometimes hard for the individual, it is best for the race, because it insures that survival of the fittest in every department. We accept and welcome, therefore, as conditions to which we must accommodate ourselves, great inequality of environment [and] the concentration of business . . . in the hands of a few.

And then, in a line that etched the phrase "gospel of wealth" into the American consciousness, Carnegie wrote:

> Such, in my opinion, is the true Gospel concerning Wealth, obedience to which is destined some day to solve the problem of the Rich and the Poor, and to bring "Peace on earth, among men Good Will."[49]

By invoking the phrase "Peace on earth, among men Good Will," Carnegie in effect suggested that the gospel of wealth would usher in the final kingdom of God. That was in 1889.

But the principles of the gospel of wealth first appeared in the public square as early as 1870, only five years after the Civil War. Henry Ward Beecher—brother of Harriet Beecher Stowe, known for her novel *Uncle Tom's Cabin*, and a preacher so well known in American life that his name was a household word—preached a sermon that turned the biblical understanding of the kingdom of

God upside down. Beecher objected to the common Christian belief that virtue required having and using little. "Far from it," he said.

> As you go toward the savage state, you go away from complexity, from multitudinous power, down toward simplicity, and when you come to the lowest state—to the simplicity of men that wear skins and leather apparel, and live in huts and caves—you come to the fool's ideal of prosperity.

On the contrary, Beecher argued, genuine Christianity requires both hard work and the production of wealth. "So then," he concluded,

> I am not afraid to rejoice, Get rich, if you can. . . . And when you shall have amassed wealth, it will be God's power, if you are wise to use it, by which you can make your home happier, the community more refined, and the whole land more civilized.
>
> And, on the whole, the general tendency of wealth is such as to lead me today to thank God for the increasing wealth of America. May it ever be sanctified. May it ever learn nobler uses, and aspire higher and higher, until the symbolism of the heavenly state, where the very streets are paved with gold, shall be reproduced in the realities and actualities of our life here on earth.

He concluded his sermon with the maxim that would become fundamental to the gospel of wealth: "The general truth will stand, that no man in this land suffers from poverty unless it be more than his fault—unless it be his sin."[50]

Over the next three decades and even into the twentieth century, many highly influential Christian preachers zealously advocated on behalf of the Gilded Age and its wealthy beneficiaries and thereby promoted the gospel of wealth. They praised the rich as moral exemplars and condemned the working poor as both slothful and undeserving.

In 1901, for example, the Reverend William Lawrence, Episcopal bishop of Massachusetts, proclaimed:

> In the long run, it is only to the man of morality that wealth comes. . . . Put two men in adjoining fields, one man strong and normal, the other weak and listless. One picks up his spade, turns over the earth, and works till sunset. The other turns over a few clods, gets a drink from the spring, takes a nap, and loafs back to his work. In a few years one will be rich for his needs, and the other a pauper dependent on the first, and growling at his prosperity.
>
> Put ten thousand immoral men to live and work in one fertile

valley and ten thousand moral men to live and work in the next valley, and the question is soon answered as to who has the material wealth. Godliness is in league with riches.[51]

Another prominent preacher, Russell Conwell of Philadelphia, traveled the country, explaining to all who heard him preach why it was their duty to get rich. "I say that you ought to get rich, and it is your duty to get rich," he intoned. "The men who get rich may be the most honest men you find in the community."[52]

Such was the outlook of these Christian patrons of wealth in the Gilded Age. And, on the whole, such was the outlook of Christian America in the northern United States. Nothing, of course, could have been more alien to the biblical vision of the kingdom of God which pronounces blessings on the poor and counsels Christians to share with those in need. For the most part, Christian America in the Gilded Age missed that message altogether.

The Social Gospel

Since so many Roman Catholics were recent immigrants who suffered under the oppressive weight of the gospel of wealth, Catholic clergy and laypersons alike saw through its hypocritical pretensions from an early date. At a time when most Protestants viewed labor unions as subversive of Christianized American culture, James Cardinal Gibbons, archbishop of Baltimore, advocated the right of Catholics to join those unions in the interest of self-protection. it is not surprising that Catholics dominated the first national labor union, the Knights of Labor, from its inception in 1869.

Protestants were much slower than Catholics to discern the vast discrepancies between the gospel of wealth, on the one hand, and the biblical vision of the kingdom of God, on the other. Among Protestants, Walter Rauschenbusch saw the problem with the gospel of wealth when he was pastor of the Second German Baptist Church in a district of New York City known as Hell's Kitchen. His work with immigrants, coupled with his reading of the biblical text, led him to provide a theological basis for an alternative to the gospel of wealth—a movement that came to be known as the social gospel.

The social gospel argued that the gospel of wealth was fundamentally misconceived. Instead of praising the rich and damning the poor, advocates of the social gospel claimed that Christians should embark on a massive ministry to the poor and to all those Jesus viewed as "the least of these." Rauschenbusch wrote several books to support this project, among them *Christianity and the Social Crisis* (1907) and *A Theology for the Social Gospel* (1917).

While Rauschenbusch wrote primarily for academics, Charles Sheldon popularized the social gospel among ordinary people with his bestselling novel *In His Steps* (1897), a book that argued that Christians should be guided by the simple question "What would Jesus do?" Sheldon's novel told the story of an upscale church—a church that was dominated by the principles of the gospel of wealth—that found itself turned upside down through an encounter with the working poor. That encounter led the church to ask, "What would Jesus do?" The answers, as one might expect, had much to do with the biblical vision of the kingdom of God and thereby led the congregation into the fold of the social gospel. That question—"What would Jesus do?"—is the same question, we recall, that Al Gore pledged would govern his policies if elected president.

Its promoters typically argued that the social gospel would Christianize the nation and usher in the kingdom of God. One of the movement's most influential advocates, Washington Gladden of Columbus, Ohio, rejected "the establishment of any form of religion by law in this land." Still, he said, "Most of us would be willing to see the nation in its purposes and policies and ruling aims becoming essentially Christian."[53] The social gospel, he claimed, would achieve precisely that objective.

Walter Rauschenbusch finally realized that the kingdom of God is by definition at least partly a future reality that can never be fully implemented on earth.[54] But as Robert Handy wrote, most other social gospellers "tended to sweep aside the qualifications and to interpret the kingdom of God as a perfect social order soon to come in history."[55] What was more, it would come through the agency of a Christianized American culture.

The social gospel in many ways fell in line with the New Testament vision of the kingdom of God. It therefore represented in certain ways the best of American Christianity. But its failure lay in its messianic nationalism—its assumption that the United States as a Christian nation would finally rejuvenate the world. Accordingly, Washington Gladden suggested that "if we want the nations of the earth to understand Christianity, we have got to have a Christianized nation to show them."[56]

One must remember, as well, that Josiah Strong, author of the enormously popular book *Our Country* (1885), was an early spokesman for the social gospel just as he was a spokesman for the doctrine of manifest destiny. Strong believed the "Anglo-Saxon race" represented "the purest Christianity [and] the highest civilization." For Christians like Strong, that race—embodied especially in the American people—had every right to "dispossess many weaker races, assimilate others, and mold the remainder."[57] They believed this precisely because they believed America to be a profoundly Christian nation.

Looking Forward

The messianic nationalism of the United States became even more pronounced in the twentieth century. Many books have told that story in substantial detail, so there is no need to repeat that information here.[58] We do need to ask, however, how American messianism, driven and sustained by fundamentalist underpinnings, functioned in the early years of twenty-first-century America.

There can be no doubt that American messianism reached an apex after the terror attack on the Pentagon and the World Trade Center on September 11, 2001. Not only was the United States wholly unprepared for that attack in terms of military intelligence; the United States was also unprepared both psychologically and spiritually.

Indeed, seldom has the United States more fully betrayed the claim that it functions as a Christian nation than in the aftermath of those attacks. Instead of asking the question, "Why do they hate us?" and listening carefully to the highly complex answers to that question our enemies might have offered; instead of seizing the opportunity to create an entirely new world order by sowing seeds of friendship instead of seeds of hate; instead of building alliances and forging bonds of reconciliation; instead of using its vast wealth to alleviate hunger, poverty, suffering, and disease around the world—instead of doing all those things one might expect a Christian nation to do, America sought vengeance and retribution and went to war—and did so almost unilaterally.

In that way, it perpetuated the age-old politics of violence and embraced the never-ending spiral of an eye for an eye and a tooth for a tooth. Through the instrumentality of war, America sought to export democracy and capitalism, to suppress global pluralism, and to redeem the world for American values. In all these ways, it lived out its messianic self-understanding, but in the process raised serious questions about its status as a Christian nation.

The truth is, the American response to 9/11 was driven by a fundamentalist vision of the world that has little in common with the historic Christian faith. What that fundamentalist vision is and how it has functioned in the United States of the twenty-first century is the story we shall tell in the final chapter.

Chapter 5

A FUNDAMENTALIST VISION
for Christian America

From the Scopes Trial to George W. Bush

Journalists and historians often use the term *fundamentalism* to describe a conservative, intolerant, and embattled form of religion that appears in many cultures and many religious traditions worldwide. In the American context, however, the term has a specific historic meaning and points to a religious movement that emerged in the United States in the early years of the twentieth century.[1]

While American fundamentalism has gone through several incarnations, it emerged during the waning years of the twentieth century as a religious and political force that could not be ignored. And by the early twenty-first century, fundamentalist movements on opposite sides of the world—an American variety, on the one hand, and an Islamic variety on the other—were locked in mortal combat.

Understanding the Fundamentalist Perspective

Fundamentalism in America today wears many faces, just as it did in the early twentieth century. Clearly, some fundamentalists in those early years were crude and unlettered. The Baltimore journalist H. L. Mencken, however, painted them all with that brush when he covered the Scopes-Monkey Trial in Dayton, Tennessee, for the *Baltimore Evening Sun* in 1925.

Of the trial itself, Mencken wrote that it "serves notice on the country that Neanderthal man is organizing in these forlorn backwaters of the land."[2] And of fundamentalists and the Genesis account of creation, he reported, "The cosmogony of Genesis is so simple that even a yokel can grasp it. . . . It offers, to an ignorant man, the irresistible reasonableness of the nonsensical. So he accepts it with loud hosannas, and has one more excuse for hating his betters."[3] No doubt there was some truth to what Mencken had to say.

On the other hand, some fundamentalists were urbane, erudite, polished, and well equipped in the tools of scholarship. A notable case in point was J. Gresham Machen, New Testament professor at Princeton Theological Seminary and founder in 1929 of Westminster Theological Seminary when Princeton refused to embrace a more conservative and orthodox form of Christianity.

Fundamentalism today reflects those same disparities, ranging from moderate to ultraconservative and from bumpkin to scholar. One characteristic, however, stood and continues to stand at the heart of all forms of fundamentalism. One could even argue that without that characteristic, fundamentalism would not exist. That characteristic is the belief that they are right and that others are simply wrong. All sorts of religions make that claim, of course, but moderate religions are at least partly open to counterarguments and competing viewpoints. Typically, fundamentalists are not. Instead, they offer claims to rectitude with a dogmatism that precludes any sort of question and any level of doubt.

One finds that trait not only among Christian fundamentalists in the United States, but also among Muslim fundamentalists in Iraq, Iran, and Afghanistan; among Hindu fundamentalists in India; and among Jewish fundamentalists in Israel. Indeed, the perspective of being right while others are wrong is a staple of fundamentalist movements and sects wherever they exist.

In the American context, that perspective combined with the fundamentalists' propensity to idealize a golden age of the past and to defend at all costs a nineteenth-century version of Christian America—a perspective we noted in the previous chapter. Together, those characteristics lent to American fundamentalism its antipluralist orientation and rendered it ill equipped to cope with complexity, with paradoxical thinking, with nuance and ambiguity, and with metaphoric and symbolic language. These are also the traits that led—and continue to lead—so many fundamentalists to divide the world so neatly into good and evil, right and wrong, ally and enemy, Christian and anti-Christian.

Because fundamentalists typically had such difficulty dealing with complexity and ambiguity, some worried that fundamentalists in positions of political power would undermine the welfare of both the nation and the world. Some thought that President George W. Bush, with his unilateral policies and his zeal to divide the world into the forces of good and the forces of evil, illustrated well the danger fundamentalism posed to the public good.[4] Others argued that fundamentalism not only threatened the nation but seriously distorted the Christian faith as well.[5] And the noted journalist Bill Moyers, observing the end-times theology that motivated so many fundamentalists in the United States, had this to say:

> There are times when what journalists see and intend to write about dispassionately sends a shiver down the spine, shaking us from our neutrality. This has been happening to me frequently of late as one story after another drives home the fact that the delusional is no longer marginal but has come in from the fringe to influence the seats of power.[6]

All these factors help explain why President Jimmy Carter could remark in his book *Our Endangered Values* on the "disturbing trend toward fundamentalism" in both politics and religion and the way "they have become increasingly intertwined."[7] Indeed, the fundamentalist movement that began in the United States in the 1910s and 1920s and then enjoyed a renaissance in the 1980s and 1990s had become by the early twenty-first century a potent force on the American political stage.

In this chapter, we will explore several aspects of American fundamentalism—its origin and development in the United States, its ideological commitments, its influence on politics and public policy in the early twenty-first century, and finally the way so many fundamentalists seek to hasten the final battle of Armageddon, the end of time, and the destruction of our planet. Through it all, we will continue to ask the question, "What does it mean when fundamentalists argue that the United States is a Christian nation or, having despaired of that proposition, seek to return the nation to its supposed Christian roots?"

The Issues That Drove American Fundamentalism

The fundamentalist movement in the United States emerged in the early twentieth century in response to several seismic shifts in American life, culture, and religion. In this context, I wish to mention four: population shifts, the emergence of industrialization and the American city, the rise of evolutionary theory, and the emergence of biblical criticism.

In the first place, fundamentalism responded to radical shifts in the population of the United States that began shortly after the Civil War. Between 1865 and 1900, at least 13.5 million immigrants settled in the United States. Almost 9 million came during the first decade of the twentieth century. We gain some understanding of the magnitude of this transition when we realize that between 1865 and 1910, the population of the United States almost doubled.

Compounding the change was the fact that so many of these new immigrants were altogether foreign to the British folkways that had helped define the United States from its inception. They hailed from Italy, Bohemia, Poland, Russia, Romania, Croatia, and other eastern European nations. And by and large, they were Catholic. There were exceptions to that rule, of course, since many came from countries that embraced Eastern Orthodox Christianity. But the crucial fact is this: these new immigrants were almost entirely alien to the world of Protestantism.

Their presence posed a significant challenge to many Christians in the United States who were dedicated to preserving a Christian America. For in their view, a Christian America was a Protestant America. Many American Protestants viewed these foreigners, therefore, as positively subversive of the kind of nation America had become during the course of the nineteenth century—and the kind of nation, in their view, it should always be.

Second, the industrialization that occurred both during and after the Civil War helped create great American cities in the northern part of the nation—Boston, New York, and Philadelphia, for example. The factories in those cities became magnets that drew not only immigrants but even those Americans whose lives had been spent in this country but on the family farm. This transition from a rural to an urban America produced vast and highly complex problems: crowded tenement buildings, long hours for workers, poverty, hunger, disease, and crime. The gospel of wealth that exalted the rich at the expense of the poor—a development we considered in the previous chapter—only compounded the dilemma.

With their backs against the wall, the working poor did what they could to protect themselves: They organized labor unions. But advocates for Christian America found the unions as threatening as the immigrants themselves, for the unions enhanced the power of these immigrants with their alien folkways, their often liberal politics, and their seemingly subversive religions.

These dramatic changes that overtook the United States at the end of the nineteenth century are crucial for understanding the rise of American fundamentalism. For these were more than changes. These were ruptures in the fabric of traditional American life—the rural, Protestant, and Anglo-American way of life—that had dominated the United States since the Second Great Awakening. Christian America—as the nineteenth century had defined Christian America—was rapidly disappearing into a vast sea of immigrants, Catholics, alien folkways, and organized labor.

Third, the late nineteenth and early twentieth centuries also witnessed startling new developments in modern science. None of those developments was more revolutionary than Charles Darwin's theory of evolution—a theory he elaborated in his book *On the Origin of Species*, published in 1859. Though Darwin never intended his book as an attack on the Bible, many American Christians understood it to be precisely that, for Darwin—they thought—had flatly denied the biblical teaching that God had created human beings in his own divine image from the dust of the earth.

But there was yet more to come, for Darwin had done more than offer a theory of biological evolution. He had also offered a whole new way—an evolutionary way—of understanding cultural and even literary development. Accordingly, German biblical scholars in the late nineteenth century applied evolutionary theories to the development of biblical texts, thereby giving birth to the discipline of biblical criticism.

Christians had believed for centuries that God had spoken the Bible into existence through authors like Moses, Isaiah, and Paul. But these new biblical scholars now suggested that specific books of the Bible—Genesis, for example—evolved over a very long time. They theorized that numerous writers over many years had written sections of text that editors finally collated into many of the books that now appear in the Bible.

For American fundamentalists, biblical criticism, evolutionary theory, and the millions of immigrants who had come to America's shores were interconnected in two compelling ways: They all were foreign born and they all were alien to the Protestant ethos that defined the United States. None could have grown from the native soil of Christian America.

Nonetheless, biblical criticism and the theory of evolution quickly found their way into American colleges, universities, and schools of theology and, as a result, into America's public schools and even some of its pulpits. Thousands of Christians understood these theories as serious attacks on the credibility and authenticity of the biblical text. The encounter with these notions in newspapers, churches, and schools, therefore, transformed many traditional Protestants into fundamentalists, fighting to save the Bible as the cornerstone for Christian America.

Significantly, fundamentalism—like the Second Great Awakening that preceded it—grew from the womb of the Reformed tradition. This does not mean that fundamentalism failed to attract Christians from many Christian traditions, Reformed and otherwise, even in its earliest years. But it found its driving force both in Reformed churches—especially Baptist and Presbyterian—and in a larger Christian culture that had been shaped by a Reformed perspective from the time of the Second Great Awakening. It is not surprising, then, that fundamentalism embraced one of the central objectives of the Reformed tradition, harking back to John Calvin in the sixteenth century—to bring all human culture under the sovereign sway of almighty God and to transform the nation into the premier outpost of His kingdom.

The Fundamentals of the Christian Faith

In the late nineteenth and early twentieth centuries, change was everywhere—from immigration to urbanization to labor strikes to evolutionary theory. But fundamentalists viewed changes of every sort through the lens of two issues: Darwinian evolution and biblical criticism. Indeed, these two issues became for fundamentalists metaphors for the age.

The seriousness of those issues and the way they seemed to threaten Christian America prompted fundamentalists to launch a campaign to defend the Bible as the word of God and America as a Christian nation—a nation based on timeless biblical truths.

But if the nation was based on timeless biblical truths, what were those truths? What propositions should be defended in this battle to save Christian civilization? The fundamentalists identified five:

the inerrancy of the Bible, the virgin birth of Jesus Christ, the substitutionary atonement on behalf of sinners, the bodily resurrection of Jesus, and Jesus' imminent premillennial return to reign on earth with his saints. The future of Christianity, they imagined, hinged on these five doctrines. If even one went down, the Christian faith—and with it, Christian civilization—would be lost. For that reason, true believers defended the "fundamentals" tooth and nail.

The irony lies in the fact that only three of their five affirmations shared common ground with the doctrines all Christians had affirmed over nineteen centuries of Christian history. The substitutionary atonement, the third item in the fundamentalist creed, argued that the death of Jesus was a substitute for the deaths of sinners—a punishment required by the justice of God. In making this affirmation, fundamentalists stood shoulder to shoulder with many orthodox Christians across the centuries including Anselm of Canterbury, Thomas Aquinas, and John Calvin.

The second and fourth items in the fundamentalist creed affirmed the virgin birth and bodily resurrection of Jesus—statements the fundamentalists shared in common with all the historic Christian creeds. However, in affirming the virgin birth and bodily resurrection of Jesus, the fundamentalists had purposes quite foreign to the purposes of the fathers of the ancient church or of Luther or Calvin or any other orthodox Christian leader prior to the twentieth century—a point that I will elaborate on shortly. For now, we need to explore the first item in the fundamentalist creed—the inerrancy of the Bible.

BIBLICAL INERRANCY

By placing the inerrancy of the Bible at the top of their list of theological affirmations, fundamentalists intended to say to the evolutionists and the biblical critics, "The Bible is inerrant and cannot be wrong. If the Bible indicates that Moses wrote Genesis, then Moses wrote Genesis, regardless of all the theories of the learned German critics. And if the Bible states that God created the heavens and the earth in seven days, then Darwin must be wrong with his diabolical theory of evolution." In other words, an inerrant Bible simply trumped all the theories of all the scientists who stood in the vanguard of the modern age. It was precisely that reduction of complex problems to simple solutions that I had in mind when I stated earlier in this chapter that fundamentalists typically were "ill-equipped to cope with complexity."

Ironically, by embracing the Bible's alleged inerrancy, the fundamentalists also transformed the Bible into something that virtually no one in the history of Christianity, prior to the twentieth century, had thought it to be: a divinely authored book of scientific truths. Further, fundamentalists typically held that the literal meaning of every biblical statement that bore on scientific questions was beyond dispute.

Earlier generations of Christians, reaching all the way back to the ancient church, had understood the Bible as a theology text— that is, a book that probed the mysteries of God and the meaning of human life in the light of God's work as creator, sustainer, and redeemer. That age-old understanding of the Bible made room for paradox, for ambiguity, and for meaningful reflection on the mysteries of God and the mysteries of the universe. It also made room for metaphor and symbolic expression—qualities essential to Christian theology if, as Christians have always claimed, God as the Infinite One is beyond human comprehension.

But the fundamentalists' understanding of the Bible as an inerrant text, both scientifically and theologically, robbed the Bible of all its symbolic and metaphoric qualities. It therefore placed God, the Bible, and the entire Christian tradition in an intellectual straightjacket. Either the Bible was true or it was false. Either you believed it or you didn't. And, of course, since the Bible always said what it meant and meant what it said, there was only one way to understand it. Such assumptions lent to American fundamentalism a rigid and brittle quality that made it uncomfortable with dialogue, ill at ease with diversity, and suspicious of pluralism.

The fundamentalists' vision for Christian America, therefore, was a vision based on what they regarded as correct beliefs, especially with respect to biblical criticism and evolutionary theory. But their preoccupation with correct beliefs lent to fundamentalism an inherently defensive nature, a reluctance to dialogue with its enemies, and a tendency to bifurcate the world into good and evil. Those whom the fundamentalists viewed as good were those who upheld God's eternal truths, at least as the fundamentalists understood those truths. And those they viewed as evil were those who did not.

This fundamentalist view of the world was a minor note in the early twentieth century since at that time fundamentalists were minor players on the national stage. By the dawn of the twenty-first century, however, fundamentalists had worked themselves into positions of significant political power, and they wielded that power to elect to national office people who shared their suspicion of diversity, their aversion to nuance, and their instinctive way of dividing the people of the world into good and evil. The overall vision remained the same; only the issues had changed. Instead of biblical criticism and evolution, the new issues were abortion, gay marriage, and their unfailing support for a war against the "evil-doers" in Iraq. But that is a story we shall tell later in this chapter.

THE SUPERNATURAL AND THE END OF THE WORLD

Earlier I suggested that when the fundamentalists affirmed the virgin birth and bodily resurrection of Jesus as indispensable teachings of the Christian faith, their purposes were foreign to those of orthodox Christians throughout the history of the Christian faith. Clearly, Christians throughout the centuries have affirmed both these doctrines. But American fundamentalists made these affirmations in the context of a world defined by the eighteenth-century Enlightenment—a world of science and rationality, radically different from the world of the first or twelfth centuries, for example, when people simply took the supernatural for granted.

By affirming these propositions, then, the fundamentalists sought to claim far more than simply the virgin birth and the resurrection of Jesus Christ. They also meant to make room for the possibility of genuine miracles in a scientific world that reduced all reality to a rational cause-and-effect relationship. And to some degree, by embracing these propositions, the fundamentalists intended to categorically reject the rational, scientific perspective on which the modern world—with its modernist outlook—had been constructed.

By affirming miracles and the supernatural, they also intended to erect the foundation for the fifth in their list of fundamentals—the imminent, premillennial return of Jesus Christ. The two words, *imminent* and *premillennial*, clearly deserve some clarification.

Both terms underscore the pessimism over the future of the world that has been so characteristic of fundamentalism. Indeed, fundamentalists believed the world had become so bad—that religious decline since the end of the Civil War had been so pronounced—that nothing could save it short of the second coming of Jesus. When they used the word *imminent*, therefore, fundamentalists meant to suggest that Jesus would come soon—a conviction comparable to that of the earliest Christian communities depicted in the documents of the New Testament.

By using the term *premillennial,* fundamentalists meant to say that Jesus would come "pre-," or prior to, the glorious millennium—the thousand-year reign of Christ over all the earth that would herald the end of the world.

But there was far more to the term *premillennial* than that. Indeed, the notion of the premillennial return of Christ went through several mutations and, in fact, there were numerous versions of how the end of the world would play itself out. Central to all those versions was a theory spun by an itinerant British preacher in the nineteenth century, John Nelson Darby, and popularized by the *Scofield Reference Bible,* an edition of the Bible compiled and annotated by Cyrus I. Scofield and published in 1909.

That theory held that the history of the world consisted of seven dispensations. The present Christian dispensation was the sixth, but would soon give way to the seventh and final dispensation when Jesus would return to earth for the "rapture"—the miraculous rescue of true and faithful Christians. Indeed, Jesus would spirit these Christians to heaven, where they would witness the terrors of the seven-year rule of the Antichrist, a period Darby called the Tribulation.

Before these events could occur, the Jews would return to their ancient homeland and rebuild their temple in Jerusalem—the single event that would trigger the Tribulation. During the course of the seven years of terror, the Antichrist would focus his wrath especially on the Jews and seek their destruction. At the end of the seven years, Jesus would return to earth, save a remnant of the Jews who had converted to Christianity, and defeat the armies of the Antichrist in the great Battle of Armageddon. Jesus' victory over the forces of evil would finally usher in the millennium—the thousand-year rule of Christ on earth—followed by the resurrection of the dead and the final judgment. [8]

While John Nelson Darby wove together a variety of proof texts to construct his understanding of premillennialism, the seven dispensations, and the rapture, the theory as Darby framed it has no basis either in scripture or in Christian history. It is true that various strands of Darby's theory have been elaborated from time to time over the course of Christian history. But Darby's full-blown version of these events was quite novel in the larger Christian context. [9] Most important, neither the word nor the concept of the rapture, as Darby understood it, ever appears in the Bible. Darby arrived at his conclusions only after piecing together a variety of unrelated biblical texts that he had strained to interpret in fresh and novel ways. Yet thousands upon thousands of fundamentalists have embraced this vision ever since the *Scofield Reference Bible* popularized it in marginal notes and glosses on the text of the King James Bible in the early twentieth century.[10]

Darby's notion of the rapture did serve one purpose: It provided the fundamentalists with an escape hatch from this world in the event that they failed to defeat the modernists, the evolutionists, and the biblical critics. For if the modernists finally managed to vanquish the fundamentalists and overwhelm the supernatural with a purely scientific worldview, Jesus would then return to earth, destroy his modernist enemies, and rescue his faithful at the end of the age.

Premillennial theory graphically underscores the essential characteristics of American fundamentalism: their conviction that they alone were right while everyone else was wrong, the extent to which they thrived on enemies, their inability to cope with complexity, their discomfort with nuance and ambiguity, and their estrangement from symbolic and metaphoric language. Indeed, theirs was a fanciful elaboration of end-times scenarios, based on a literal and twisted reading of symbolic and metaphoric texts, and designed to assure themselves that they would finally triumph over their enemies and those they viewed as the enemies of God.

Fundamentalism and Christian America

If premillennial theology helped define the character of fundamentalism, it also undermined the fundamentalists' conviction that the United States was a Christian nation, at least in the movement's early years. Indeed, prior to World War I, fundamentalists were convinced that Christian America had been lost. The problems, they thought, were too overwhelming. The unrelenting wave of immigrants had robbed the nation of its noble Protestant character, the dignity of work had given way to labor unions and bloody strikes, the cauldron of the American city was sucking the life out of traditional morality, biblical criticism had undermined the authority of the Bible in American culture, and the theory of evolution had opened the door to hedonism of every kind by debasing the very nature of humanity. There was nothing they could do, most fundamentalists believed at the time, but wait for Jesus to return to earth, destroy the wicked, and rescue his saints.

In their earliest years, therefore, fundamentalists took refuge in the biblical vision of the kingdom of God. Many refused to fight for their country, becoming pacifists instead. Indeed, many refused even to vote, claiming primary citizenship in the kingdom of God, not in the United States. In any event, they reasoned, Jesus would come again soon. Why, then, should they become embroiled in a battle to save the sinking ship of civilization?[11]

By the close of World War I, fundamentalists almost completely reversed their stance on these issues. Throughout the course of America's involvement in that conflict, the federal government waged an intense propaganda campaign to encourage—indeed, to compel—all Americans to support the war. And for those who refused to conform or who publicly criticized the war effort, the Espionage and Sedition Acts authorized hefty fines and lengthy prison terms. It is little wonder that by war's end, fundamentalists found ample reason to reverse their ideological course.

Obviously, they could never concede that they might have buckled under government pressure. They desperately needed some compelling justification for this radical about-face. And they found it when they compared the promise of American civilization with the popular stereotypes of German culture. They came to believe, as George Marsden explains, that "Americans had just fought a war that could be justified only as a war between civilization and barbarism."[12] And standing at the very heart of Germany's barbaric behavior—or so the fundamentalists believed—were the twin theories of evolution and biblical criticism. If those two theories could undermine German culture, they could do the same in the United States.

Fundamentalists now had all the more reason to wage war against these diabolical theories of the modern world. Almost overnight, therefore, they committed themselves to the recovery of Christian America and the renewal of Christian civilization in the United States. And Christian America, as they envisioned it, would become a profoundly anti-modern nation, deeply suspicious of scientific theories that seemed to contradict literal readings of the biblical text.

By the time World War I had come to an end, fundamentalism had little in common with its nineteenth-century predecessor, the Second Great Awakening. It is true that both movements sought to propagate the gospel through evangelism and both were committed to a vision of Christian America. But while the Second Great Awakening had fought for the abolition of slavery, fundamentalism fought for a nation free from Darwin's theory of evolution. While the Second Great Awakening had fought for prison reform, fundamentalism fought to defend an inerrant Bible. And while the Second Great Awakening had fought for the creation of common schools throughout the nation, fundamentalism fought to free those schools from scientific theories that failed to conform to a literal reading of the biblical text.

The truth is, the agenda the fundamentalists embraced following World War I not only separated them from their fellow evangelicals of a hundred years before; it also separated them from the biblical vision of the kingdom of God that they, themselves, had embraced in earlier years. For the New Testament's description of the kingdom of God has nothing to do with biblical inerrancy or fanciful theories about when and how the second coming of Jesus might occur. Instead, the biblical vision of the kingdom of God has everything to do with how the followers of Jesus should treat their sisters and their brothers in *this* world.

Obviously, when one moves from the early twentieth to the early twenty-first century, the issues have changed dramatically. But the seminal characteristics of fundamentalism—hostility to pluralism, paradox, and nuanced understandings of important ideas; rejection of ambiguity and preoccupation with the war between good and evil; a fixation on enemies; and opposition to key ideas of modern science—have remained constant as fundamentalism has morphed from one incarnation to another over the course of more than a century.

The Demise of Fundamentalism: 1925

As far as the general public was concerned, early twentieth-century fundamentalism met an early demise when, in effect, it was placed on trial in a sweltering courtroom in the summer of 1925 in the small southern town of Dayton, Tennessee. The defendant, as far as the court was concerned, was a schoolteacher named John Scopes, who defied the state's law against teaching evolution in his classroom. But the reporters who covered that spectacle—among them H. L. Mencken, whom we quoted earlier in this chapter—placed the entire fundamentalist movement on trial before the American public when they portrayed its adherents and defenders as backwoods ignoramuses.

It made no difference that the Great Commoner, William Jennings Bryan—a three-time Democratic nominee for the presidency of the United States and former secretary of state under Woodrow Wilson—prosecuted Scopes on behalf of the state of Tennessee. Menc-

ken portrayed Bryan as fully as deluded as those on whose behalf
he prosecuted John Scopes.[13] Once Bryan "had one leg in the White
House and the nation trembled under his roars," Mencken wrote.
But in the heat of the trial, Mencken suggested that Bryan was

> a tinpot pope in the coca-cola belt and a brother to the forlorn pas-
> tors who belabor half-wits in galvanized iron tabernacles behind
> the railroad yards. His own speech was a grotesque performance
> and downright touching in its imbecility. Its climax came when
> he launched into a furious denunciation of the doctrine that man
> is a mammal. It seemed a sheer impossibility that any literate
> man should stand up in public and discharge such nonsense. Yet
> the poor fellow did it.

Of Bryan's argument, Mencken wrote, "All the familiar contentions
of the Dayton divines appeared in it—that learning is dangerous,
that nothing is true that is not in the Bible, that a yokel who goes to
church regularly knows more than any scientist ever heard of."

Clearly, Mencken's strategy was to paint the great defender of
fundamentalism with the same brush of imbecility with which he
painted fundamentalists themselves. Thus, he wrote:

> Bryan has been roving around in the tall grass for years and he
> knows the bucolic mind. He knows how to reach and inflame
> its basic delusions and superstitions. He has taken them into his
> own stock and adorned them with fresh absurdities. Today he may
> well stand as the archetype of the American rustic. His theology is
> simply the elemental magic that is preached in a hundred thousand
> rural churches fifty-two times a year.[14]

Large sections of the American public outside Dayton, Tennessee, devoured these accounts, fully convinced that fundamentalists
were nothing short of lunatics. The court finally ruled that John
Scopes was guilty. But that verdict made little difference since the
defendant in the public eye—the fundamentalist movement—had
been dealt a stunning defeat.

Little wonder, then, that after the trial, the fundamentalist
movement retreated from the public square and became a little-
noticed and little-understood subculture in American life. In effect,
fundamentalists gave up on America once again. If the American
public could delight in the caustic, ungodly excesses of the likes
of H. L. Mencken, the fundamentalists reasoned, there was little
hope that the United States would become a Christian nation any
time soon. For the most part, then, they preached and prayed in

their cultural ghetto for the next fifty years, exhorting one another to keep the faith when the whole world seemed to have turned against them.

After World War II, significant segments of fundamentalism morphed into a kinder, gentler form of the Christian faith under the leadership of revivalist Billy Graham. In effect, Graham was calling fundamentalists back to the evangelical spirit of the nineteenth century, reflected in the Second Great Awakening, and many who made that transition considered themselves evangelicals, not fundamentalists.

In addition to a kinder, gentler spirit, many of these evangelicals also sought to recapture the spirit of social concern that had characterized the Second Great Awakening. For example, Carl F. H. Henry, the first editor of the flagship evangelical magazine, *Christianity Today*, published in 1947 *The Uneasy Conscience of Modern Fundamentalism*, a book that summoned fundamentalists to social and intellectual engagement with the larger world.[15]

The Rebirth of Fundamentalism: The 1970s and 1980s

Although significant segments of fundamentalism had morphed into evangelicalism after World War II, the old-time fundamentalism reemerged in the early 1970s, this time in response to civil unrest and social dislocations at least as severe as the cultural crises that prompted the original version of the movement in the early twentieth century.

While many of the issues that spurred the revival of fundamentalism in the 1970s were unique to that period, one persisted from the late nineteenth and early twentieth centuries: the issue of immigration. A hundred years before, as we have seen, immigrants poured into the United States from Italy, Russia, and Eastern Europe, thereby subverting the Protestant America that the Second Great Awakening had worked so hard to construct.

In the 1960s and 1970s, the United States experienced another great wave of immigration. But these newer immigrants were not only foreign to the Protestant agenda; they were foreign to any kind of Christian agenda whatsoever. They came from places like Thailand, Cambodia, and South Vietnam; India, Pakistan, and Nepal; Lebanon, Iran, and Egypt. And they brought their religions with them: Islam, Buddhism, Hinduism, and many other religious traditions largely alien to most Americans at that time.[16]

While this new wave of immigration was not the immediate catalyst for the revival of American fundamentalism, it formed an important backdrop to that revival. At the very least, it spoke loudly to fundamentalists that the diversity they found so objectionable had come to their shores in ways they could never have imagined just a few years earlier. And it alerted them to the fact that any hope they may have had for the renewal of Christian America was now at risk. If they intended to recreate the Christian nation their forebears from the nineteenth century had constructed, time was running out.

For several years after these immigration patterns began, fundamentalists were reluctant to stare them in the face and cope with their implications. But they could not remain passive when, in the context of the Vietnam War and the civil-rights movement, some of their own sons and daughters—or children of friends and neighbors—joined the hosts of young people who now rejected traditional American Christianity as the tool of an oppressive establishment and embraced these new and exotic religions instead.

From the perspective of these young radicals, Christianity had failed in dismal ways, and a Christian America, by definition, was an unjust and immoral America. From their perspective, they saw proof of that contention every night as television screens across the land portrayed the reluctance of white Americans to treat their African-American brothers and sisters in just and equitable ways. They encountered additional proof in the nightly reports of the death and destruction the American military rained down on North and South Vietnam. And when they heard Christian preachers and other representatives of America's Christian establishment condemn the freedom movement and its leaders like Martin Luther King Jr., Stokely Carmichael, or Malcolm X, or when those same preachers lent support to America's war in Vietnam, many of these young people abandoned Christianity and turned to eastern religions that struck them—rightly or wrongly—as less compromised, less tainted with injustice, and less stained with the blood of war.

Patriotism suffered the same fate as large numbers of America's youth viewed the war in Vietnam as little more than an exercise in American imperialism, pursued—they believed—for the sake of commerce and economic profit. Traditional morality also fell on hard times as the countercultural revolution morphed into a sexual revolution and a culture devoted to psychotropic drugs.

During those years, the nation splintered into hardened ideological silos. Those who supported the war viewed those who opposed it as subversive, unpatriotic, and even anti-American. At the same time, those who rejected the war viewed its supporters as deluded at best and fascist at worst. The nation also experienced serious ideological ruptures over the civil-rights movement. Some supported complete freedom and equality for blacks, while others fought to maintain white privilege, and still others viewed the freedom movement as a Communist plot to undermine the social fabric of American society.

Robert N. Bellah has suggested that divisions in American society at that time were so deep and so entrenched that the very fabric of American culture threatened to unravel.[17] At the very least, the two decades of the 1960s and 1970s comprised a period of enormous upheaval in American life—upheaval at least as wrenching as the seismic shifts that characterized the several decades that led up to the birth of fundamentalism in the early twentieth century.

As we have observed, fundamentalist movements almost always respond to social upheaval by seeking to restore the tranquility—whether real or imagined—of an earlier age. It is hardly surprising, then, that Christian fundamentalism resurfaced in the United States in the aftermath of the chaos that engulfed the nation in the 1960s and 1970s. Those who led that movement summoned America to return to its alleged Christian roots in the hope that the United States might become a Christian nation yet once again.

No one did more to articulate that vision early on than a Baptist preacher in Lynchburg, Virginia, named Jerry Falwell. President Richard Nixon inspired Falwell when he pointed in 1969 to a great "silent majority" of Americans who supported the war in Vietnam and refused to join hands with the growing counterculture movement. Playing off Nixon's term "silent majority," Falwell and other conservative Christian leaders like Paul Weyrich and Richard Viguerie later claimed that a great "moral majority" would lend its support to a renewed and determined effort to Christianize American life, culture, and politics.

And they were right. For throughout the nation, fundamentalists had labored in their cultural and religious ghettoes for more than fifty years—ever since they had suffered defeat at the hands of American journalists in 1925. Falwell and his colleagues intended to summon these people out of their cultural isolation, to mobilize them for active involvement in American politics, and in that way, to renew the vision of Christian America that had dominated the nineteenth century. In pursuit of that vision, they created in 1979 a religiopolitical organization called the Moral Majority.

Within the next few years, other fundamentalist leaders created similar organizations. James Dobson, a well-known Christian psychologist and radio personality, launched his Family Research Council in 1981. And in 1989 Pat Robertson organized his Christian Coalition.

The issues these latter-day fundamentalists embraced obviously differed from the issues that drove the movement in the early twentieth century. Still, these newer fundamentalists betrayed the same sorts of commitments that have driven fundamentalist movements wherever they have appeared: a tendency to divide the world into good and evil coupled with the belief that they alone were right while others were wrong, a preoccupation with their enemies, a profound distrust of pluralism, an inability to deal in meaningful ways with complexity, nuance, or ambiguity, and a deep suspicion of many of the findings of modern science.

These latter-day fundamentalists differed profoundly in other ways, both from leaders of the Second Great Awakening and from leaders of the original fundamentalist movement some seventy-five years before. For leaders of those pioneering movements sought to build a Christian America chiefly through persuasion—through the power of preaching, for example, and through prayer—and in the case of the Second Great Awakening, through extensive social reform.

It is obviously true that in the nineteenth century, some pressed for a Christian amendment to the Constitution and for Sabbath legislation. And it is true that fundamentalists in the early twentieth century pressed for laws against the teaching of evolution. Still, those two movements, by and large, sought to Christianize the nation mainly through spiritual means. But when fundamentalism reemerged in the late 1970s and 1980s, it did something relatively new. It entered foursquare into the political arena and sought to achieve its objectives *chiefly* through the exercise of political power.

The latter-day fundamentalists, therefore, pressured senators and representatives at every level of government for legislation favorable to prayer in America's public schools, for legislation that would ban abortion under all circumstances, and for legislation that would substitute the Genesis account of creation for evolutionary science in public classrooms. At the same time, they sought to use the political process to undermine measures favorable to diversity and pluralism: the Equal Rights Amendment, gay rights, and even the U.S.-Soviet SALT treaties.

They eventually brought enormous pressure to bear on federal, state, and local judges who refused to hand down rulings favorable to their agendas. James Dobson, for example, blasted the United States Supreme Court for its failure to implement aspects of the fundamentalist agenda. The court, he claimed, was "unaccountable," "out of control," "a despotic oligarchy," and for forty years had been conducting a "campaign to limit religious liberty."[18] If these fundamentalists had succeeded with all the legislation they either supported or opposed—and had they succeeded in intimidating not only legislators, but judges as well—they would have created a virtual Christian establishment, the very thing the nation's Founders so much feared and opposed.

And yet when we use the word *Christian* to describe the initiatives these latter-day fundamentalists promoted—or to describe the Christian America they sought to create—we must use that term advisedly, especially when we keep in mind the biblical vision of the kingdom of God that we explored in chapters 2 and 3 of this book. That kingdom, we recall, exalted the poor, comforted those who mourned, lifted up the dispossessed, ministered to the suffering, fed the hungry, cared for those in prison, and found a place for the marginalized very close to the heart of God. But the latter-day fundamentalists paid virtually no attention to these issues. Indeed, they often advocated measures that stood diametrically opposed to the Christian message they claimed to serve.

Nothing made that point more clearly than the resignation in November 2006 of Rev. Joel C. Hunter from the presidency of Pat Robertson's Christian Coalition. Hunter, pastor of an evangelical megachurch in Longwood, Florida, had indicated he hoped to expand the agenda of the Christian Coalition from a preoccupation with abortion and gay marriage to include the reduction of poverty and global warming—issues Hunter viewed as central to the biblical vision. No sooner had Hunter taken office than the board of the Christian Coalition asked him to resign. According to Hunter, the board informed him, "This just isn't for us. It won't speak to our base, so we just can't go there."[19]

Indeed, the very origins of latter-day fundamentalism as an organized political movement betray it as thoroughly estranged from the biblical vision of the kingdom of God, even at its inception. As Randall Balmer and William C. Martin tell the story, the political movement popularly styled "the religious right" first coalesced in the mid-1970s to support the longstanding practice of racial segregation and discrimination on the part of many so-called Christian schools.[20]

In 1975 the Internal Revenue Service sought to rescind the tax-exempt status of Bob Jones University because the school forbade interracial dating. The United States Supreme Court had ruled in its landmark decision of 1954, *Brown v. Board of Education*, that segregation in America's public schools was illegal. It took Bob Jones University sixteen years after that to open its doors to African American students who were married. And not until 1975—fully twenty years after the *Brown v. Board of Education* decision—would Bob Jones University admit African American students who were single. And even then, the school refused to allow interracial dating.

The IRS based its case against Bob Jones University on a 1972 district court ruling in *Green v. Connally* that stipulated that any institution that engaged in racial segregation had, by definition, forfeited its standing as a charitable institution and was therefore ineligible for tax-exempt status. When the IRS informed the school that its tax-exempt status was on the line over its discriminatory policies, fundamentalist leaders around the country took note. Indeed, they viewed the federal ruling against Bob Jones University not as an opportunity to comply with the biblical mandate for justice and equality, but as an assault on the prerogatives of the fundamentalist subculture to bar black citizens from full participation in their schools. It was around this issue that the latter-day fundamentalists first coalesced as anything like a coherent political force.

Paul Weyrich, a fundamentalist organizer who had been trying to galvanize like-minded Christians into an active political force for many years, made this truth abundantly clear. Weyrich had floated as potential rallying points such issues as school prayer, abortion, and the proposed Equal Rights Amendment, but in every case he had failed. He later explained, "What galvanized the Christian community was not abortion, school prayer, or the ERA. I am living witness to that because I was trying to get those people interested in those issues and I utterly failed. What changed their mind was Jimmy Carter's intervention against the Christian schools, trying to deny them tax-exempt status on the basis of so-called de facto segregation."[21] Of course, it was not Jimmy Carter who authorized this "intervention against the Christian schools," since Carter was not president when these "interventions" occurred.

Of all the political initiatives the fundamentalists launched, by far the most important was their attempt to control the entire political process by electing to office candidates who supported their so-called Christian agenda. Since the 1980s, they have actively

supported conservative candidates—almost always Republicans—
for political office at the federal, state, and local levels, working on
the assumption that Christian legislators would pass laws in sync
with a Christian vision for America. They drew up "report cards"
on both candidates and actual officeholders, grading them on their
compliance with a host of measures the fundamentalists wanted
to see enacted into law. And they distributed those report cards
through fundamentalist churches throughout the United States.
In this way, the sprawling network of fundamentalist churches
became a significant power bloc in American politics.

At this point we must be clear that the power bloc the fundamentalists had created went far beyond fundamentalist churches to
encompass many evangelical Christians as well. Fundamentalists
and evangelicals believed many of the same points of doctrine—both
believed in a literal reading of the Bible, for example—but parted
company mainly over manners and demeanor. While fundamentalists thrived on enemies, evangelicals did not. While fundamentalists were often defensive, negative, and mean-spirited, evangelicals
were often more open to differing points of view—or at least more
willing to listen to others with a different perspective. In a word,
the difference between fundamentalists and evangelicals was the
difference between Jerry Falwell and Pat Robertson, on the one
hand, and Billy Graham, on the other.

It should also be said that some evangelicals embraced perspectives completely foreign to fundamentalist ideology. These more
progressive evangelicals sought to articulate a vision for social reform based on the biblical understanding of the kingdom of God—
the vision we explored in chapters 2 and 3 of this book. The most
obvious examples of such a progressive variety of evangelicalism
were Tony Compolo, author, lecturer, and professor emeritus at
Eastern College; Brian D. McLaren, author and founding pastor of
Cedar Ridge Community Church in Spencerville, Maryland;[22] Jim
Wallis and his *Sojourners* network;[23] and Ron Sider and his Evangelicals for Social Action.[24]

Still and all, many evangelicals had far more in common with
fundamentalism than they did with Wallis or Sider. Like their fundamentalist brothers and sisters, therefore, these evangelicals seldom identified war, or torture, or hunger, or poverty as issues that
demanded attention from the Christian community. Instead, they
responded with special passion to the two issues that dominated

both their own discourse and that of the fundamentalists—abortion and gay marriage.

By the dawn of the twenty-first century, those issues allowed fundamentalists to bring large numbers of evangelicals into the political power bloc they had organized. And when that power bloc flexed its muscle, it was able to effectively control one major political party and shape significant segments of the federal government around its "Christian" agenda.

Indeed, by 2004, this fundamentalist-evangelical power bloc effectively controlled the Republican Party, the House of Representatives, and the Senate. That fact became evident in the report cards—technically called Congressional Scorecards—issued by the leading fundamentalist advocacy group, the Christian Coalition. Those report cards graded members of the House on thirteen issues and members of the Senate on six. Forty-two members of the Senate earned an A+—a 100 percent score on all six issues, and 163 members of the House earned an A-—a 90 percent score on all thirteen issues on which they were graded. And the Christian Coalition gave 45 senators and 186 congressional members a rating of 80 percent or better. Those numbers suggest that the political organizing on which the fundamentalists had embarked in 1979 and 1980 had paid off handsomely and that, by 2004, they were well on their way toward transforming the United States into their version of Christian America.

Fundamentalism and George W. Bush

But the fundamentalist power bloc achieved its most significant victory when it helped elect George W. Bush to two successive terms as president of the United States. According to Election Day exit polls from 2004, when Bush ran for his second term as president, 23 percent of all voters claimed to be "evangelical Christians"— a catch-all term that embraced conservative Protestants of every stripe, including hard-core fundamentalists.[25] An analyst for the nonpartisan Cook Political Report suggested that at least a third of Republican voters were conservative Christians.[26]

Either way, research conducted by the Pew Research Center for the People and the Press suggested that 78 percent of evangelicals and fundamentalists gave their votes to Bush in 2004. That number is especially striking when one bears in mind that when Bush ran in

2000, he won only 68 percent of the evangelical and fundamentalist vote—still a hefty majority, but 10 percent less than he would receive in 2004.[27]

How can we explain this extraordinary level of support that fundamentalist and evangelical Christians gave to George W. Bush, first in 2000 and then again in 2004? The culture wars that James Davidson Hunter and Robert Wuthnow have described so well obviously played a significant role in the 2000 presidential election, as liberals, on the one hand, and fundamentalists and evangelicals, on the other, struggled to define the soul of the United States.[28]

In the heat of that struggle, the majority of fundamentalists and evangelicals viewed George W. Bush as one of them. He was, after all, a born-again Christian, converted by the evangelical preacher and pastor to presidents, Billy Graham. And though he belonged to a mainline denomination whose theology ranged from moderate to liberal—the United Methodist Church—Bush had far more in common with fundamentalism than he did with his denomination.[29] Fundamentalists and evangelicals understood that well, and when they voted for George W. Bush in 2000, they voted to place in the White House a Christian whose theology, style, and demeanor reflected familiarity with—and even affection for—a fundamentalist-evangelical perspective and worldview.

Then, only months after George W. Bush had been elected president of the United States, September 11, 2001, came crashing into the American consciousness. Terrorists had destroyed one of the central financial centers of the United States—the Twin Towers of the World Trade Center, had done significant damage to the nerve center for American military operations—the Pentagon, and apparently had planned to fly a fourth airplane into the White House—home of the president of the United States.

As we explored the emergence of American fundamentalism in the early twentieth century and its reemergence in the 1970s and 1980s, we saw how radical social dislocations, seismic changes in cultural traditions, or significant threats to cultural stability invariably help create—or help intensify—fundamentalist activity. By the time the tragic events of September 11, 2001, occurred, fundamentalists in the United States had been organizing and building a power bloc for some twenty years. But the events of September 11 intensified their efforts and accentuated their characteristics—their distrust of diversity, their discomfort with change, their suspicion of nuance and ambiguity, their hostility toward enemies, and their fascination with the radical divide that they believed separated good from evil.

In his response to the terrorist attacks of September 11, 2001, George W. Bush embraced many of those same characteristics and revealed that he, himself, was also a fundamentalist, if not in terms of many traditional theological categories, at least in the way he understood the struggle between good and evil, America's role in that struggle, and America's relationship to God—points we shall elaborate in substantial detail in the next several pages.

More than anything else, these characteristics, coupled with the stand Bush had taken in America's culture wars—his stand on abortion and gay marriage, for example—help explain why, by 2004, so many evangelical and fundamentalist voters viewed George W. Bush as God's anointed. As Bush neared the end of his first term in office, for example, John Hope from Rockville, North Carolina, affirmed, "I think it was by the grace of God that he is in office."[30] At a Bush reelection rally, Gary Walby from Destin, Florida, told the president, "This is the very first time that I have felt God was in the White House." And Hardy Billington of Poplar Bluff, Missouri, told a crowd at another Bush reelection rally, "God uses the president to keep evil down, to see the darkness and protect this nation. . . . God gave us this president to be the man to protect the nation at this time." Reporter Ron Suskind observed that these were sentiments "shared by millions of Bush supporters."[31]

Those supporters obviously included fundamentalist leaders. Jerry Falwell, for example, wrote in the July 1, 2004, issue of his e-mail newsletter, "For conservative people of faith, voting for principle this year means voting for the re-election of George W. Bush." He continued, "I believe it is the responsibility of every political conservative, every evangelical Christian, every pro-life Catholic, every traditional Jew, every Reagan Democrat, and everyone in between to get serious about re-electing President Bush."[32]

And after Bush had been reelected in 2004, Bob Jones III, president of Bob Jones University—the same institution whose ban on interracial dating triggered the creation of fundamentalism as a national political force—wrote a letter to the president that read, in part,

> In your re-election, God has granted America—though she doesn't deserve it—a reprieve from the agenda of paganism. You have been given a mandate. We the people expect your voice to be like the clear and certain sound of a trumpet. Because you seek the Lord daily, we who know the Lord will follow that kind of voice eagerly.

Don't equivocate. Put your agenda on the front burner and let it boil. You owe the liberals nothing. They despise you because they despise your Christ. Honor the Lord, and He will honor you. . . .

It is easy to rejoice today, because Christ has allowed you to be His servant in this nation for another presidential term. Undoubtedly, you will have opportunity to appoint many conservative judges and exercise forceful leadership with the Congress in passing legislation that is defined by biblical norms regarding the family, sexuality, sanctity of life, religious freedom, freedom of speech, and limited government. You have four years—a brief time only—to leave an imprint for righteousness upon this nation that brings with it the blessings of Almighty God. . . .

Pull out all the stops and make a difference. If you have weaklings around you who do not share your biblical values, shed yourself of them. Conservative Americans would love to see one president who doesn't care whether he is liked, but cares infinitely that he does right.[33]

The courtship between the fundamentalists and George W. Bush was hardly a one-sided affair. He courted them fully as much as they courted him, a process documented in *Tempting Faith*, a report by David Kuo, former second-in-command in Bush's faith-based office and special assistant to the president from 2001 to 2003. In June 2004, for example, the *New York Times* reported that "the Bush campaign is seeking to enlist thousands of religious congregations around the country in distributing campaign information and registering voters." Luke Bernstein, the Bush campaign coordinator in Pennsylvania, confirmed that report: "The Bush-Cheney '04 national headquarters in Virginia has asked us to identify 1,600 'Friendly Congregations' in Pennsylvania where voters friendly to President Bush might gather on a regular basis."[34]

Later Kuo reported how the Bush administration cynically used America's conservative Christians as pawns in the game of amassing political power. According to Kuo,

National Christian leaders received hugs and smiles in person and then were dismissed behind their backs and described as "ridiculous," "out of control," and just plain "goofy." The leaders spent much time lauding the president, but they were never shrewd enough . . . to wonder whether they were just being used. They were.[35]

The Bush campaign not only sought to co-opt fundamentalist and evangelical churches in the president's reelection bid. It also asked Catholic churches to hand over copies of parish directories in order to enlist potential supporters.[36]

In its continuing effort to cement the alliance between George W. Bush and religiously conservative voters, the Bush campaign also sought to portray Democrats as hostile both to the Bible and to people of religious faith. It sent mass mailings in September 2004 to residents of two states—Arkansas and West Virginia—to warn them that "'liberals' seek to ban the Bible."[37] And the Senate majority leader at that time, Senator Bill Frist, warned that Democratic senators who opposed judicial nominees favored by many evangelical and fundamentalist Christians were engaged in "an assault on people of faith."[38]

Efforts like these, aimed at co-opting churches and people of faith for blatantly political purposes, stood squarely in the Constantinian tradition that we discussed in chapters 3 and 4 of this book. Nonetheless, millions of fundamentalist and evangelical Christians viewed George W. Bush as God's anointed to implement "biblical norms" in the public square—to borrow a phrase from Bob Jones III—and to continue the work of creating a Christian America. We now must ask, what did Christian America look like during his years as president of the United States?

Since the preeminent initiative of Bush's presidency was the war on terror, fought on the battlefields of both Afghanistan and Iraq, and since he won such wide approval from the fundamentalist-evangelical community even after those wars had been raging for several years—indeed, after thousands upon thousands of Iraqi civilians had been killed—it seems fair to assume that the fundamentalists who helped to elect him viewed war-making—even preemptive war-making—as a central component of Christian America, or at least as something thoroughly compatible with their vision for Christian America.

In fact, Jim Lobe reported in 2002, when the war was still in the planning stage, that "some 69 percent of conservative Christians favor military action against Baghdad, 10 percentage points more than the U.S. adult population as a whole." That report appeared under the headline, "Conservative Christians Biggest Backers against Iraq."[39]

By April 2003, a month after the United States launched its preemptive strike against Iraq, the decision to invade that nation drew support from an astounding 87 percent of all white evangelical Christians, even though Iraq had done nothing to harm the United States. By June 2006, when the war was rapidly losing popularity in the country's general population, some 68 percent of white evangelical Christians still supported the American occupation of Iraq.[40]

From the war's inception, influential Christian preachers whipped up support among the faithful. Charles Stanley, pastor of the First Baptist Church in Atlanta, affirmed, "We should offer to serve the war effort in any way possible. . . . God battles with people who oppose him, and fight against him and his followers." Others, including Franklin Graham, son of Billy Graham, and Marvin Olasky, editor of the *World* magazine, suggested that the war would open up a whole new field for converting Muslims to the Christian faith. Still others, like Tim LaHaye, coauthor of the bestselling *Left Behind* series of end-times books, suggested that by virtue of the war, Iraq would become "a focal point of end-times events."[41]

It is certainly true that some evangelicals urged a more restrained approach to international conflict. Thus, the National Association of Evangelicals issued in 2004 a landmark document on civic engagement that urged Christians to "engage in practical peacemaking" and "non-violent conflict resolution."[42] Yet the very year that document appeared, a sizable majority of fundamentalist and evangelical Christians voted to return George W. Bush to the White House and expressed strong support for the president's war in Iraq. The inability of moderate evangelicals to provide meaningful leadership and direction on issues like war and peace finally prompted Ron Sider to lament the political disarray among evangelical Christians in his book *The Scandal of Evangelical Politics.*[43]

In 2008, as George W. Bush was nearing the end of his second term in office, two important books appeared in America's bookstores, both suggesting that evangelical Christians—especially younger evangelical Christians—had wearied of the fundamentalist agenda in American politics, and that the religious right had lost its grip on conservative Christians. Indeed, these books pointed to a strong, more moderate evangelical subculture that had never identified with the fundamentalist political agenda and that was poised to provide meaningful leadership for American evangelicalism in the years to come. Those two books were Jim Wallis's *Great Awakening: Reviving Faith and Politics in a Post-Religious Right America* and David Gushee's *Future of Faith in American Politics: The Public Witness of the Evangelical Center.*[44] It is too soon to know whether these books offered an accurate assessment of American evangelicalism or merely reflected wishful thinking on the part of their authors.

Fundamentalists, George W. Bush,
and the Great American Myths

Since evangelical and fundamentalist Christians were so favorable to America's preemptive war against Iraq, and since that war—especially as a "preemptive war"—was so foreign not only to American tradition but also to the biblical witness, we must wonder what factors prompted these people to so completely abandon the biblical principles they claimed to support.

The fact is, when supporting America's wars, evangelical and fundamentalist Christians imagined that they were completely faithful to the Bible. They were able to make this extraordinary leap since, in addition to the myth that America is a Christian nation, they embraced other myths that placed the United States completely inside the biblical text. And while many pundits poked fun at George W. Bush for his butchery of the English language, no one articulated those myths better than he. In the next few pages, we shall explore those myths in some detail, especially as they were embraced by George W. Bush, but also as they were embraced by his fundamentalist followers.

Those myths included (1) the conviction that, of all the nations of earth, God chose the United States for a special mission in the world—a notion we described in chapter 1 as *the myth of the chosen nation*; (2) the conviction that while other nations are rooted in ambiguity and tainted by compromise, corruption, and evil, the United States was fundamentally good and altogether innocent—a notion we shall designate as *the myth of the innocent nation*; and (3) the conviction that the United States would usher in a final golden age of peace, justice, and democracy for all humankind—a notion we shall designate as *the myth of the millennial nation*.

Each of these myths located the United States at the center of the biblical saga and each suggested that the United States was acting out the biblical story in these latter days. Each, therefore, simply reinforced for American fundamentalists their conviction that the United States was, indeed, a Christian nation.

The fact is, each of those myths has a long and venerable history and has been a staple in American life since the birth of the nation—a point I elaborate in my book, *Myths America Lives By*. But after September 11, 2001, George W. Bush and his fundamentalist supporters absolutized these myths in ways that allowed no room for ambiguity, for nuance, or for paradox. In their view, America embraced the right, her enemies embraced the wrong, and God stood on the side of the United States, leading her in the redemption of the world.

We now must explore in some detail the way George W. Bush embraced each of these myths.

THE MYTH OF THE CHOSEN NATION

In his Second Inaugural Address, delivered in January 2005, President George W. Bush rejected the suggestion that he considered the United States a chosen nation. "We go forward with complete confidence in the eventual triumph of freedom," he said, "not because we consider ourselves a chosen nation; God moves and chooses as He wills."

Despite that statement, in countless contexts—including the Second Inaugural itself—Bush argued that since God ordained freedom as the natural birthright of every man, woman, and child in the world, the mission of the United States is to extend that freedom around the globe. Indeed, in that same Second Inaugural Address, Bush affirmed that "freedom is the permanent hope of mankind" and that "history has a visible direction, set by liberty and the Author of liberty." For that reason, he said, advancing liberty "is the mission that created our Nation."[45] The inescapable conclusion is this: God chose the United States to advance his will for the world. If we offered the most innocuous interpretation of Bush's words possible, it would be this: The United States has rightly discerned God's will for the world and seeks to act as God's agent in that regard. Either way, it is clear that Bush believed that American foreign policy was a response to a divine directive.

In his 2003 State of the Union Address, Bush declared, "Americans are a free people who know that freedom is the right of every person and the future of every nation. The liberty we prize is not America's gift to the world; it is God's gift to humanity." He later told Bob Woodward that "I was the person who wrote that line. . . . And it became part of the jargon."[46]

In defending his decision to launch a war against Iraq, Bush returned to that theme time and again. In a speech to the National Endowment for Democracy in November 2003, he claimed that "liberty is both the plan of Heaven for humanity, and the best hope for progress here on earth." In that same speech, he told his audience that "the advance of freedom is the calling of our time,

. . . the calling of our country, . . . the design of nature, . . . [and] the direction of history." And in his State of the Union Address for 2004, he claimed, "The cause we serve is right, because it is the cause of all mankind."

If we consider these assertions at face value, we must conclude that, in making these claims, Bush stood squarely in the Jeffersonian tradition. For Jefferson also believed that "all men are created equal and are endowed by their Creator with certain inalienable rights, among which are life, liberty, and the pursuit of happiness." These "inalienable rights," Jefferson claimed, were both "inalienable" and "self-evident" since Almighty God—described by Jefferson as "Nature's God"—had woven these rights into the very fabric of nature. So if Jefferson pointed to "Nature and Nature's God" as the guarantor of human liberty, Bush spoke of liberty as "the design of nature," "the direction of history," "God's gift to humanity," and "the cause of all mankind."

But there was one crucial difference between Bush, on the one hand, and most Americans in the nation's early years on the other. That difference lay in the role they thought America should play with respect to these ideals. Simply put, most Americans of the early nineteenth century believed the United States would renovate the world through example alone. Lyman Beecher, perhaps the best known preacher in the early nineteenth century, spoke for many when he suggested that the light of the American experiment would "throw its beams beyond the waves; it will shine into darkness there and be comprehended; it will awaken desire and hope and effort, and produce revolutions and overturnings, until the world is free."[47]

But George W. Bush, convinced that God had chosen the United States for this special mission in the world, promoted freedom with force—with guns, planes, and bombs. He then claimed he was doing the will of God. "Going into this period [of war with Iraq]," he later told Bob Woodward, "I was praying for strength to do the Lord's will."[48] When Woodward asked if he had consulted his father, the former president of the United States, before he ordered the invasion of Iraq, Bush responded, "He is the wrong father to appeal to in terms of strength. There is a higher father that I appeal to."[49]

And in January 2004—a month when Iraq Body Count reported that some 60,000 Iraqi civilians had died as a direct result of the U.S.-led military intervention in that country[50]—Bush proclaimed in his State of the Union Address that:

The cause we serve is right, because it is the cause of all mankind. The momentum of freedom in our world is unmistakable—and it is not carried forward by our power alone. We can trust in that greater power who guides the unfolding of the years. And in all that is to come, we can know that His purposes are just and true.

If we place these words in their proper context—America's war in Iraq—they suggest that God served the United States as the Supreme General of its military operation in that country, snuffing out the lives of Iraqi civilians by the hundreds and the thousands in order to make them free, and destroying a nation's culture so that God's own system of freedom and democracy might prevail in that part of the world. This is the obvious meaning of the myth of the chosen nation as framed by George W. Bush. It should be clear by now how Bush both absolutized and subverted the myth of the chosen people—a myth that historically had only required that the American nation serve as a model of freedom to the rest of the world.

David Domke has suggested that by dealing in absolutized myths, Bush emerged as the prototypical fundamentalist, sharing far more in common with the enemies he fought than with the nation he sought to serve. Thus, Domke wrote,

One is hard pressed to see how the perspective of Osama bin Laden, that he and his followers are delivering God's wishes for the United States (and others who share western customs and policies), is much different from Bush's perspective that the United States is delivering God's wishes to the Taliban or Iraq. Clearly, flying airplanes into buildings in order to kill innocent people is an indefensible immoral activity. So too, some traditional allies told the Bush administration, is an unprovoked pre-emptive invasion of a sovereign nation.

Domke concluded that "Fundamentalism in the White House is a difference in degree, not kind, from fundamentalism exercised in dark, damp caves."[51]

In *Myths America Lives By*, I explored the myth of the chosen nation in substantial detail. I also explored another myth that we will not consider in depth in this book—the myth of "nature's nation." By "nature's nation," I meant a nation rooted and grounded in the laws of nature. The myth of nature's nation called and beckoned men and women to the fountain of freedom, but it never forced them. At the heart of nature's nation are "self-evident truths" and "inalienable rights"—notions Bush made foundational to his war in Iraq.

By introducing the element of force, and by suggesting that God had authorized that force and had called the United States to implement that force, George W. Bush subverted one of the great legacies of the American people—the notion guaranteed by the Declaration of Independence that while all men are entitled to liberty, they are also entitled to life. In this way, he virtually destroyed the myth of nature's nation and placed in its stead the nonsensical and oxymoronic notion that God forces all human beings to be free.

The irony that any nation might deliver freedom to another people by raining on that people an awesome display of death and destruction was apparently lost on George W. Bush. So was the irony that God would sustain and sponsor the death and destruction one nation would inflict on another. And so was the irony that God might serve the nationalistic and patriotic purposes of any nation. But appreciation of irony, like the appreciation of nuance, was never a strength of any fundamentalist movement—a point we have noted time and again throughout the course of this text. In like manner, appreciation of irony was never a strength of George W. Bush.

One final aspect of George W. Bush's use of the myth of the chosen nation deserves our attention, and that is the way he sought to Christianize that myth. As we have noted, the nation's founders grounded the "inalienable rights" of "all men" in "Nature's God," that is, the God all human beings can discern in nature. Nature's God, therefore, would serve men and women of all religions and of no religion at all. It would serve not only Christians, but also Jews, Muslims, Hindus, Buddhists, and adherents of countless other religious traditions. And while atheists might not recognize God in nature, "Nature's God" was intended to serve them as well, insofar as "Nature's God" guaranteed to "all men" those "inalienable rights."

But in an effort to appeal to his evangelical and fundamentalist base, George W. Bush went out of his way to place "Nature's God" in an explicitly Christian context. He did this by ripping passages of scripture out of their New Testament contexts and applying them to the United States of America. In this way, he seemed to suggest that the God who chose America for a special mission in the world was not "Nature's God," as Jefferson clearly indicated in the Declaration of Independence, but the God Christians knew as "the God and Father of our Lord and Savior, Jesus Christ."

Thus, for example, just one year after the attacks of 9/11, Bush made his familiar pitch that American ideals are "the hope of all mankind." And then he said, "That hope drew millions to this harbor. That hope still lights our way. And the light shines in the darkness. And the darkness will not overcome it. May God bless America."[52]

The "light that shines in the darkness," according to the Gospel of John in the Christian New Testament, is neither America nor American ideals, but Jesus the Christ. Thus, the text of John 1:4–5 reads as follows: "In him was life, and that life was the light of men. The light shines in the darkness, but the darkness has not overcome it."

Apparently neither George W. Bush nor his millions of fundamentalist and evangelical supporters saw a great deal of difference between Jesus Christ as the light of the world and the United States as the light of the world. If his evangelical and fundamentalist supporters had discerned that difference, they would surely have responded in outrage to this misuse of the biblical text—a misuse so severe that many Christians might well have thought it blasphemous. The fact that they never condemned the president for this serious misuse of the biblical text suggests that they viewed his rhetoric as altogether appropriate in the context of Christian America.

Or again, in his State of the Union Address of 2003, Bush affirmed that "there's power, wonder-working power, in the goodness and idealism and faith of the American people." Bush ripped that phrase, "There's power, wonder-working power," from a Christian hymn written by Lewis E. Jones in 1899 and entitled "There's Power in the Blood." The lyrics go like this:

> Would you be free from the burden of sin?
> There's power in the blood, power in the blood;
> Would you o'er evil a victory win?
> There's wonderful power in the blood.
> There is power, power, wonder-working power
> In the blood of the Lamb;
> There is power, power, wonder-working power
> In the precious blood of the Lamb.[53]

Again, one wonders whether George W. Bush or his fundamentalist and evangelical supporters saw a great deal of difference between the power the Christian tradition attributes to the blood of Jesus Christ and the power that resides in the goodness of the American people. The logic Bush employed seemed to suggest that

Americans were good since America was a Christian nation, sustained and redeemed by the blood of Jesus Christ.

Bush borrowed language from another Christian hymn for the title of his campaign autobiography, *A Charge to Keep: My Journey to the White House*. While many Americans would find the words, "a charge to keep," fairly innocuous, fundamentalist and evangelical Christians would not. For Christians have been singing the hymn "A Charge to Keep I Have" since 1762, when the great Methodist hymn-writer, Charles Wesley, first composed it. The words of the first stanza go like this:

> A charge to keep I have,
> A God to glorify,
> A never-dying soul to save,
> And fit it for the sky.[54]

But George Bush pirated these venerable Christian words and applied them to his own personal political ambitions.

Or again, in his effort to encourage Americans to fight terror, on the one hand, and "promote freedom around the world," on the other, Bush used the words from Julia Ward Howe's "Battle Hymn of the Republic" that we explored in some detail in the introductory chapter. Thus, in his Easter message of 2002, only months after 9/11, Bush stated, "In the wake of great evil . . ., Americans responded with strength, compassion, and generosity. As we fight to promote freedom around the world and to protect innocent lives in America, we remember the call of 'The Battle Hymn of the Republic': As He died to make men holy, let us live to make men free."[55]

Of course, only a fool would fail to recognize that at one level, this reference was nothing more than a play for votes. In fact, in the mid-1980s, shortly after Bush had experienced a born-again conversion, his father assigned him a role as campaign liaison to the fundamentalist and evangelical community in the United States. The man his father assigned to advise him in that capacity was Doug Wead, an Assemblies of God minister and a well-known Republican operative. Wead counseled Bush to "signal early and often" by lacing his speeches with allusions to the Bible and other well-known Christian literature.[56]

But his use of Christian language in his presidential rhetoric was more than a play for votes. As a fundamentalist Christian, Bush—like his evangelical and fundamentalist base—thoroughly confused the Christian view of reality with the purposes of the

United States. After all, from their perspective, the United States really was a Christian nation.

THE MYTH OF THE INNOCENT NATION

Time and again in this chapter, we have seen that one of the hallmarks of fundamentalists in every culture is their inability to nuance arguments, to embrace ambiguity, or to work with complexity, and their tendency to reduce highly complex problems to overly simple solutions. They routinely divide the world, therefore, into absolute good, which they embody, versus absolute evil embodied by their enemies.

Inevitably, the contrast between good and evil that fundamentalists celebrate in the best of times is rendered even starker during times of war. Indeed, Christ Hedges observed that "the moral certitude of the state in wartime *is* a kind of fundamentalism [italics mine]." He elaborated: "War makes the world understandable, a black and white tableau of them and us. It suspends thought, especially self-critical thought. All bow before the supreme effort."[57]

The war George W. Bush oversaw in Iraq clearly conformed to that assessment, for in the context of the war, the president repeatedly claimed that the United States was altogether good and innocent while its enemies were utterly evil and outside the pale of redemption.[58] Only two weeks after September 11, 2001, Bush explained his vision of the world to employees of the FBI:

> I see things this way. The people who did this act on America, and who may be planning further acts, are evil people. They don't represent an ideology, they don't represent a legitimate political group of people. They're flat evil. That's all they can think about, is evil. And as a nation of good folks, we're going to hunt them down, and we're going to find them, and we will bring them to justice.[59]

Key members or former members of the Bush administration also picked up on this theme. David Frum, former special assistant to Bush, and Richard Perle, former chairman of Bush's Defense Policy Board, published a book with the absolutist title, *An End to Evil: How to Win the War on Terror.*[60]

From Bush's perspective, the terrorists were not only evil; they were essentially subhuman creatures who lacked the universal human ability to experience emotional pain and hurt. One senior aid to the president reported in 2005, "He [Bush] told me . . . that the fundamental difference between us and them is that we hurt when people die and they don't."[61]

Having portrayed the terrorists as intrinsically evil and less than human, Bush argued time and again that the task facing the United States was the eradication of evil from the face of the earth. Only three days after 9/11, from the pulpit of America's National Cathedral in Washington, D.C., he told the nation, "Our responsibility to history is already clear: To answer these attacks and rid the world of evil." On October 4, 2001, Bush explained to the employees of the Labor Department that "now is the time to root out evil." In a speech at the United States Military Academy on June 1, 2002, Bush declared, "There can be no neutrality between justice and cruelty, between the innocent and the guilty. We are in a conflict between good and evil, and America will call evil by its name."[62] And in his State of the Union Address for 2003 he argued that the task facing the United States was to "confound the designs of evil men."

Out of this ideological context, Bush delivered his famous ultimatum to the nations of the world that "every nation, in every region, now has a decision to make. Either you are with us, or you are with the terrorists."[63] That statement left no room for any nation to nuance or qualify its response in any way at all. In effect, Bush had divided the entire world into opposing camps of good and evil. It was also out of this context that Bush delivered his famous statement that identified North Korea, Iraq, and Iran as members of "an axis of evil, aiming to threaten the peace of the world."[64]

If America's enemies were evil, Bush made it clear that the American nation and the American people were altogether good. The United States, he said, was "the greatest force for good in history." Americans, he said, were "the hardest working people in the world," and America was "the greatest country, full of the finest people, on the face of the earth." In fact, he said, America was "built on fundamental values that rejects [sic] hate, rejects [sic] violence, rejects [sic] murderers, rejects [sic] evil."

This is why he could claim that even though the United States had launched a preemptive invasion of Iraq, "we are not conquerors; we're liberators."[65] And this is why—as we noted in chapter 3—Defense Secretary Donald Rumsfeld could respond to a question from a foreign reporter about American empire building: "We don't seek empires. We're not imperialistic. We never have been. I can't imagine why you'd even ask the question."[66]

The presumption of American innocence prevented not only President Bush but virtually his entire administration from asking in a sustained and serious way the one question that should have been asked after the terrible events of September 11, 2001: "Why do they hate us?" Had that question been asked, and had Americans been willing to listen carefully and thoughtfully to the answers, the American response to those tragic events might have been radically different. As Geiko Müller-Fahrenholz, a German observer of America's War on Terror, has pointed out, "President Bush, unashamedly Christian in his public confessions, might have led his nation in a way that reflected the gospel's potential for reconciliation and a reconstruction of world politics."[67]

As it was, the president registered bewilderment at the very suggestion that anyone could possibly hate the United States: "How do I respond when I see that in some Islamic countries there is vitriolic hatred for America? I'll tell you how I respond: I'm amazed. . . . I just can't believe it. Because I know how good we are, and . . . we're fighting evil."[68] Over the next several months and years, Bush consistently responded to the question "Why do they hate us?" with the claim that terrorists hate freedom. "Americans are asking: Why do they hate us?" Bush told a joint session of Congress only days after 9/11 had occurred. "They hate what we see right here in this chamber—a democratically elected government. Their leaders are self-appointed. They hate our freedoms—our freedom of religion, our freedom of speech, our freedom to vote and assemble and disagree with each other."[69]

As time went on, key Bush supporters also embraced the fundamentalist division of the world into radical good and radical evil, always affirming that the United States was the moral beacon for the world. William Kristol, editor of the neoconservative publication *The Weekly Standard*, for example, suggested that Europe was unfit to lead the world because it was "corrupted by secularism." Nor could the developing nations lead the world, because they were "corrupted by poverty." Only the United States, Kristol thought, offered a "moral framework" commensurate with the requirements for leading a new world order. Kristol therefore asked, "Well, what's wrong with dominance, in the service of sound principles and high ideals?"[70]

Since Kristol spoke for countless fundamentalist and evangelical Christians who viewed the United States not only as a moral nation but as a Christian nation as well, it is fair to refer his question to the one text that all Christians view as authoritative—the New Testament. From the perspective of that text, there's a great deal wrong with "dominance in the service of sound principles and high ideals." As we saw in chapter 3, the New Testament exalts the poor and the powerless but consistently stands in judgment on those imperial powers that seek to dominate others.

The fact that those powers imagine they serve "sound principles and high ideals" finally makes no difference, for what the imperial powers may regard as "high ideals," the powerless may regard as tools of oppression. Henri Nouwen captured this irony well. "We keep hearing . . . that having power—provided it is used in the service of God and your fellow human beings—is a good thing," Nouwen wrote. "With this rationalization, crusades took place; inquisitions were organized; Indians were enslaved; positions of great influence were desired; [and] Episcopal palaces, splendid cathedrals, and opulent seminaries were built."[71]

But there is more. For in the human quest for power and dominance, human beings have already sacrificed their "sound principles and high ideals." From the biblical perspective, all human ideals and actions are inevitably corrupted by self-interest and greed—qualities that simply define the human condition. Whoever claims, therefore, that he or she embraces an adequate "moral framework" while others are "corrupted" has failed to discern the essential human condition. Most of all, that person has failed to discern the truth about herself or himself—that any claim to moral superiority is, in fact, an implicit admission that just the reverse is true. This is precisely why Jesus taught that the person who is zealous to remove the splinter from another's eye should first remove the log from his own.

Nothing more clearly flies in the face of the claim that the United States is a Christian nation than the nation's inability to grasp this teaching that stands at the heart of the biblical text. That teaching simply means that there is no such thing as an innocent human being and, therefore, no such thing as an innocent nation. It also means that any attempt to divide the world into competing camps of good and evil is finally self-deceptive and illusionary. Most of all, it means that any nation that assumes the cloak of innocence will inevitably fail to recognize its own high crimes. How could it be otherwise, for an innocent nation can do only good, and deeds that might be crimes when committed by others are thought to be free of guilt when committed by a nation that views itself as innocent by definition.

This is the biblical idea that George W. Bush failed to grasp when he proclaimed, "To answer these attacks and rid the world

of evil . . . we will export death and violence to the four corners
of the earth in defense of this great nation."[72] The assumption of
American innocence allowed the United States to torture its enemies and to justify that crime as altogether right and appropriate.
After all, torture was legitimate when employed "in the service of
sound principles and high ideals." The assumption of innocence
allowed the United States to unlawfully seize individuals merely
suspected of terrorist connections and to extradite those individuals
to nations that would torture them *on behalf of* the United States.
But, of course, those actions were also "in the service of sound
principles and high ideals." The assumption of innocence allowed
the United States to detain terror suspects without either charging
those suspects with a crime or trying them in a court of law—once
again "in the service of sound principles and high ideals." The assumption of innocence allowed the United States to take the lives
of thousands upon thousands of Iraqi civilians. Through it all, the
United States carefully nurtured its own illusion of innocence by
reasoning that those lives had been sacrificed "in the service of
sound principles and high ideals."

Finally, an assumption of innocence allowed the Bush administration to deceive the American people as they sought to make its case
for invading Iraq. We noted in chapter 3 that William Stringfellow,
in his analysis of the book of Revelation, concluded that the practice
of deceit was central to Babylon, the symbol of imperial power. In
a Babylonian world, Stringfellow wrote, "the truth is usurped and
displaced by a self-serving version of events or facts, with whatever
selectivity, distortion, falsehood, manipulation, exaggeration, evasion, [or] concoction necessary to maintain the image or enhance the
survival or multiply the coercive capacities of the principality."[73]

In January 2008, two nonprofit journalism organizations—the
Center for Public Integrity, working with the Fund for Independence
in Journalism—issued a report on the extent of deception employed
by the Bush administration. That study counted "935 false statements" that "were part of an orchestrated campaign that effectively
galvanized public opinion and, in the process, led the nation to war
under decidedly false pretenses." It concluded that "the cumulative
effect of these false statements—amplified by thousands of news
stories and broadcasts—was massive, with the media coverage creating an almost impenetrable din for several critical months in the
run-up to war."[74]

But even before this report was issued, Bill Moyers had explained how "our press largely surrendered its independence and its skepticism to join with our government in marching to war." Indeed, Moyers claimed that the Bush administration "needed a compliant press to pass on their propaganda as news," and his report documented the many ways in which the news agencies in this country cheerfully complied. But, of course, all that deception was also placed "in the service of sound principles and high ideals."[75]

In the face of these terrible ironies, the question one must ask is this: At what point does an innocent nation, intent upon resisting violence with violence—and sustaining that violence with deceit—finally embody the evil it seeks to oppose?

Cornel West has suggested that "violence is readily deployed by those who cloak themselves in innocence."[76] That is only part of a much larger truth. The fact is, presumptions of innocence *inevitably* beget violence against "evildoers." Geiko Müller-Fahrenholz makes the point like this:

> The war on terrorism is the logical expression of these fundamentalist fixations. The clear-cut options it pretends to offer are the product of a radical reduction of global complexities and injustices to a good-versus-evil dichotomy, which produces a mindset that allows no serious consideration of alternatives. As a result, authoritarian forms of leadership prevail, and massive violence is inevitable. . . . The war that President Bush has launched against Saddam Hussein's Iraq is a clear product of this fundamentalist dilemma.[77]

In this way, Christian America—the nation so many wished to identify with the Prince of Peace—became an agent of violence that turned the meaning of the Christian religion on its head.

THE MYTH OF THE MILLENNIAL NATION

We turn now to the third of the three myths we promised to consider—the myth of the millennial nation. In its classic American form, that notion holds that the United States will usher in a golden age of peace, justice, and democracy for all humankind. In recent years many American fundamentalists have transformed that vision into one of global death and annihilation. How such a dramatic ideological reversal could occur is the story we will explore in this section.

The myth of the millennial nation finds its deepest roots in the ancient Jewish anticipation that someday

The wolf will live with the lamb,
The leopard will lie down with the goat,
The calf and the lion and the yearling together,
And a little child will lead them. (Isaiah 11:6)

The central theme in this vision is clearly the kingdom of God—a kingdom of peace and universal tranquility. In the early nineteenth century, this vision inspired the noted folk painter Edward Hicks (1780–1849) to portray that ideal in his famous painting "The Peaceable Kingdom." Hicks created more than a hundred versions of that painting. In one of them he depicted on the left side of the canvas a youthful United States and on the right side the peaceable kingdom where the lamb, the lion, the wolf, and the child lie down in peace together. The questions Hicks sought to raise in this painting were these: Could the United States embody that peaceable kingdom? Indeed, could the United States help to make the kingdom of God a reality for all humankind?

In the early nineteenth century—the period when Hicks did his work—another biblical text helped shape the popular belief that the United States would usher in a golden age of peace and justice for all humankind. That text was Revelation 20:1–3, which reads as follows:

And I saw an angel coming down out of heaven, having the key to the Abyss and holding in his hand a great chain. He seized the dragon, that ancient serpent, who is the devil, or Satan, and bound him for a thousand years. He threw him into the Abyss, and locked and sealed it over him, to keep him from deceiving the nations anymore until the thousand years were ended. After that, he must be set free for a short time.

Many understood this passage to teach that someday the devil—the source of all evil, all war, and all injustice—would be bound for a thousand years, that is, for a millennium. During that period, the earth would become the peaceable kingdom of God where the wolf and the lion would lie down with the lamb and the child.

The Millennial Nation: The Classic American Vision

From an early date—even before the birth of the nation—Americans identified the building of the kingdom of God with the progress of the Christian faith in the American colonies. No one stated that vision more clearly than Jonathan Edwards, who, during the course of the Great Awakening (1734–43), suggested that "this new world is probably now discovered, that the new and most glorious state of God's church on earth might commence there; that God might in it begin a new world in a spiritual respect, when he creates the *new heavens and new earth.*"[78]

After the American Revolution and well into the nineteenth century, others sounded the same refrain—that the United States would usher in the kingdom of God. By now, the values embodied in the Declaration of Independence exerted a powerful influence on the way Americans understood that kingdom. The kingdom of God, most Americans now believed, was no longer simply a kingdom of peace; it was also a kingdom of equality and universal liberty for all humankind. Most also believed that God would use the United States to make that kingdom a global reality.

The popular preacher in early nineteenth-century America, Lyman Beecher, expressed that conviction well. The United States would lead the world, Beecher proclaimed in 1835, until "the world's hope is secure. The government of force will cease, and that of intelligence and virtue will take its place; and nation after nation cheered by our example, will follow in our footsteps, till the whole earth is free."[79]

The Millennial Nation: The Fundamentalist Vision

Ironically, at the very time that Beecher was offering these predictions and so many Americans were following his lead, another preacher—this time in Ireland—was working out a radically different understanding of those biblical texts that informed the American vision of the kingdom of God. This other preacher was a disgruntled priest from the Church of Ireland who later joined a sect called the Brethren. His name was John Nelson Darby—the man we met earlier in this chapter. As we have seen, Darby's prophetic calculations exerted an extraordinary influence on American fundamentalism, and by the early twenty-first century, his vision would even help shape the foreign policy of the United States.

While the classic American vision for the kingdom of God— a vision embraced by Jonathan Edwards and Lyman Beecher and countless Americans in between—had been hopeful, positive, and optimistic, the vision Darby laid out was dour, negative, and pessimistic. In a word, Darby had abandoned hope for this world. As long as this earth was unredeemed, it could never become the stage for the kingdom of God, he argued. Further, there was nothing humans could do to hasten that final golden age. Instead, Darby taught, only God could redeem this corrupt and sinful world, and he would do so at the second coming of Jesus Christ.

Darby's vision was hardly novel in Christian history, but he added some elements that were. The most important of Darby's inventions were "the rapture," "the tribulation," and the centrality of the Jewish people—and the state of Israel—to end-time events. Indeed, in Darby's imaginative vision, the end-time events could not transpire apart from the restoration of Israel to its promised land.[80]

Because his vision proved so crucial to large swaths of American fundamentalism, we should briefly rehearse his vision. According to Darby, Jesus would "rapture" true believers away from the earth prior to the appearance of the Antichrist, a satanic figure who would tyrannize the world for seven years—the period of "the Tribulation." The Antichrist would target his fury especially against the Jews and their Israeli state. Finally, the forces of the Antichrist would gather from all corners of the world in one last attempt to destroy the Jewish people in the great battle of Armageddon, a cataclysmic war that would take place at the end of the seven years of tribulation. Jesus would then return with his saints to defeat the Antichrist and his followers. Indeed, he would cast them all into a lake of fire and hurl Satan into a bottomless pit. Along with his saints, Jesus would then rule the earth for a thousand years from Solomon's temple, restored to its ancient grandeur in the city of Jerusalem.[81]

Darby's vision might have died a natural death had it not been for Cyrus Scofield, who popularized Darby's fanciful ideas in the notations of his *Scofield Reference Bible*, published in 1909. That Bible became a bestseller in the United States, and through that Bible, Darby's views exerted an extraordinary influence on the fundamentalist movement taking root in America at that time. It should not be surprising that American fundamentalists found Darby's views compelling, since they shared his dour and pessimistic view of the world. According to historian Timothy Weber, by World War I Darby's views "had become nearly synonymous with [American] fundamentalism."[82]

Hal Lindsey further popularized Darby's views in his book *The Late Great Planet Earth*, published in 1970. That book argued that Israel's stunning victory over Egypt, Jordan, and Syria in the Six-

Day War was a clear fulfillment of prophecy. True to Darby's vision, Lindsey suggested that the end of the world was near and that Jesus would rapture true believers before the great Tribulation—a terrible time of plagues, famines, and wars. After the Tribulation, Jesus would return to earth and rule with his saints for a thousand years.

Lindsey's book eventually sold more than 35 million copies and helped to confirm Darby's visionary, apocalyptic perspective in the minds of America's fundamentalists. Virtually all the major preachers in the fundamentalist orbit soon embraced Darby's perspective, and many of those preachers—Oral Roberts, Rex Humbard, Kenneth Copeland, Jimmy Swaggart, Jerry Falwell, and Jim Bakker among them—heralded the gospel of the end of the world on prime-time television.[83]

In more recent years, the *Left Behind* series of prophetic novels, authored by Tim LaHaye and Jerry Jenkins, did yeoman's work to promote Darby's visionary, apocalyptic ideas. By April 2007, sixteen novels in this series had appeared, and each had sold more than 3 million copies.[84] The publisher, Tyndale House, even produced a video game in which young Christians could act out the apocalyptic struggle between believers and unbelievers.

The Role of Israel in Rapture Theology

In 1948 one key component of Darby's visionary scheme became reality when Israel proclaimed itself a state and a homeland for dispersed Jews throughout the world. Then, when Israel defeated Egypt, Jordan, and Syria in the famous Six-Day War of 1967, many fundamentalists viewed that war as a prelude to the final battle of Armageddon. From their perspective, God's righteous decrees, uttered in biblical prophecy, were fulfilling themselves before their very eyes. They therefore threw their complete and unwavering support behind Israel, without considering what that unqualified stand for Israel might mean for suffering and poverty-stricken people in the Arab world or for injustice for the Palestinian people. All that mattered was that Christians in the United States stand with God in this final, end-times scenario. The fundamentalist leader John Hagee offered, for example, this ultimatum:

> Christians and Jews, let us stand united and indivisible on this issue. There can be no compromise regarding the city of Jerusalem,

not now, not ever. We are racing toward the end of time, and Israel lies in the eye of the storm. . . . Israel is the only nation created by a sovereign act of God, and He has sworn by His holiness to defend Jerusalem, His Holy City. If God created and defends Israel, those nations that fight against it fight against God.[85]

Jerry Falwell concurred, "When you go back to the pharaohs, the Caesars, Adolf Hitler and the Soviet Union, all those who dared to touch the apple of God's eye—Israel—have been punished by God. America has been blessed because she has blessed Israel."[86] And the Christian writer Kay Arthur claimed that if forced to choose between Israel and America, "I would stand with Israel, stand with Israel as a daughter of the King of Kings, stand according to the word of God."[87]

Since 1970, millions of fundamentalist Christians have organized on behalf of Israel. In 2003, for example, the International Fellowship of Christians and Jews announced a drive to enlist one hundred thousand churches and a million Christians as part of their "Stand for Israel" campaign. They also sought to build meaningful lines of communication with the federal government and to shape American foreign policy. Participants in the 2002 IFCJ convention, for example, heard from Attorney General John Ashcroft and members of the U.S House of Representatives Tom Delay (R-Tex.) and Tom Lantos (D-Calif.). In gratitude for their work on behalf of Israel, the IFCJ bestowed on Delay and Lantos the first Friends of Israel awards. It is difficult to know the extent to which George W. Bush may have shared the apocalyptic visions espoused by millions of fundamentalist Christians in the United States, but as Bill Moyers noted, "he would not be president without them."[88]

Former president Jimmy Carter lamented the "strong influence of some Christian fundamentalists on U.S. policy in the Middle East." He elaborated on this point in his book, *Our Endangered Values*:

Their agenda calls for a war in the Middle East against Islam (Iraq?) and the taking of the entire Holy Land by Jews (occupation of the West Bank?), with the total expulsion of all Christians and other gentiles. . . . Based on these premises, some top Christian leaders have been in the forefront of promoting the Iraqi war, and make frequent trips to Israel, to support it with funding, and lobby in Washington for the colonization of Palestinian territories. Strong pressure from the religious right has been a major factor in America's quiescent acceptance of the massive building of Israeli settlements and connecting highways on Palestinian territory in the West Bank.[89]

Not only did fundamentalists seek to influence government policy toward Israel, but, on certain occasions at least, the federal government welcomed their perspectives. Hal Lindsey, for example, consulted at the American Air War College and the Pentagon, explaining to military planners the implications of his *Late Great Planet Earth* for the Arab–Israeli conflict and the politics of the entire Middle East.[90] In light of the conflagration sure to come, Lindsey encouraged in 1980 a massive buildup of American military might. He wrote "that the Bible supports building a powerful military force. And the Bible is telling the U.S. to become strong again."[91]

In the meantime, the Israeli government courted its friends in the American fundamentalist network. Noted preachers like Jerry Falwell, Pat Robertson, and Oral Roberts led "Christian tour groups" to holy and historic sites in Israel. And Prime Minister Menachem Begin met with fundamentalist leaders from the United States on numerous occasions, even allowing them to instruct him in Bible prophecy.[92]

But fundamentalists in the United States were a fragile reed on which Israel might lean. As Geiko Müller-Fahrenholz pointed out,

> The gathering of the Jews in their Promised Land is nothing but a precondition for the Second Coming of Christ. They are counting on 144,000 Jews to accept Jesus as their Messiah; the rest belong to the *massa perditionis*—the condemned masses. When the real Messiah comes, the land of Israel will be turned into the final battlefield, where all the armies of the earth will converge. This, then, is the "final solution": the state of Israel will disappear . . . [and] all Jews who have not accepted Christ will . . . be annihilated.[93]

Or, as Bill Moyers has summarized the visions for the future that many rapture theologians entertain,

> Once Israel has occupied the rest of its "biblical lands," legions of the Antichrist will attack it, triggering a final showdown in the valley of Armageddon. As the Jews who have not been converted are burned, the Messiah will return for the Rapture. True believers will be transported to heaven where, seated at the right hand of God, they will watch their political and religious opponents writhe in the misery of plagues—boils, sores, locusts, and frogs—during the several years of the tribulation that follows.[94]

Islam As Antichrist

If Israel is the centerpiece in the end-times drama foretold by rapture theology, the other crucial player is the Antichrist—that demonic figure who resists the will of God and persecutes both Christians and Jews.

For many years, rapture theologians identified the Soviet Union as the Antichrist. But after September 11, 2001, they became quite certain that the Antichrist was closely connected with the Arab world and the Muslim religion. Two years after 9/11, Richard Cizik, vice president of the National Association of Evangelicals, reported to the *New York Times* that "evangelicals have substituted Islam for the Soviet Union. The Muslims have become the modern-day equivalent of the Evil Empire."[95]

Indeed, some rapture theologians made that suggestion long before that date. The historian Paul Boyer, for example, reports the following:

> "The Arab world is an Antichrist-world," wrote Guy Dury in "Escape from the Coming Tribulation" (1975). "God says he will lay the land of the Arabs waste and it will be desolate," Arthur Bloomfield wrote in *Before the Last Battle—Armageddon*, published in 1971 and reprinted in 1999. "This may seem like a severe punishment, but . . . the terms of the covenant must be carried out to the letter."[96]

At the very least, the events of September 11, 2001, prompted many fundamentalists and evangelicals to conclude that Islam is an evil religion. Only two months after those attacks, Franklin Graham, son of evangelist Billy Graham, called Islam "a very evil and wicked religion." Two years later, a national poll suggested that roughly two-thirds of evangelical leaders thought Islam "a religion of violence" intent on "world domination."[97]

Many fundamentalist leaders therefore welcome war with the Islamic world and, for that reason, support American military involvement in the Middle East. The contest over the Dome of the Rock, an Islamic holy site, illustrates the issue. The Dome sits on the site of Solomon's Temple, and many fundamentalists believe that the Second Coming of Jesus is contingent on the reconstruction of that temple. Some, therefore, have advocated destroying the Dome of the Rock. When asked if such an action might trigger World War III, a Christian tour leader in Israel responded, "We are near the End Times. . . . Orthodox Jews will blow up the mosque and this will provoke the Muslim world. It will be a cataclysmic holy war with Israel. This will force the Messiah to intervene."[98]

This is the context Bill Moyers had in mind when he reported that for some fundamentalists, "The invasion of Iraq was a warm-up act, predicted in the book of Revelation, where four angels 'bound in the great river Euphrates' will be released 'to slay the third part of man.'" For these people, Moyers continued, "A war with Islam in the Middle East is not something to be feared but welcomed—an essential conflagration on the road to redemption."[99]

A Fundamentalist View of the Millennium: What Difference Would It Make?

We now must ask what difference it would make for public policy at home and foreign policy abroad if millions of Americans embraced rapture theology.

The truth is that millions of American fundamentalists *have* embraced rapture theology, and that reality can hold enormous consequences for American public and foreign policy. First, rapture theology projects the United States into a pivotal role in the final dissolution of the earth. On the one hand, rapture theologians have embraced the Darbyite notion that God will smite unbelievers at the end of time—the notion promoted by Hal Lindsey's *Late Great Planet Earth* and the *Left Behind* series by Jenkins and LaHaye. But they also subscribe to the classic American understanding that the United States is the vessel through which God will hasten His millennial kingdom in the coming golden age—the notion held by American Christians like Jonathan Edwards and Lyman Beecher.

The resulting vision has nothing to do with either peace (the biblical vision) or freedom (the classic American vision). Instead, it holds—to put it bluntly—that God will use the United States to smite the Antichrist and other enemies of righteousness at the end of time, preparing the way for the millennial reign of Christ and His saints. And God will use the United States in this way precisely because of this country's history as a Christian nation. This is why Tim LaHaye, coauthor of the bestselling series of end-times books, could lend such strong support to the American invasion and occupation of Iraq. By virtue of that war, LaHaye believed, Iraq would become "a focal point of end-times events"[100]—a belief we noted earlier in this chapter.

Second, we have seen that rapture theology encourages war with the Islamic world. It also opens the door for nuclear holocaust. Rapture theologians have always held that God will destroy his enemies at the end of time in the great Battle of Armageddon, a battle prophesied—they believe—in the book of Revelation. Since World War II, they have increasingly identified Armageddon with nuclear

weaponry, thereby lending to the prospects of global nuclear annihilation a certain biblical inevitability. As one prophecy writer put
it, "The holocaust of atomic war would fulfill the prophecies."[101]
Historian Timothy Weber writes that, in recent years, not all rapture
teachers "agreed on when or how nuclear war would come, but
they all agreed that the divine plan included widespread nuclear
annihilation."[102]

They also agreed on something else—that Christians will escape this awful calamity. After all, before the nuclear conflagration, God—they claim—will rapture Christians away from the
earth to the heavenly realms. There, they will calmly witness the
nuclear annihilation that God will visit on unbelievers.[103] Listen,
for example, to John Hagee, a rapture theologian and pastor of the
17,000–member Cornerstone Church in San Antonio, Texas:

> *Believers in Christ will escape doomsday!* Mark it down, take it
> to heart, and comfort one another with these words. Doomsday
> is coming for the earth, for nations, and for individuals, but those
> who have trusted in Jesus will not be present on earth to witness
> the dire time of tribulation.[104]

The public policy implications of a belief like this are immense,
for if fundamentalists believe that God has foreordained a nuclear
conflagration that they themselves will escape, they might very well
welcome that event—indeed, they might well encourage it—as the
fulfillment of the will of God for the destruction of the world.

Third, rapture theology severs the prophetic nerve that is central to the biblical tradition. Here, I use the word *prophetic*, not in
the sense of predicting the future, but in the context of the eighth-
century BCE Hebrew prophets who spoke on behalf of social justice,
especially for the marginalized and the poor. Rapture theology severs that nerve by consistently prizing prophecy-as-prediction over
prophecy-as-ethical-challenge. Put another way, in the world of
rapture theology, the prophetic timetable imposed on the biblical
text almost always trumps biblical teachings on peace, justice, and
the kingdom of God.

Thus, in the world of rapture theology, support for Israel always
crowds out the question of justice for impoverished and oppressed
Palestinians. And when government officials and advisers advocate
preemptive strikes against other nations, rapture theology guaran-
tees that millions of Christians will not resist. And why should
they resist, since God has chosen the United States to hasten the

world's final consummation, since any given war may well be the war God will use to hasten the millennial reign of Christ, and since God has promised to rescue Christians from the final tribulation in any event?

In her major study *The Rapture Exposed*, Barbara Rossing compared rapture theology with the central teachings of the biblical text and concluded that "this theology is not biblical."[105] The truth is, rapture theology is not only unbiblical; it is *anti*-biblical, for rapture theology implicitly rejects the biblical vision of the kingdom of God that we explored in the second and third chapters of this book.

If the biblical vision of the kingdom of God exalts the poor at the expense of the rich, rapture theology exalts only Christians—and fundamental, born-again Christians at that—at the expense of everyone else. If the biblical vision of the kingdom of God promises justice for the oppressed, rapture theology promises greater oppression for those who don't conform to the prophetic timetable the rapture theologians have imposed on the biblical text. If the biblical vision of the kingdom of God resists imperial powers, rapture theology exalts imperial powers as long as they conform to an imagined prophetic script. And if the biblical vision of the kingdom of God nurtures the paths of peace, rapture theology celebrates apocalyptic violence.

When all is said and done, rapture theology is little more than the myth of Christian America writ in violent, apocalyptic terms.

Conclusions

Obviously, there is a sense—and, in fact, a profound sense—in which America is a Christian nation. After all, some 76 percent of the American people claim to be Christian in one form or another. But the Christian character of the United States is comparable to the Christian character of the Roman Empire after Constantine or the Holy Roman Empire in the sixteenth century. Christian trappings abound, but if one compares, for example, the Christian dimensions of the Holy Roman Empire with the teachings of Jesus, the differences are stunning.

Jesus counseled peace, but the empire practiced violence. Jesus counseled humility, but the empire engaged in a ruthless pursuit of power. Jesus counseled concern for the poor, but the empire practiced exaltation of the rich. Jesus counseled modesty, but the empire practiced extravagance. Jesus counseled simple living, but the empire encouraged luxurious living for those with the means to embrace that way of life. And while Jesus counseled forgiveness and love for one's enemies, the empire practiced vengeance.

Like that ancient empire, the United States abounds in Christian trappings. And yet the United States embraces virtually all the values that have been common to empires for centuries on end. It pays lip service to peace but thrives on violence, exalts the rich over the poor, prefers power to humility, places vengeance above forgiveness, extravagance above modesty, and luxury above simplicity. In a word, it rejects the values of Jesus.

How, then, can we claim that the United States is a Christian nation?

NOTES

Introduction

1. www.theocracywatch.org/texas_gop.htm, accessed October 10, 2008. Kevin Phillips asserts that the "Christian nation" platform of the Texas Republican Party was only one of several, mainly in the South and the West. See his *American Theocracy* (New York: Viking, 2006), 232–33.

2. Richard T. Cooper, "General Casts War in Religious Terms," www. commondreams.org/headlines03/1016–01.htm, accessed March 28, 2008.

3. Susan Jacoby, *Freethinkers: A History of American Secularism* (New York: Metropolitan Books, 2004), 353.

4. Sermon by Franklin Graham, inaugural prayer service for President George W. Bush, Washington D.C., January 21, 2001, in http://www.angelfire .com/in/HisName/inauguralsermon.html, accessed March 28, 2008.

5. Stanley Fish, "Religion without Truth," *New York Times*, May 31, 2007, A27.

6. Chris Hedges, "Christianizing US History," *The Nation* 286 (January 28, 2008), 23.

7. John McCain, interview with beliefnet.com, October 1, 1007, http:// www.beliefnet.com/Video/News-and-Politics/John-McCain-2008/John -Mccain-Constitution-Established-A-Christian-Nation.aspx, accessed October 24, 2008.

8. First Amendment to the Constitution of the United States of America.

9. Christian Smith, *Christian America? What Evangelicals Really Want* (Berkeley: University of California Press, 2000), 199.

10. Gregory A. Boyd makes this point quite forcefully in his book, *The Myth of a Christian Nation: How the Quest for Political Power Is Destroying the Church* (Grand Rapids, Mich.: Zondervan, 2005).

11. Tony Norman, "If Ann Coulter's a Christian, I'll Be Damned," *Pittsburgh Post-Gazette*, http://www.post-gazette.com/pg/06160/696887–153 .stm, accessed February 4, 2008.

12. Ann Coulter, *Godless: The Church of Liberalism* (New York: Crown Forum, 2006), 99–146; quotes are from 3, 8, and 22, respectively.

13. Coulter, "This Is War" in "National Review Online," September 13,

2001, at http://www.nationalreview.com/coulter/coulter.shtml, accessed March 28, 2008.

14. For a summary of some of these concerns on the part of the Moral Majority, see John C. Bennett, "Assessing the Concerns of the Religious Right," *Christian Century* 98 (October 14, 1981), 1018–22.

15. A. H. Lewis, *A Critical History of the Sabbath and the Sunday in the Church* (New York, 1886), 495–96, cited in Robert T. Handy, *A Christian America: Protestant Hopes and Historical Realities* (New York: Oxford University Press, 1971), 100.

16. Jacoby, *Freethinkers*, 105–6.

17. Martin E. Marty, *Righteous Empire: The Protestant Experience in America* (New York: Dial Press, 1970), 249.

18. Marty, *Righteous Empire*, 94–95.

19. Ezra Stiles Ely, *The Duty of Freemen to Elect Christian Rulers . . .* (Philadelphia, 1828), pp. 12, 14, cited in Handy, *Christian America*, 50.

20. For more information on House Resolution 888, see Hedges, "Christianizing US History," 23–24.

21. On this point, see Sidney E. Mead, "From Coercion to Persuasion: Another Look at the Rise of Religious Liberty and the Emergence of Denominationalism," in *The Lively Experiment: The Shaping of Christianity in America* (New York: Harper and Row, 1963), 16–37.

22. *Church of the Holy Trinity v. United States*, 143 U.S. 226 (1892), as quoted by Joseph Tussman, ed., *The Supreme Court on Church and State* (Oxford, U.K.: Oxford University Press, 1962), 41.

23. Robert N. Bellah, "Civil Religion in America," *Daedalus* 96 (Winter 1967), 7. A more recent take on the idea of America's civil religion—though it avoids using that term—is David Gelernter, *Americanism: The Fourth Great Western Religion* (New York: Doubleday, 2007).

24. Geiko Müller-Fahrenholz, *America's Battle for God: A European Christian Looks at Civil Religion* (Grand Rapids, Mich.: Eerdmans, 2007), 19.

25. For a discussion of these cultic dimensions of America's civic faith, see Bellah, "Civil Religion in America," 11.

26. For the text of "The Battle Hymn of the Republic," along with an analysis, see David Hackett Fischer, *Liberty and Freedom: A Visual History of America's Founding Ideas* (Oxford, U.K.: Oxford University Press, 2005), 331–32.

27. Winthrop S. Hudson, *The Great Tradition of the American Churches* (New York: Harper and Row, 1953), 108.

28. Handy, *Christian America*, 123.

Chapter 1. Christian America As God's Chosen People

1. "We All Must Learn to Forgive, Clergy Say," *Harrisburg Patriot-News*, October 6, 2006, A5.

2. On Amish forgiveness in the context of this tragic incident, see Donald Kraybill, David Weaver-Zercher, and Steven M. Nolt, *Amish Grace: How Forgiveness Transcended Tragedy* (San Francisco: Jossey-Bass, 2007).

3. "Amish Forgive, 'Keep On Going,'" *Harrisburg Patriot-News*, October 31, 2006, B1–2.

4. Sally Kohn, "What the Amish Are Teaching America," *alternet.org*, October 10, 2006, at http://www.alternet.org/story/42773, accessed November 5, 2006.

5. Will Herberg, *Protestant, Catholic, Jew*, rev. ed. (Garden City, N.Y.: Doubleday, 1960), 2.

6. Bill McKibben, "The Christian Paradox: How a Faithful Nation Gets Jesus Wrong," *Harper's Magazine* (August 2005), 31.

7. Stephen Prothero, *Religious Literacy: What Every American Needs to Know—and Doesn't* (San Francisco: HarperSanFrancisco, 2007), 30, 36.

8. David E. Wells, *No Place for Truth; or, Whatever Happened to Evangelical Theology?* (Grand Rapids, Mich.: Eerdmans, 1993), 4.

9. Thomas Hooker, *The Danger of Desertion, a farewell sermon preached immediately before his departure* [1633] *out of old England* (London, 1641), in Winthrop Hudson, ed., *Nationalism and Religion in America* (New York: Harper and Row, 1970), 25.

10. D. James Kennedy, *What If America Were a Christian Nation Again?* (Nashville, Tenn.: Thomas Nelson, 2003), 10–11.

11. William Tyndale, "A Prologue into the Fifth Book of Moses Called Deuteronomy," in Tyndale, trans., *Tyndale's Old Testament*, 1530, ed. David Daniell (New Haven, Conn.: Yale University Press, 1992), 256.

12. Tyndale, "W. T. unto the Reader," in Tyndale, *Tyndale's New Testament*, 1534, ed. David Daniell (New Haven:, Conn.: Yale University Press, 1989), 4.

13. Tyndale, "The Prologue to the Prophet Jonas," 1531, in Tyndale, *Tyndale's Old Testament*, 634–35.

14. John Winthrop, *A Model of Christian Charity*, in http://religiousfreedom.lib.virginia.edu/sacred/charity.html, accessed March 22, 2007.

15. Abraham Keteltas, "God Arising and Pleading His People's Cause," 1777, in Hudson, *Nationalism and Religion in America*, 49, 52; and Nicholas Street, "The American States Acting over the Part of the Children of Israel in the Wilderness and Thereby Impeding Their Entrance into Canaan's Rest," 1777.

16. Irving L. Thompson, "Great Seal of the United States," *Encyclopedia Americana* (1967), 13:362.

17. John Cushing, "A Discourse Delivered at Ashburnham, July 4, 1796," in Hudson, *Nationalism and Religion in America*, 18.

18. Herman Melville, *White Jacket; or, The World in a Man-of-War* (Boston: St. Botolph Society, 1892), 144.

19. Cited in William G. McLoughlin Jr., *Billy Graham: Revivalist in a Secular Age* (New York: Ronald Press, 1960), 48, 142–43.

20. Roger Williams, *The Bloudy Tenent of Persecution for the Cause of Conscience*, in *American Christianity: An Historical Interpretation with Representative Documents*, vol. 1, 1607–1820, ed. H. Shelton Smith, Robert T. Handy, and Lefferts A. Loetscher (New York: Scribner's, 1960), 153.

21. Most scholars agree that the book of Isaiah contains material by multiple authors and that this particular passage appears in "Third Isaiah." No

good purpose will be served, however, by importing questions of authorship into this present text. Throughout this book, therefore, I will refer to all passages from the biblical text of Isaiah with the traditional designation, Isaiah.

22. James A. Michener, *The Covenant* (London: Mandarin, 1992).

23. *Congressional Record* 33 (Washington, D.C.: Government Printing Office, 1900), 711.

24. Richard T. Hughes, "Poking Holes in the 'Just War Theory,'" *Harrisburg Patriot-News*, October 19, 2004.

25. Letter dated October 26, 2004.

Chapter 2. The Witness of the Hebrew Bible

1. John Dominic Crossan, *God and Empire: Jesus against Rome, Then and Now* (San Francisco: HarperSanFrancisco, 2007), 116–17.

2. On different interpretations of the metaphor "kingdom of God," see Glen H. Stassen and David P. Gushee, *Kingdom Ethics: Following Jesus in Contemporary Context* (Downers Grove, Ill.: InterVarsity Press, 2003), 19–31; and George Eldon Ladd, *The Gospel of the Kingdom: Scriptural Studies in the Kingdom of God* (Grand Rapids, Mich.: Eerdmans, 1959), 13–23.

3. Crossan, *God and Empire*, 116.

4. For classic treatments of the early nineteenth-century vision, so common in the United States, that this country was itself the kingdom of God, or would usher in that kingdom, see H. Richard Niebuhr, *The Kingdom of God in America* (New York: Harper and Row, 1937), 141–63; and Ernest Tuveson, *Redeemer Nation: The Idea of America's Millennial Role* (Chicago: University of Chicago Press, 1980).

5. Alexander Campbell, "An Oration in Honor of the Fourth of July," 1830, in *Popular Lectures and Addresses* (St. Louis: John Burns, 1861), 374–75.

6. Walter Brueggemann, *The Prophetic Imagination* (Minneapolis: Fortress Press, 1978), 33.

7. Brueggemann, *Prophetic Imagination*, 30.

8. Gordon Brubacher, "Just War and the New Community: The Witness of the Old Testament for Christians Today," *Princeton Theological Review*, 12 (Fall 2006), 19. I am especially indebted to Brubacher for helping me discern the ethical distance between Israel's early history and the witness of the Hebrew prophets who worked in the eighth and subsequent centuries BCE. I am also indebted to Brubacher for calling my attention to the witness against war and violence and the strong stand for peace and peace-making that are so characteristic of those prophets.

9. Ibid.

10. Crossan, *God and Empire*, 94.

11. Brubacher, "Just War," 23.

12. Crossan, *God and Empire*, 132.

13. Brubacher, "Just War," 24.

Chapter 3. The Witness of the New Testament

1. Donald Kraybill, *The Upside-down Kingdom*, 25th anniversary ed. (Scottdale, Pa.: Herald Press, 2003.

2. See also Kraybill's earlier book, *Our Star-Spangled Faith* (Scottdale, Pa.: Herald Press, 1976).

3. See, for example, Warren Carter, *Matthew and the Margins: A Sociopolitical and Religious Reading* (Maryknoll, N.Y.: Orbis, 2000); *Matthew and Empire: Initial Explorations* (Harrisburg, Pa.: Trinity Press, 2001); and *What Are They Saying about Matthew's Sermon on the Mount?* (New York: Paulist Press, 1994). See also Richard A. Horsley, *Jesus and Empire: The Kingdom of God and the New World Disorder* (Minneapolis: Fortress Press, 2003); Horsley, *Religion and Empire: People, Power, and the Life of the Spirit* (Minneapolis: Fortress Press, 2003); and Richard A. Horsley and Neil Asher Silberman, *The Message and the Kingdom: How Jesus and Paul Ignited a Revolution and Transformed the Ancient World* (Minneapolis: Fortress Press, 1997). See also Barbara R. Rossing, *The Rapture Exposed: The Message of Hope in the Book of Revelation* (New York: Basic Books, 2004). And finally, see Crossan, *God and Empire*, and Crossan and Jonathan L. Reed, *In Search of Paul: How Jesus's Apostle Opposed Rome's Empire with God's Kingdom* (San Francisco: HarperSanFrancisco, 2004).

4. Horsley and Silberman, *Message and the Kingdom*, 10–12.

5. Horsley, *Jesus and Empire*, 13.

6. Ronald Steel, *Pax Americana* (New York: Viking Press, 1967), 16–18 and vii.

7. Ronald Reagan, "Remarks at the Annual Washington Conference of the American Legion," February 22, 1983, quoted in Andrew J. Bacevich, *The New American Militarism: How Americans Are Seduced by War* (New York: Oxford University Press, 2006), 185.

8. David Frum and Richard Perle, *An End to Evil: How to Win the War on Terror* (New York: Random House, 2003), 279; remarks by the president at graduation exercise at United States Military Academy, June 1, 2002 (http://www.whitehouse.gov/news/releases/2002/06/20020601-3.html, accessed August 19, 2002); and Donald Rumsfeld at press conference, April 23, 2003, quoted in Rahul Mahajan, *Full Spectrum Dominance: U.S. Power in Iraq and Beyond* (New York: Seven Stories Press, 2003), 9.

9. George W. Bush, "Inaugural Address," *New York Times*, January 20, 2005 (http://www.nytimes.com/2005/01/20/politics/20BUSH-TEXT.html, accessed February 23, 2005).

10. Section III, "Strengthen Alliances to Defeat Global Terrorism and Work to Prevent Attacks against Us and Our Friends," in "The National Security Strategy of the United States of America," http://www.whitehouse.gov/nsc/print/nssall.html, accessed March 13, 2004.

11. "Remarks by Al Gore," as prepared, New York University, May 26, 2004, http://www.moveonpac.com/goreremarks052604.html, accessed December 12, 2005.

12. Section IX, "Transform America's National Security Institutions to

Meet the Challenges and Opportunities of the Twenty-First Century," in "National Security Strategy of the United States."

13. Excerpts from 1992 draft "Defense Planning Guidance," www.pbs .org/wgbh/pages/frontline/shows/iraq/etc/wolf.html, accessed March 26, 2008.

14. Charles Krauthammer, "The Unipolar Moment," *Foreign Affairs* 70 (special issue, 1990/91), quoted in David Ray Griffin, *Christian Faith and the Truth behind 9/11* (Louisville, Ky.: Westminster John Knox Press, 2006), 88.

15. Krauthammer, "Universal Dominion: Toward a Unipolar World," *National Interest* (Winter 1989), 47–49; and "Bless Our Pax Americana," *Washington Post*, March 22, 1991.

16. Griffin, *Christian Faith and the Truth behind 9/11*, 88.

17. Andrew J. Bacevich, *American Empire: The Realities and Consequences of U.S. Diplomacy* (Cambridge, Mass.: Harvard University Press, 2002), 44.

18. Griffin, *Christian Faith and the Truth behind 9/11*, 94.

19. "Secretary Rumsfeld Interview with the New York Times," *New York Times*, October 12, 2001.

20. George W. Bush, introductory section, "National Security Strategy of the United States."

21. Jonathan Freedland, "Is America the New Rome?" *Guardian* (September 11, 2002), G2: 2–5.

22. Joseph S. Nye Jr., "American Power and Strategy after Iraq," *Foreign Affairs* (July–August 2003), 60, quoted in Griffin, *Christian Faith and the Truth behind 9/11*, 106.

23. Krauthammer, "The Bush Doctrine," *Time* (March 5, 2001); and Krauthammer, quoted in Emily Eakin, "All Roads Lead to D.C.," *New York Times*, Week in Review, March 31, 2002.

24. Bacevich, *American Empire*, 244.

25. Gary Dorrien, *Imperial Designs: Neoconservatism and the New Pax Americana* (New York: Routledge, 2004). Also writing from a more liberal perspective, Jack Nelson-Pallmeyer wondered whether it would be possible to save Christianity from complicity with American imperial designs: *Saving Christianity from Empire* (New York: Continuum, 2005). Liberal observers have commented on the emerging American empire for many years. For a list of some of these observers, along with their books and articles, see David Ray Griffin, John B. Cobb Jr., Richard A. Falk, and Catherine Keller, *The American Empire and the Commonwealth of God: A Political, Economic, Religious Statement* (Louisville, Ky.: Westminster John Knox, 2006), 161, n. 22. Chapter 1 of this book—"America's Non-Accidental, Non-Benign Empire" by David Ray Griffin—is one of the best short summaries of the emergence of the United States into an imperial power that I have read.

26. Cited in Richard W. Van Alstyne, *The Rising American Empire* (New York: Norton, 1974), 159.

27. http://globalresearch.ca/index.php?context=va&aid=5564, accessed January 23, 2008.

28. Lee Camp, *Mere Discipleship: Radical Christianity in a Rebellious World* (Grand Rapids, Mich.: Brazos Press, 2003), 42.

29. Crossan, *God and Empire*, 107–8 and 141; and Crossan and Reed, *In Search of Paul*, 11.

30. Crossan, *God and Empire*, 107.

31. Eldridge Cleaver, *Soul on Ice* (New York: Dell, 1968), 31–39.

32. There is considerable debate among scholars over the sources for the Sermon on the Mount and how much or how little of this sermon comes from Jesus himself. My concern in this book, however, is not to explore the various aspects of this debate, but simply to ask how the Sermon on the Mount, as it appears in Matthew, helps us understand the meaning of the kingdom of God. For a survey of the issues in identifying sources for Matthew's Sermon on the Mount, see Warren Carter, *What Are They Saying about Matthew's Sermon on the Mount?* (New York: Paulist Press, 1994), 12–26.

33. Carter, "Power and Identities: The Contexts of Matthew's Sermon on the Mount" in David Fleer and Dave Bland, eds., *Preaching the Sermon on the Mount: The World It Imagines* (St. Louis: Chalice Press, 2007), 14.

34. Brueggemann, *Prophetic Imagination*, 45.

35. Ibid., 41.

36. Ibid., 45.

37. Carter, *Matthew and the Margins: A Sociopolitical and Religious Reading* (Maryknoll, N.Y.: Orbis, 2000), 131.

38. Horsley and Silberman, *Message and the Kingdom*, 10.

39. Ibid., 9.

40. Michael Himes, *Doing the Truth in Love: Conversations about God, Relationships and Service* (New York: Paulist Press, 1995), 51.

41. Kurt Vonnegut, *A Man without a Country* (New York: Random House Trade Paperbacks, 2007), 13–14.

42. Roland Bainton, *Christian Attitudes toward War and Peace: A Historical Survey and Critical Re-Evaluation* (Nashville, Tenn.: Abingdon, 1960), 64.

43. Crossan and Reed, *In Search of Paul*, 336.

44. Crossan, *God and Empire*, 94. Italics in original.

45. Lareta Finger, "Paul's Ephesian Letter As a Challenge to Empire," unpublished plenary speech at biennial conference of the Ecumenical and Evangelical Women's Caucus, July 2006, Charlotte, North Carolina, pp. 7–8. I am grateful to Finger, my colleague at Messiah College, and to Stuart Love, my former colleague at Pepperdine University, for helping me to understand the importance of the household codes as the context for these passages.

46. Brian J. Walsh and Sylvia C. Keesmaat, *Colossians Remixed: Subverting the Empire* (Downers Grove, Ill.: InterVarsity Press, 2004), 208.

47. Celsus cited by Origen, *Contra Celsum*, 8:68, in *Ante-Nicene Fathers*,

4, ed. Alexander Roberts and James Donaldson (1885; repr. Peabody, Mass.: Hendrickson, 1999), 665.

48. Bainton, *Christian Attitudes toward War and Peace*, 68.

49. Tertullian and Cyprian quotations cited in Bainton, *Christian Attitudes toward War and Peace*, 77.

50. On the alleged necessity for war, see Daniel C. Maguire, *The Horrors We Bless: Rethinking the Just-War Legacy* (Minneapolis: Fortress Press, 2007).

51. Chris Hedges, *War Is a Force That Gives Us Meaning* (New York: Public Affairs, 2002), 84.

52. Hedges, *War Is a Force That Gives Us Meaning*, 28 and 13.

53. The standard account of the transition from the commitment to nonresistance that dominated the church during its first three centuries to just war theory is Bainton, *Christian Attitudes toward War and Peace*. See esp. pp. 53–100.

54. John Yeatts, *Believers Church Bible Commentary: Revelation* (Scottdale, Pa.: Herald Press, 2003), 357.

55. Letter dated October 26, 2004.

56. Crossan, *God and Empire*, 94–95.

57. Crossan, *God and Empire*, 227.

58. William Stringfellow, *An Ethic for Christians and Other Aliens in a Strange Land* (Waco, Tex.: Word Books, 1973), 16, 14.

59. Martin Luther King Jr., "A Time to Break Silence," 1967, in James M. Washington, ed., *I Have a Dream: Writings and Speeches That Changed the World* (San Francisco: HarperSanFrancisco, 1986), 142.

60. Stringfellow, *Ethic for Christians*, 92–93.

61. Ibid., 81.

62. Ibid., 51.

63. Ibid., 51.

64. Ibid., 98–99.

65. Ibid., 100.

66. Ibid., 32.

67. Ibid., 51.

Chapter 4. Why Do We Think of America as a Christian Nation?

1. Theodore Dwight Bozeman makes this argument in *To Live Ancient Lives: The Primitivist Impulse in Puritanism* (Chapel Hill: University of North Carolina Press, 1988).

2. Numerous recent books explore the religion of America's Founding Fathers. See, for example, David L. Holmes, *The Faiths of the Founding Fathers* (Oxford, U.K.: Oxford University Press, 2006); Jon Meacham, *American Gospel: God, the Founding Fathers, and the Making of a Nation* (New York: Random House, 2006); Edwin S. Gaustad, *Faith of the Founders: Religion and the New Nation 1776–1826* (Waco, Tex.: Baylor University Press, 2004); Frank Lambert, *The Founding Fathers and the Place of Religion in America* (Princeton, N.J.: Princeton University Press, 2003); and Daniel

L. Dreisbach, Mark D. Hall, and Jeffry H. Morrison, eds., *The Founders on God and Government* (New York: Rowman and Littlefield, 2004).

3. Thomas Jefferson to Benjamin Waterhouse, June 26, 1822, in Norman Cousins, ed., *"In God We Trust": The Religious Beliefs and Ideas of the American Founding Fathers* (New York: Harper, 1958), 160–61.

4. John Adams to Thomas Jefferson, September 14, 1813, in Lester J. Cappon, ed., *The Adams–Jefferson Letters* (New York: Simon and Schuster, 1971), 373.

5. Letter from Benjamin Franklin to Ezra Stiles, March 9, 1790, in Cousins, *"In God We Trust,"* 42.

6. Cited in Henry F. May, *The Enlightenment in America* (Oxford, U.K.: Oxford University Press, 1976), 335.

7. Thomas Jefferson to Jared Sparks, November 4, 1820, in Cousins, *"In God We Trust,"* 156.

8. Thomas Jefferson to Miles King, September 26, 1814, in Cousins, *"In God We Trust,"* 144–45.

9. Thomas Jefferson to James Smith, December 8, 1822, in Cousins, *"In God We Trust,"* 159.

10. John M. Mason, *The Voice of Warning, to Christians, on the Ensuing Election of a President of the United States* (New York, 1800), 20, cited in G. Adolf Kock, *Religion of the American Enlightenment* (New York: Thomas Y. Crowell, 1968), 271.

11. Sidney E. Mead, *The Lively Experiment: The Shaping of Christianity in America* (New York: Harper and Row, 1963), 38–54; and Martin E. Marty, *The Infidel: Free Thought and American Religion* (New York: World, 1961).

12. George Duffield Jr., "The God of Our Fathers, an Historical Sermon," January 4, 1861 (Philadelphia, 1861), 15.

13. Pat Robertson, *The New World Order* (Dallas: Word Publishing, 1991), 246.

14. David Barton, *The Myth of Separation: What Is the Correct Relationship between Church and State?* (Aledo, Tex.: WallBuilder Press, 1989). On Barton's theory of church-state separation, see Deborah Caldwell, "David Barton and the 'Myth' of Church-State Separation," http://www.beliefnet.com/Search/Site.aspx?q=david+barton, accessed October 26, 2008.

15. Chris Vaughn, "A Man with a Message; Self-Taught Historian's Work on Church-State Issues Rouses GOP," *Fort Worth Star-Telegram*, May 22, 2005, in http://www.baylor.edu/pr/bitn/news.php?action=story&story=34559, accessed March 26, 2008.

16. "David Barton," in http://www.speroforum.com/site/wiki.asp?id=DavidBarton, accessed February 5, 2008; http://www.beliefnet.com/News/Politics/2004/10/David-Barton-The-Myth-Of-Church-State-Separation.aspx?p=1; and http://www.positiveatheism.org/writ/founding.htm, accessed October 10, 2008.

17. D. James Kennedy with Jerry Newcombe, *What If America Were a Christian Nation Again?* (Nashville, Tenn.: Thomas Nelson, 2003), 4.

18. Mark A. Noll, Nathan O. Hatch, and George M. Marsden, *The Search for Christian America* (Colorado Springs, Colo.: Helmers and Howard, 1989), 81, 88–93.

19. Mark D. Hall, "James Wilson: Presbyterian, Anglican, Thomist, or Deist? Does It Matter?" in Dreisbach, Hall, and Morrison, eds., *The Founders on God and Government*, 181–205.

20. Noll, Hatch, and Marsden, *Search for Christian America*, 133–34, 107.

21. Mark A. Beliles and Stephen K. McDowell, *America's Providential History* (Charlottesville, Va.: Providence Foundation, 1989), 178.

22. Henry Fielding, *The History of Tom Jones* (New York: Modern Library Edition), 84.

23. Jonathan Edwards, "Some Thoughts concerning the Present Revival of Religion in New England" (New York: S. Converse, 1830), 128–33.

24. Abraham Keteltas, "God Arising and Pleading His People's Cause . . ., a sermon preached October 5, 1777, in . . . Newburyport" (Newburyport, Mass., 1777), in Hudson, *Nationalism and Religion in America*, 49, 52–53.

25. Samuel Sherwood, *The Church's Flight into the Wilderness* (New York, 1776), 39–49.

26. Martin E. Marty, *Righteous Empire: The Protestant Experience in America* (New York: Dial Press, 1970), 38.

27. Timothy Dwight, "A Discourse on Some Events of the Last Century," delivered January 7, 1801, in *American Christianity: An Historical Interpretation with Representative Documents*, ed. H. Shelton Smith, Robert T. Handy, and Lefferts A. Loetscher, vol. 1 (New York: Scribner's, 1960), 533, 537–38.

28. For a succinct description of these efforts, see Thomas Askew and Richard Pierard, *The American Church Experience* (Grand Rapids, Mich.: Baker, 2004), 86–90.

29. Marty, *Righteous Empire*, 127ff.

30. Ibid., 15.

31. Ibid., 89, 15, and 90 (quote).

32. David Walker, *Walker's Appeal . . . to the Colored Citizens of the World*, 2nd ed. (1830; repr., Nashville, Tenn.: James C. Winston, 1994), 49 and 55.

33. Frederick Douglass, *Narrative of the Life of Frederick Douglass, an American Slave, Written by Himself* (1845; rev. ed., New York: Signet Books, 1968), 120.

34. Cited in Marty, *Righteous Empire*, 49.

35. For all these myths, see my *Myths America Lives By* (Urbana: University of Illinois Press, 2003), chapters 1, 2, and 4.

36. John L. O'Sullivan, quoted in *New York Morning News*, December 27, 1845.

37. Horace Greeley, letter in *New York Tribune*, June 1859, reprinted in James Parton, *Life of Andrew Jackson* (New York: Mason Brothers, 1861), I:401n.

38. O'Sullivan, quoted in *New York Morning News*, December 27, 1845.

39. H. V. Johnson, *Congressional Globe*, 30th Cong., 1st sess. (Washington, D.C.: Blair and Rives, 1848), appendix, 379.

40. William McKinley quoted in *Congressional Record*, 55th Cong.,

3d sess., 2518, cited in Albert K. Weinberg, *Manifest Destiny: A Study of Nationalist Expansionism in American History* (1935; repr., Chicago: Quadrangle Books, 1963), 294.

41. Josiah Strong, *Our Country* (1885), in Hudson, *Nationalism and Religion in America*, 115–16.

42. Strong, *The New Era* (New York, 1893), 81, cited in Handy, *Christian America*, 105–6; *Christian Index* (August 3, 1899), quoted in Rufus B. Spain, *At Ease in Zion: A Social History of Southern Baptists* (Nashville, Tenn.: Vanderbilt University Press, 1977), 126, cited in Handy, *Christian America*, 128.

43. James H. King, "The Christian Resources of Our Country," in *National Perils and Opportunities: The Discussions of the General Conference, held in Washington, D.C., . . . 1887, under the Auspices and Direction of the Evangelical Alliance* (New York, 1887), 272, cited in Handy, *Christian America*, 106.

44. Lewis French Stearns, *The Evidence of Christian Experience* (New York, 1890), 366, cited in Handy, *Christian America*, 121–22.

45. Sidney E. Gulick, *The Growth of the Kingdom of God* (New York, c. 1897), 316, cited in Handy, *Christian America*, 123.

46. *Official Report of the Proceedings and Debates of the Twenty-Third General Conference of the United Brethren in Christ*, 1901, 24, cited in Handy, *Christian America*, 127.

47. General James Rusling, "Interview with President William McKinley," *The Christian Advocate*, Feb. 22, 1903, p. 17; reprinted in Daniel Schirmer and Stephen Rosskamm Shalom, eds., *The Philippines Reader* (Boston: South End Press, 1987), pp. 22–23.

48. James Henderson Berry, *Congressional record*, 55th Cong., 3rd sess., vol. 32, pt. 2 (Washington, D.C.: Government Printing Office, 1899), 1299.

49. Andrew Carnegie, "Wealth" [1889], in *The Role of Religion in American Life: An Interpretive Historical Anthology*, ed. Robert A. Mathisen (Dubuque, Iowa: Kendall/Hunt, 1994), 168, 173.

50. Quoted in Henry F. May, *Protestant Churches and Industrial America* (New York: Harper and Row, 1967), 69.

51. William Lawrence, "The Relation of Wealth to Morals" (1901), in Conrad Cherry, ed., *God's New Israel: Religious Interpretations of American Destiny*, rev. ed. (Chapel Hill: University of North Carolina Press, 1998), 250–52.

52. Russell Conwell, *Acres of Diamonds* (1890; repr., New York: Harper and Row, 1905), 18.

53. Washington Gladden, *The Church and the Nation* (n.p.: Christian Home Missionary Society, 1905), 4.

54. Walter Rauschenbusch, *A Theology for the Social Gospel* (New York, 1917), 139.

55. Handy, *Christian America*, 141.

56. Gladden, *The Church and the Kingdom* (New York, 1894), 11.

57. Strong, *Our Country*, quoted in Hudson, *Nationalism and Religion in America*, 115–16.

58. See, for example, Geiko Müller-Fahrenholz, *America's Battle for God:*

A European Christian Looks at Civil Religion (Grand Rapids, Mich.: Eerdmans, 2007); John Shelton Lawrence and Robert Jewett, *The Myth of the American Superhero* (Grand Rapids, Mich.: Eerdmans, 2002); and Hughes, *Myths America Lives By.*

Chapter 5. From the Scopes Trial to George W. Bush

1. There is a wealth of literature both on fundamentalist sects, groups, and movements worldwide and on fundamentalism in the American context in particular. On the phenomenon of fundamentalism, see Martin E. Marty and R. Scott Appleby, eds., *Fundamentalisms Observed (The Fundamentalism Project)* (Chicago: University of Chicago Press, 2004). On fundamentalism in America, see George M. Marsden, *Fundamentalism and American Culture: The Shaping of Twentieth-Century Evangelicalism, 1870–1925* (New York: Oxford University Press, 1980).

2. H. L. Mencken, "Homo Neanderthalensis," *Baltimore Evening Sun*, June 29, 1925; article in http://www.positiveatheism.org/hist/menck01.htm#SCOPES1, accessed March 28, 2008.

3. Mencken, "Battle Now Over, Mencken Sees; Genesis Triumphant and Ready for New Jousts," *Baltimore Evening Sun*, July 18, 1925; article in http://www.positiveatheism.org/hist/menck04.htm#SCOPESA, accessed April 7, 2006.

4. David Domke, *God Willing? Political Fundamentalism in the White House, the "War on Terror," and the Echoing Press* (London: Pluto Press, 2004).

5. Randall Balmer, *Thy Kingdom Come: An Evangelical's Lament: How the Religious Right Distorts the Faith and Threatens America* (New York: Basic Books, 2006).

6. Bill Moyers, "A Shiver down the Spine," 2004, 2005, in Moyers, *Moyers on America: A Journalist and His Times* (New York: Anchor Books, 2005), 3.

7. Jimmy Carter, *Our Endangered Values: America's Moral Crisis* (New York: Simon and Schuster, 2005), 31.

8. On Darby and his theories, see the magisterial history of end-times prophecies in the United States, Paul Boyer's *When Time Shall Be No More: Prophecy Belief in Modern American Culture* (Cambridge, Mass.: Belknap Press, 1992), 86–90

9. Boyer, *When Time Shall Be No More*, 88.

10. The standard work exposing the notion of rapture as a fraud if measured by Christian scripture and history is Rossing, *Rapture Exposed.*

11. On fundamentalist pacifism and the allegiance of Christian fundamentalists to the kingdom of God, see Marsden, *Fundamentalism and American Culture*, 143–48. During World War I, professors Shailer Mathews and Shirley Jackson Case of the University of Chicago Divinity School attacked the fundamentalists in print over this very issue. Mathews and Case both complained that the fundamentalists' allegiance to the kingdom of God and their resulting pacifism undermined the Allied war effort. Again, see Marsden, *Fundamentalism and American Culture*, 145–47.

12. Marsden, *Fundamentalism and American Culture*, 149.

13. In his book *A Godly Hero: The Life of William Jennings Bryan* (New York: Anchor Books, 2007), Michael Kazin has demonstrated how skewed Mencken's judgments actually were.

14. Mencken, "Malone the Victor, Even Though Court Sides with Opponents, says Mencken," *Baltimore Evening Sun*, July 17, 1925, article in http://www.positiveatheism.org/hist/menck04.htm#SCOPES19, accessed April 7, 2006.

15. Carl F. H. Henry, *The Uneasy Conscience of Modern Fundamentalism* (1947; repr. Grand Rapids, Mich.: Eerdmans, 2003).

16. On the religious impact of immigration into the United States from Southeast Asia, the Middle East, and other parts of the world many traditional Americans would find exotic, see Diana Eck, *A New Religious America: How a "Christian Country" Has Become the World's Most Religiously Diverse Nation* (San Francisco: HarperSanFrancisco, 2002).

17. Robert N. Bellah, *The Broken Covenant: American Civil Religion in Time of Trial*, 2nd ed. (Chicago: University of Chicago Press, 1992), 1.

18. Carter, *Our Endangered Values*, 62.

19. "Pastor Chosen to Lead Christian Coalition Steps Down in Dispute over Agenda," *New York Times*, November 28, 2006. Hunter subsequently published an important book that laid out his vision for the kinds of issues the Christian community ought to embrace: Joel C. Hunter, *A New Kind of Conservative* (Ventura, Calif.: Regal, 2008).

20. William C. Martin, *With God on Our Side: The Rise of the Religious Right in America*, rev. ed. (New York: Broadway Books, 2005), 168–73; and Balmer, *Thy Kingdom Come*, 13–17.

21. Martin, *With God on Our Side*, 173.

22. Both Compolo and McLaren have written popular books on their own, but they jointly wrote *Adventures in Missing the Point: How the Culture-Controlled Church Neutered the Gospel* (Grand Rapids, Mich.: Zondervan/Youth Specialties, 2006).

23. See, for example, Jim Wallis, *God's Politics: Why The Right Gets It Wrong and the Left Doesn't Get It* (San Francisco: HarperSanFrancisco, 2005).

24. Ron Sider, *Rich Christians in an Age of Hunger: Moving from Affluence to Generosity* (Nashville, Tenn.: W Publishing, 2005).

25. Hedges, *American Fascists: The Christian Right and the War on America* (New York: Free Press, 2008), 23.

26. "Right Is Might for GOP's Aspirants," *Los Angeles Times*, March 25, 2006.

27. Ibid.

28. James Davison Hunter, *Culture Wars: The Struggle to Define America* (New York: Basic Books, 1991); and Robert Wuthnow, *The Struggle for America's Soul: Evangelicals, Liberals, and Secularism* (Grand Rapids, Mich.: Eerdmans, 1989).

29. See on this point David Aikman, *A Man of Faith: The Spiritual Journey of George W. Bush* (Nashville, Tenn.: W Publishing, 2004), p. 81.

30. Wyatt Olson, "Onward Christian Soldiers: TV Preacher D. James Kennedy and His Religious Cohorts Want to 'Reclaim America for Christ'—and the GOP," *Church and State*, 57, no. 1 (January 2004): 10.

31. Ron Suskind, "Without a Doubt," *New York Times Magazine* (Oc-

tober 17, 2004), http://www.cs.umass.edu/~immerman/play/opinion05/
WithoutADoubt.html, accessed October 26, 2008.

32. David Domke, "God's Will, According to the Bush Administration,"
http://www.counterpunch.org/domke09102004.html, accessed October 10,
2005.

33. Letter to George W. Bush from Bob Jones III; This letter was originally
posted on the Bob Jones University website but has since been removed. A
copy currently can be found at http://www.danjor.com/wordpress/?p=604,
accessed October 11, 2008.

34. "Bush Campaign Seeks Help from Thousands of Congregations,"
New York Times, June 3, 2004.

35. David Kuo, *Tempting Faith: An Inside Story of Political Seduction*
(New York: Free Press, 2006), 229–30.

36. Kevin Phillips, *American Theocracy* (New York: Viking, 2006),
212.

37. "Republicans Admit Mailing Campaign Literature Saying Liberals
Will Ban the Bible," *New York Times*, September 24, 2004.

38. Carter, *Our Endangered Values*, 62.

39. Jim Lobe, "Conservative Christians Biggest Backers of Iraq War," *Common Dreams News Center*, http://www.commondreams.org/headlines02/
1010-02.htm, October 10, 2002, accessed November 12, 2005.

40. Charles Marsh, "Wayward Christian Soldiers," *New York Times*,
January 20, 2006.

41. Ibid.

42. "For the Health of the Nation: An Evangelical Call to Civic Responsibility," p. 11, found at http://www.nae.net/images/civic_responsibility2
.pdf, accessed March 31, 2008. This document may also be found in the
appendices of David P. Gushee, *The Future of Faith in American Politics:
The Public Witness of the Evangelical Center* (Waco, Tex.: Baylor University
Press, 2008), 223–34.

43. Ronald J. Sider, *The Scandal of Evangelical Politics: Why Are Christians Missing the Chance to Really Change the World?* (Grand Rapids,
Mich.: Baker Books, 2008).

44. Jim Wallis, *The Great Awakening: Reviving Faith and Politics in a
Post-Religious Right America* (New York: HarperOne, 2008); and Gushee,
Future of Faith in American Politics.

45. Bush, Second Inaugural Address, January 20, 2005, http://www
.whitehouse.gov/news/releases/2005/01/20050120–1.html, accessed March
26, 2008.

46. Bob Woodward, *Plan of Attack* (New York: Simon Schuster, 2004),
89.

47. Lyman Beecher, "The Memory of Our Fathers" (Dec. 22, 1827), in
Hudson, *Nationalism and Religion in America*, 104–5.

48. Woodward, *Plan of Attack*, 379.

49. Ibid., 421.

50. See database for January 2004 at http://www.iraqbodycount.org, accessed January 26, 2004.

51. Domke, "God's Will, According to the Bush Administration."

52. Bush, "Presidential Address to the Nation Marking the Observance of
the September 11 Attacks," September 11, 2002, in Bush, *We Will Prevail:*

President George W. Bush on War, Terrorism, and Freedom (New York: Continuum, 2003), 183.

53. Lewis E. Jones, "There's Power in the Blood," http://library.timelesstruths.org/music/There_Is_Power_in_the_Blood/, accessed October 26, 2008.

54. Charles Wesley, "A Charge to Keep I Have," http://www.hymnsite.com/lyrics/umh413.sht, accessed October 26, 2008.

55. Bush, "Presidential Easter Message," March 27, 2002, in *We Will Prevail*, 140.

56. Bruce Lincoln, "Bush's God Talk," *Christian Century* (October 5, 2004), 22.

57. Hedges, *War Is a Force That Gives Us Meaning*, 147, 10.

58. On Bush's propensity to divide the world into good and evil, see Peter Singer, *The President of Good and Evil: Questioning the Ethics of George W. Bush* (New York: Penguin Group, 2004).

59. "Excerpted Remarks by the President from Speech to Employees at the Federal Bureau of Investigation," September 25, 2001, in Bush, *We Will Prevail*, 22.

60. David Frum and Richard Perle, *An End to Evil: How to Win the War on Terror* (New York: Ballantine Books, 2003).

61. John Barry, Richard Wolffe, and Evan Thomas, "War of Nerve," *Newsweek* (July 4, 2005), 25.

62. "Remarks by the President from a Speech at National Day of Prayer and Remembrance Ceremony," National Cathedral, Washington D.C., September 14, 2001, in Bush, *We Will Prevail*, 5; "Excerpted Remarks by the President from Speech to the Employees of the Department of Labor," October 4, 2001, in Bush, *We Will Prevail*, 30; and "Excerpted Remarks by the President from Speech at the Graduation Exercises of the United States Military Academy," June 1, 2002, in Bush, *We Will Prevail*, 161.

63. Bush, "Presidential Address to a Joint Session of Congress," September 23, 2001, in Bush, *We Will Prevail*, 15.

64. Bush, "Excerpted Remarks from President's State of the Union Address," January 29, 2002, in Bush, *We Will Prevail*, 108.

65. Bush, "Radio Address by the President to the Nation," August 31, 2002, at http://www.whitehouse.gov/news/releases/2002/08/print/20020831.html, accessed March 12, 2004; "State of the Union Address," 2004, http://www.whitehouse.gov/news/releases/2004/01/20040120-7.html, accessed October 26, 2008; "Excerpted Remarks by the President from Speech at Massachusetts Victory 2002 Reception," October 4, 2002, in Bush, *We Will Prevail*, 191; "Excerpted Remarks by the President from Speech Unveiling 'Most Wanted' Terrorist List," FBI Headquarters, October 10, 2001, in Bush, *We Will Prevail*, 38; and "Excerpted Remarks by the President from Speech to Citizens and Military Personnel in North Carolina," March 15, 2002, in Bush, *We Will Prevail*, 136.

66. Rumsfeld at press conference, April 23, 2003, quoted in Mahajan, *Full Spectrum Dominance*, 9.

67. Müller-Fahrenholz, *America's Battle for God*, 95.

68. Bush, "President Holds Prime Time News Conference," October 11, 2001, White House release, http://www.whitehouse.gov/news/releases/2001/10/20011011-7.html, accessed February 6, 2006.

69. Bush, "Presidential Address to a Joint Session of Congress," September 23, 2001, in Bush, *We Will Prevail*, 14. For other examples of Bush's use of this theme, see Bush, "Presidential Address to the Nation," September 11, 2001, in Bush, *We Will Prevail*, 2; and Bush, "Remarks by the President from a Speech at National Day of Prayer and Remembrance Ceremony," National Cathedral, Washington D.C., September 14, 2001, in Bush, *We Will Prevail*, 7.

70. Reported by Jim Wallis in *God's Politics*, 138.

71. Henri J. M. Nouwen, *In the Name of Jesus: Reflections on Christian Leadership* (New York: Crossroad, 1989), 76.

72. Michael O. Hill, "Mine Eyes Have Seen the Glory: Bush's Armageddon Obsession Revisited," *Counter Punch* (January 4, 2003), located at http://www.gainesvillehumanists.org/apocalypse.htm, accessed March 26, 2008.

73. William Stringfellow, *An Ethic for Christians and Other Aliens in a Strange Land* (Waco, Tex.: Word Books, 1973), 98–100.

74. Charles Lewis and Mark Reading-Smith, "False Pretenses," Center for Public Integrity website, http://www.publicintegrity.org/WarCard/, accessed March 26, 2008.

75. Bill Moyers in "Bill Moyers Journal: Buying the War," PBS, April 25, 2007.

76. Cornel West, *Democracy Matters* (New York: Penguin Press, 2004), 7.

77. Müller-Fahrenholz, *America's Battle for God*, 137.

78. Jonathan Edwards, "Some Thoughts concerning the Present Revival of Religion in New England" (New York: S. Converse, 1830), 128–33.

79. Lyman Beecher, "A Plea for the West" (1835), in *God's New Israel: Religious Interpretations of American Destiny*, rev. ed., ed. Conrad Cherry (Chapel Hill: University of North Carolina Press, 1998), 130.

80. Boyer, *When Time Shall Be No More*, 89.

81. In addition to Boyer's *When Time Shall Be No More*, noted above, see also Timothy Weber, *On the Road to Armageddon: How Evangelicals Became Israel's Best Friend* (Grand Rapids, Mich.: Baker Academic, 2004), 25.

82. Weber, *On the Road to Armageddon*, 13.

83. Ibid., 191–92.

84. For an estimate of sales for the first nine volumes, see Weber, *On the Road to Armageddon*, 194.

85. John Hagee in *Final Dawn over Jerusalem* (Nashville, Tenn.: Thomas Nelson, 1998), cited in Paul Boyer, "When U.S. Foreign Policy Meets Biblical Prophecy," *AlterNet*, February 20, 2003, found at http://www.alternet.org/story/15221/?page=2, accessed March 10, 2004.

86. Cited in Weber, *On the Road to Armageddon*, 220.

87. Cited in Chris Hedges, "Feeling the Hate with the National Religious Broadcasters," *Harpers* 310 (May 2005), 59.

88. Moyers, "Shiver down the Spine," 9.

89. Carter, *Our Endangered Values*, 114.

90. Weber, *On the Road to Armageddon*, 197.

91. Hal Lindsey, *The 1980s: Countdown to Armageddon* (King of Prussia, Pa.: Westgate Press, 1980), 165.

92. Weber, *On the Road to Armageddon*, 229 and 221–22.

93. Müller-Fahrenholz, *America's Battle for God*, 40–41.

94. Moyers, "Shiver down the Spine," 5–6.

95. "Seeing Islam As 'Evil Faith,' Evangelicals Seek Converts," *New York Times*, May 27, 2003.

96. Boyer, "When U.S. Foreign Policy Meets Biblical Prophecy."

97. Esther Kaplan, *With God on Their Side: George W. Bush and the Christian Right* (New York: New Press, 2004), 13, 22.

98. Weber, *On the Road to Armageddon*, 252–53.

99. Moyers, "Shiver down the Spine," 6.

100. Marsh, "Wayward Christian Soldiers," *New York Times*, January 20, 2006.

101. Cited in Boyer, *When Time Shall Be No More*, 125.

102. Weber, *On the Road to Armageddon*, 202. For a thorough review of the way rapture theologians have linked Armageddon to nuclear annihilation, see Boyer, *When Time Shall Be No More*, 115–51. See also Grace Halsell, *Forcing God's Hand: Why Millions Pray for a Quick Rapture—and Destruction of Planet Earth*, rev. ed. (Beltsville, Md.: Amana, 2003).

103. Boyer, *When Time Shall Be No More*, 126.

104. Cited in Rossing, *Rapture Exposed*, 3.

105. Rossing, *Rapture Exposed*, 1–2, 99.

INDEX

and support from conservative Christians, 157–60; and Thomas Jefferson, 165

Calvin, John, 28, 108–9
Calvinists, 107–9
Camp, Lee: and *Mere Discipleship*, 58
Campbell, Alexander, 32
Cane Ridge Revival, 121
Carmichael, Stokely: and Freedom Movement, 151
Carnegie, Andrew, 130
Carter, Jimmy: and fundamentalist influence on American Middle East policy, 180; and *Our Endangered Values*, 138, 180
Carter, Warren, 52, 65, 66
Castro, Fidel, 55
Celsus, 89
Center for Public Integrity: and report on deception of Bush administration, 174
Cheney, Dick: and "Defense Planning Guidance," 55, 56
chosen people: biblical idea of, 25–28
Christian Amendment Association, 8
Christian amendment to Constitution, 7–8
Christianity and the Social Crisis (Walter Rauschenbusch), 133
Christianity Today, 150
Christian nation platforms, 187n1
Civil Religion: idea of, 11–12
Cizik, Richard, 182
Cleaver, Eldridge: and *Soul on Ice*, 64
Clinton, Bill, 57
Compolo, Tony, 156
Confederate States of America: constitution of, 7
Constantine (Roman emperor), 90, 105, 107
Constitution of United States: and Christian America, 114–18; and disestablishment, 2; and God, 7

Conwell, Russell, 132
Copeland, Kenneth: and dispensational premillennialism, 179
Coulter, Ann, 5–6; and *Godless: The Church of Liberalism*, 5; and Muslims, 5
Covenant, The (James Michener), 28
Crossan, John Dominic, 31–32, 36–37, 45, 52, 60, 62, 77, 78, 82, 97
Cushing, John: and America as new Israel, 24
Cyprian: and non-violence, 89

Darby, John Nelson: and dispensational premillennialism, 145–46, 177–78
Darwin, Charles: and fundamentalism, 140–41; and *On the Origin of Species*, 140
Day, Dorothy, 107
Dean, Howard, 17
Declaration of Independence, 110–14
"Defense Planning Guidance," 55, 56
Deism: and Declaration of Independence, 110–14
Delay, Tom: and International Fellowship of Christians and Jews, 180
Diem, Ngo Dinh, 55
Dobson, James: and Family Research Council, 153; and United States Supreme Court, 154
Domitian (Roman emperor), 92
Domke, David, 166
Dorrien, Gary, 57
Douglass, Frederick: and Christian America, 124
Dutch East India Company, 28
Dwight, Timothy, 121–22
Dyess Air Force Base, 58

Edwards, Jonathan, 120, 177
Ely, Ezra Stiles: and Christian political party, 8–9

empire, American, 52–58
An End to Evil: How to Win the War on Terror (David Frum and Richard Perle), 170
Ethic for Christians and Other Aliens in a Strange Land (William Stringfellow), 98–102
Evangelicals: and their relation to fundamentalism, 156; and support for George W. Bush, 157–59; and support for Iraq War, 161–62
Evangelicals for Social Action: and Ron Sider, 156

Falwell, Jerry, 9; and Christian tours of Israel, 181; and David Barton, 115; and dispensational premillennialism, 179; and George W. Bush, 159; and Israel, 180; and Moral Majority, 6, 152
Finney, Charles G., 122, 123
Forbes, Congressman Randy: and American Religious History Week, 9
Fordice, Kirk, 2
Founders, American: and vision for America, 109–18
Franklin, Benjamin: and Christian religion, 111–12; and America as chosen, 24
Frist, Bill, 161
Frum, David: and denial of American imperialism, 54; and *An End to Evil: How to Win the War on Terror*, 170
Fundamentalism, 136–57; and biblical inerrancy, 142–44; demise of, 148–50; and dispensationalism, 145, 177–79; and the end of the world, 144–46; and George W. Bush, 157–76; and influence over American government, 157; and its issues, 139–46; literature on, 198n1; and premillennial thinking, 144–45, 177–85; and rebirth of, 150–57; and Second Great Awakening, 118–19, 147–48, 153; and support for George

W. Bush, 157–59; and support for Iraq War, 161–62; and war with Islamic world, 181–85
Fund for Independence in Journalism: and report on deception of Bush administration, 174
Future of Faith in American Politics: The Public Witness of the Evangelical Center (David Gushee), 162

Gibbons, James Cardinal, 132
Gilded Age, 129, 131
Gingrich, Newt: and David Barton, 115
Gladden, Washington, 133
Godless: The Church of Liberalism (Ann Coulter), 5
Gore, Al, 2
Gospel of Wealth, 129–32
Graham, Billy, 158; and the American covenant, 25, 150
Graham, Franklin: and Islam as evil religion, 182; and support for Iraq War, 162
Great Awakening, 120
Great Awakening: Reviving Faith and Politics in a Post-Religious Right America (Jim Wallis), 162
Greeley, Horace, 125
Green v. Connally: and Bob Jones University, 155
Griffin, David Ray, 56
Guardian, 57
Gulick, Sidney E., 127–28
Gushee, David: and *Future of Faith in American Politics: The Public Witness of the Evangelical Center*, 162

Hagee, John: and Christians escaping doomsday, 184; and Israel, 179–80
Handel, George Frideric: and "The Messiah," 44
Handy, Robert T., 13, 133
Harrisburg Patriot-News, 29, 96
Hatch, Nathan, 116, 117